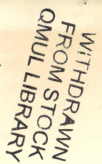

WITHDRAWN
FROM STOCK
QMUL LIBRARY

QMW L

D1766320

23 1196165 5

DATE DUE FOR RETURN

0 2 APR 2002

2 3 OCT 2002

2004

1 6 JAN 2004

-2 APR 2004

108142
18·9·74

FACTIONS NO MORE

There will indeed be this difference, amongst others, between the parties of a free government and the factions of an arbitrary one—for factions I must call them, by way of distinction: the former will subsist long together, contend and struggle, and mutually distress, and by turns almost overpower one another, but not entirely; the latter will soon destroy, or be destroyed. . . .

John Somers Cocks, M.P., 1792

FACTIONS NO MORE

Attitudes to
Party in Government and Opposition
in Eighteenth-Century England

Extracts from Contemporary Sources

J. A. W. GUNN

Professor of Political Studies
Queen's University Ontario

FRANK CASS : LONDON

WESTFIELD
UNIV.
LONDON
COLLEGE

First published in 1972 by
FRANK CASS AND COMPANY LIMITED
67 Great Russell Street, London WC1B 3BT

This collection and Introduction Copyright
© 1971 J. A. W. GUNN

All Rights Reserved

ISBN 0 7146 2595 7

Printed in Great Britain by
THE GARDEN CITY PRESS LIMITED
Letchworth, Hertfordshire
SG6 1JS

For ELEANOR

CONTENTS

PREFACE

It has often been said that no one before Burke had much of interest to say about political parties, and it was my dissatisfaction with this judgment that accounts for this book. Some few scholars —David Thomson, Caroline Robbins and Archibald Foord—have done much to uncover the presence of early sentiments favourable to party, and I hasten to acknowledge my debt to their writings. However, the conventional wisdom has still not been amended significantly. Perhaps it is because eighteenth-century England has been well served by modern political historians, save for one major oversight: they have chosen to disregard its ample polemical literature and the ideas to be found there.

This is unfortunate, for the century had some splendid pamphleteers and journalists and many competent ones. Their writings presented the arguments and prejudices deemed appropriate for public consumption, thus supplying an excellent index of prevailing attitudes. In fact, I am disposed to think that the neglected literature of political controversy is superior for some purposes either to private correspondence (the stock-in-trade of the political historian) or to formal treatises of political philosophy. The first is too specific and limited in its concerns to capture ideas about party, the second too elevated and abstract.

Allowing for the manifest differences between parties then and now, an inquiry into eighteenth-century attitudes towards parties can still cast light on the difficult business of sustaining limited social conflict. For not only was the acceptance of party reflected in institutions which have persisted to this day, but it has also come to figure as a cardinal assumption of western political science.

In choosing to reproduce extracts from seventy-four works, I have had to discard at least as many more promising items. Some of these are mentioned in my introductory essay, while others appear as brief quotations introducing the various sections, or in the notes. Although familiar names, such as Bolingbroke and Burke, are represented, the bulk of the extracts are those by writers either relatively obscure or unidentified. Major figures, whose works are readily accessible, appear only in order to provide convenient reference-points for the rest. For the purpose of my argument, the obscure works are the significant ones, since ignorance of their existence has caused historians to underestimate the frequency with which party conflict was defended, even early in the century.

This book was already in the press before I was able to consult Alan Beattie's valuable collection of documents and commentary, *English Party Politics, Volume I, 1660-1906* (London, 1970). Of the writings reproduced there, only the major figures—Burke, Bolingbroke, Hume and Perceval—are included in this volume. For the reason already noted, I have decided to retain my selection from these works.

In a book primarily concerned with political ideas, I have tried to keep bibliographical material to a minimum consistent with saying, as accurately as possible, who wrote what. Spelling, capitalization and punctuation are unchanged, except in the few items taken from modern editions. In referring to the works reproduced in the text, I have made free use of short titles; complete information on each appears at the beginning of the extract. The table of contents makes certain assumptions about authorship which are defended in the notes.

The job of bringing together materials has been made pleasant by the co-operation of a number of libraries—The British Museum, The Bodleian, London University Library, The Library of Congress, Yale University Library, The Redpath Library at McGill and The Douglas Library at my own university. Research grants from The Canada Council allowed me to make several trans-Atlantic research trips, and to that unfailing friend of Canadian scholarship I record my gratitude. I wish too to thank Professor Maurice Goldsmith of the University of Exeter, whose enthusiasm did much to turn an idea into a book, and Mr. Alastair Everitt, whose judicious and tactful editorial advice smoothed away many difficulties. During the latter stages of preparing the manuscript, I have benefited from the cheerful industry of Miss Ellen Henderson, my research assistant. My wife assisted me with some translations from German. However, it is for numerous other forms of assistance and forbearance that this book is dedicated to her.

Kingston, Ontario
August, 1970

INTRODUCTION

Conflict is central to human society as we know it; aggressive behaviour has even been labelled as instinctive—a claim difficult to support but significant of the human condition. The management of political conflict, by contrast, relies on devices culturally acquired and precariously maintained. The acceptance by government and governed of a legitimate opposition party is unknown to unsophisticated societies and alien to a number of powerful modern ideologies. An institutionalized opposition does have a place in the major strand of the modern democratic tradition, where it serves as the cornerstone and guarantor of many of the benefits of a free society. Continuity in government—that quality which has eluded both hereditary kingship, with its minorities and wars of succession, and modern dictatorship—is in theory assured through the peaceful transfer of power from government to opposition. Political scientists frequently describe civil liberties both as the requirement of peaceful party competition and as a valued by-product of that competition. Similarly, material prosperity and the existence of resources outside immediate government control have been cited as essential for effective opposition, while these conditions are also attributed, in part, to that opposition. For these reasons no one factor is more often paraded as a shibboleth of democratic respectability than the existence of a genuine opposition party.

Although perhaps vital to a functioning democracy, notions about party and opposition rarely figure, curiously enough, among the guiding ideas of the liberal-democratic tradition. Liberty, justice and equality—not to mention representation, the majority, and the separation of powers—all have their intellectual histories; but party seems to be an institution singularly bereft of intellectual parentage. This may be attributed in some measure to the fact that legitimate political opposition is not so profound an idea as to attract the attention of philosophers—being highly specific in terms of institutions, it seems scarcely to be an idea at all. Furthermore, recognized opposition arose in eighteenth-century England, among a people not noted for making matters deeper than they actually were and possessing a talent for avoiding precise theoretical statements of their political arrangements. One should perhaps add that the eighteenth century is a period of English history in which the quality of political thought has been dismissed, by Sir Leslie Stephen and others, as inconsequential.

Intellectually untidy, the acceptance of party has offered little emotional satisfaction to the partisan, be he defender of the *status quo,* radical or revolutionary. War is more often deemed a natural response to frustration. Similarly, that desert called "peace" is easily comprehended and satisfies, at least, the victors. However, the ethic of limited strife, the only scheme consistent with a functioning party system, is accepted only with difficulty—a difficulty more emotional than intellectual. To partisans it offers so little since it withholds complete success; both the "order" of the conservative and the demands of the "people", as reified by early radicals, have opposed the notion. The builders of utopias, with the honourable exception of Harrington, had no place for anything so cluttered, so persistently unresolved, as party competition, for it seemed to be the enemy of all who wished to be permanently, universally and gloriously right. Practical men of affairs, who knew at first hand of the mechanics of party, were still not usually transformed into defenders of parties as such. The natural desire was not to dignify the struggle, but to win it. Thus the people closest to the political scene were afflicted by this tension between involvement in conflict and an understanding of the general process. The latter demands the perspective of the spectator rather than the player. Even those writers who best sublimated partisanship in the interests of understanding the processes of government had their difficulties with party and opposition. For in the eighteenth century most descriptions of political life were confined to the formal mechanics of the constitution, an undertaking which was generally inaccurate because unmindful of extra-constitutional processes. Thus it was not until the twentieth century that scholars seriously examined the structure of political parties. The study of opposition has been even more neglected, perhaps owing to the fact that American political vocabulary—the language of twentieth-century political science—stresses the majority-minority party distinction rather than that of government and opposition. Indeed, the term "opposition" was perhaps more familiar in America of the early nineteenth century than it is today.[1]

THE ENGLISH EXPERIENCE

Despite all barriers, some societies have indeed come to accept opposition and parties; and, as might be expected, the successful experiment got well under way in eighteenth-century England. More surprising, perhaps, is the discovery that the development of these institutions was accompanied by a considerable amount of theoretical debate about their usefulness and rectitude. Understandably, party and opposition came first and political philosophy followed, for unlike some other questions of political thought, those concerned with party necessarily responded only to actual political practice. Many thinkers have no doubt pondered the nature of justice without having necessarily experienced the essence of it; but widespread debate about party could only be the product of the clash of particular parties on issues of the day. This necessary bow to reality means that behind many of the century's theoretical debates lurked the immediate and narrow ambitions of men hungry for office or anxious to retain it. A firm grasp of this truth is quite compatible, however, with taking the ideas of the time seriously. Political ideas are the children of interest, not truths derived from unworldly contemplation. No matter how responsive political argument might be to the calls of interest, it remains true that the actors in English public life had to adjust their notions of propriety to the scene before them—and the scene was remarkably new.

The fact of party and opposition emerged slowly, bringing with it the germ of a quite extraordinary and novel perspective on conflict. The lasting importance of this idea is that it can be divorced from particular men and measures to serve as a useful model for other political systems still without institutionalized opposition. The literature of political development has taught us that there is something magic about the first society to undergo any major stage of development—such as England's groping towards the invention of limited party conflict. Lacking both the wings and shackles given to latecomers, such a society must come to terms with questions which will arise again and again in other times and places. Men still ask, and sometimes with anguish, how to tame party without killing it; or, as in Turkey, Yugoslavia and Tanzania, they ponder whether to tolerate more than one. England first produced answers to such problems, sufficient at least for *its* needs. Englishmen tried, as we shall see, to find historical antecedents for their situation, but really there were none.

A further point needs emphasis in this connexion. Neither party nor opposition needed general acclaim or understanding in order to exist—Minerva's owl was late, as usual. However, an acceptance of party was a most significant stage in its development. Party made respectable was something different from parties which were perceived as temporary aberrations from a normal and healthy unanimity, and this remains true even if the respectable parties acted in the same way as disreputable factions. When Englishmen came to accept party, new forces were created within the political culture. The "what happened?" of history is most helpfully answered by explaining what people *thought* they were doing. When people accepted party conflict, the change was analogous to the waining of the millennial hope—imperfect reality had to be taken as the model of an imperfect future. Although ideas about party in government and opposition could never have prospered in isolation from events, the direction of influence was also reversed, with political activity responding to the realm of ideas. Eighteenth-century writers and politicians dared at times to defend parties because they had them and, having once defended them, continued to do so when the parties in opposition seemed to be in danger of extinction, as was the case at mid-century.

Similarly, it can be argued that contemporary descriptions of eighteenth-century parties often assumed a two-party struggle of Whig and Tory which is difficult to reconcile with the facts of politics in most decades of the century. The very party labels, such as "Tory" or "Jacobite", were applied to opponents in an effort to discredit them, and so produced a model of politics by which the citizen was invited to orient himself among the chaotic, shifting battle lines of actual political activity. In more ways than one these ideas and stereotypes about parties assisted in ensuring their survival. The expectations in peoples' minds, then, had a considerable role in maintaining the presence of party as a dominant factor throughout the history of the period, and no explanation of the unprecedented emergence of legitimate parties can exclude the changing opinions and prejudices of the time.

The Whigs and Tories were born of genuine philosophical disagreement, but with the erosion of their differences, they survived their early years largely by accident. While later political systems have banned opposition or, incredibly, have octroyed it by government fiat, Britain did neither. Through a fortuitous combination of events, the Whigs, by doctrine a party meant for opposition, came to court for much of the century. The Tories, on the other hand, lost power in 1714 and thereafter those recognizable as Tories languished long years in opposition, despite the unsuitability of their original principles to the role of a country party. This paradoxical state of affairs did much to force both camps into a common political idiom, and, since passive obedience and the claims of prerogative could find no influential home under such conditions, the idiom was Whiggish. The attenuation of party doctrinal differences through the assimilation of all acceptable positions to a basic Whiggism provided the necessary consensus within which the politically active population could safely quarrel. The events of the century have been felicitously summarized as being the process

• •

whereby the Whig party twice "gave life to its own shadow and bred that curious doppelganger, a constitutional opposition."[2] Thus Englishmen resisted any stifling homogeneity and, safe within the emerging consensus, retained sufficient fuel for conflict. Generations of eighteenth-century political writers, unembarrassed by the bonds uniting members of the political elite, insisted that politics was an affair of Whigs and Tories and cheerfully exaggerated the dangers in their opponents' beliefs.

This they could easily do because a number of the bonds securing stability were quite overlooked in the current opinions that were hostile to party competition. Eighteenth-century politics, in the early decades at least, was an activity in the process of becoming more aristocratic and this in itself was a restraint on divisive conflict. Parliament had by now emerged as the focus of political ambition, thus insuring that competition would grow up within the moderating conventions of that body rather than being rampant "without doors". There were, naturally, some contested elections, but the civilized traditions of Parliament undoubtedly did much to prevent the violence accompanying conflict in other societies. The ruinous regional and ethnic divisions which clouded political development on the Continent were also muted in Britain. When Scotland, for instance, impinged on English politics, the effect seems to have been to unite Englishmen, but rarely was regionalism a major issue. Furthermore, England was independent, always subject to fears of invasion, but spared the emergence from colonial status which poses such difficulties to the growth of constitutional opposition. The relation of the parties to other major groups in the community, such as religious bodies, contributed to limited conflict, but more of this later. Finally, in the crucial years the parties were fairly equal in strength and so neither could expect easily to subdue the other. The Civil War of the seventeenth century had, after all, been inconclusive, except that its aftermath led most Englishmen to accept the monarchy. Dr. Robert Wallace once defended parties in a free government with the observation that while they were no doubt turbulent at times, one could not expect to have just enough of anything and no more. In retrospect, England appears to have come remarkably close to that elusive condition.

In the reigns of William and Anne one heard much of party and little of opposition. This was a time when most ministries were composed both of Whigs and Tories, with royal favour being registered by shifting the balance one way or the other. Much political literature defined the differing principles of the two parties, but it was not always possible to discern Whig or Tory as permanent and coherent units of action, if only because men of both persuasions responded at times to another axis—that of Court and Country. The endless scholarly debate about the relative signifi-cance of this line of cleavage as opposed to that of Whig and Tory has, at least, established that on some issues there was little party cohesion, whatever the stirrings of party loyalty; on the other hand studies of division lists and of activity in the constituencies equally indicate that party was far from being a negligible consideration.[3] The presence of a Country tradition suggests an opposition of sorts, but one which lacked policies. Rather, its members saw themselves as preserving the heritage of English freedom against all assaults of prerogative. Gaining some of its greatest ornaments from men un-concerned with attaining office, the Country tradition provided a home for opponents of corruption and standing armies who de-fended their actions from the rich heritage of the right of resistance rather than any presumptions about forming an alternative govern-ment. Robert Harley might thus refer to opposition as a personal and temporary choice dictated by particular issues, as when he warned that under certain circumstances he might be "provok'd into an Opposition".[4] Now, a mature opposition is one with an acknowledged function and operative most of the time, and a modern system of political parties suggests something far more than the coteries of great men. In the early eighteenth century, England had neither party nor opposition in highly developed form and furthermore, the fluid nature of political life meant that the most respectable basis for opposition, the Country tradition, was a cause different from either Whig or Tory parties. This gap between party and opposition was to be reflected in political ideas for a long time to come.

However complex the actual state of politics, Englishmen found themselves with parties and had to reach some judgement about them. This then was a time when men wondered in what respects, if any, a world inhabited by Whig and Tory might differ from that of Guelf and Ghibelline, the factions of the ancient world or con-temporary European conditions.[5] It was a time too of partisanship, and a pamphlet of 1717, attributed to Matthew Tindal, even sug-gests in the fashion of W. S. Gilbert that everyone adhered to one or another of the parties. Another measure of this feeling came when John Toland reinterpreted Solon's maxim about the *incivisme* of the neutral in time of trouble to insist that in the England of his day all men despised the trimmer.[6]

So strong was the hold of party labels on informed opinion that ordinary vocabulary and political theory alike retained the simple Whig-Tory dichotomy even at the accession of George III, the period plumbed by Sir Lewis Namier's magisterial denial of the relevance of party denominations. Reflective Englishmen might well consult the ancients, and others, because they found themselves committed in large numbers to roles which were forbidden by traditional morality and political wisdom. Many roles, such as that of party follower, were blithely played by those unaware of their significance, but the place of party in early-eighteenth-century thought presented a standing invitation to all to explain why they were so fiercely committed to bodies which seemed to threaten the peace of the state. Traditional political wisdom gave little comfort to the supporters of party, and so the most ardent partisans were normally confined to the expectation that all party distinctions would come to be dissolved in the triumph of their own persuasion. This sentiment was rooted in both parties owing to the rough equality of strength enjoyed by Whigs and Tories until the death of Anne. In this climate of opinion, even Charles Davenant's cruel portrait of the slippery careerist, Tom Double, could bring the retort that his industrious self-promotion was far better than irrational party rage —a conclusion sweetened for many by the fact that such court sycophants strengthened the ministry.[7]

THE CASE AGAINST PARTY

Parties were unacceptable to conventional opinion for a number of reasons. The ample traditional literature on the evils of sedition testified to the overriding importance of national unity at all costs. Nor was the insight with which writers and statesmen perceived the sources of division any indication of approval. Francis Bacon had contemplated an impressive range of potential cleavages without deviating from his insistence that one must understand the disease the better to apply a cure. Courtly cabals might be set at one another's throats as the only feasible alternative to having a king take sides, but this was a far cry from the legitimation of party, however narrowly based. The cultivation of faction was one of the known techniques of preserving one-man rulership, and it might, within the prevailing orthodoxy, go so far as to shore up the weaker faction in the state. England's long-standing international role as the holder of the balance of Europe had sensitized political thinkers to the attraction of a policy of *tertius gaudens,* and the same technique was recognized as having a domestic, short-term application. Country Tories and Old Whig enemies of corruption were adamantly against governing by parties and advocated that ruler's rising above contending parties; to follow the tactics of divide and rule as the normal diet of the constitution was widely condemned as Jesuitical.

An early age would have been inclined to add that such refined statecraft was "Machiavellian" and a few do so still.[8] But Englishmen of the eighteenth century were beginning to know their Machiavelli, and so he appears rather infrequently in discussions of party. For Machiavelli differed profoundly from the majority of political sages by denying the usefulness of factions in a principality, where the making of factions was but the irresponsible resort of a weak prince. In counselling the rulers of monarchies to avoid such dissensions, Machiavelli had added that some divisions were appropriate in the sort of mixed government that eighteenth-century England seemed to be; however, this also raised difficulties, as we shall see.[9]

One reason why the international balance of power did not more strongly commend itself to the treatment of domestic conflict was that the very conditions of a successful international posture were predicated upon internal unity. Thus Bolingbroke, an advocate of the balance of power in Europe, saw no need for a permanent equivalent at home. The politically articulate members of the English polity had long claimed that it was unique in its isolation and so, protected from invasion by the sea, was far less subject to foreign influences than were other European powers. Released from certain external pressures, generations of Englishmen had taken seriously the judgement of the Duke of Rohan, penned in the 1630s, that England could never die except by its own hand, and the surest form of self-murder was the failure to maintain a common front facing Europe. This advice was still quoted well into the second half of the eighteenth century, and rarely were the champions of unity without an example of wars or delicate negotiations which would suffer through disunion. Whig and Tory, Court and Country, and such time-bound distinctions as "English" and "Hanoverian" were all in turn, and sometimes simultaneously, pilloried as the harbingers of diplomatic and economic ruin, demoralization of the armed forces, defeat abroad, and disorder at home.[10] Not even Machiavelli was of any help in answering such charges, for he too had disowned those party struggles which brought with them foreign complications. The hospitality extended by France to the Jacobites dramatized the connexion between party contentions and foreign affairs, and no minister of the Crown was unaware of the advantages of branding opposition forces as having designs against the house of Brunswick.

Walpole expressed this convenient ministerial position when he portrayed his government as the defender of the Hanoverian line against a menacing swarm of Jacobites and Republicans. As early as 1733 John, Lord Hervey, could observe that there were no considerable opponents of the government but other Whigs, and he was no friend to opposition.[11] Nevertheless, while republicanism was obviously an insignificant threat, the bogey of Jacobitism lingered on and with it the argument that disunion might bring the enemies of the succession to power. By 1767 the Jacobite menace could finally provoke the kind of mirth reserved earlier in the century for talk of republicanism, and one writer, with more wit than Latin, observed that the Pretender's cause was certainly spent, there being no reports of any Charlobites in the land. The constraints imposed by foreign involvements were never absent, however, and this reason for unity trumpeted by ministers and proclaimed in speeches from the Throne seems to have caused concern to men who otherwise found good reasons for admiring a state with parties.[12] If parties were to be squared with Britain's place in the world it could best be done, not by disowning Rohan and his message, but by denying that parties prevented the necessary degree of unity. Even some strongly anti-party writings thus admitted that their effect could not be as virulent as commonly supposed, or the nation would long ago have disappeared.[13]

Quite apart from the dangers which conflict posed to the safety of the state, the motives of party men were subject to suspicion. Party was widely equated with "interest", and this for several reasons. Those connexions, otherwise called parties, were sometimes known as "interests"; influential politicians were spoken of as having an interest in their localities, and party members, especially the leaders, were conveniently seen as primarily concerned with promoting their private interests at the expense of the public. Preoccupied, in the words of Halifax, with catching prizes, or with exacting a purely private revenge, individuals were infected with that most dreaded of social diseases—party-madness. It may seem odd, at first glance, why this should be so, since the eighteenth century understood self-interest very well, and, on the whole, refused to condemn it out of hand. Rational self-interest, when directed to securing material prosperity, or better still, preserving what one had, was well launched towards its rendezvous with the public good. But there was something about party which gave offence to the basic individualism of the age, for parties involved something less than the reasonable pursuit of personal satisfaction. Once entwined in the schemes of party, men gave up their reason and consciences to the party managers, staking their personal comfort in an unrestrained effort to satisfy ambitions not properly their own. The ethics of individualism figured in the numerous suggestions about the benefits of a virtuous emulation between subjects, but this normally only made the case for all-party ministries, in the expectation that parties might thereby expire.

An important part of the liberal tradition was its notorious hostility to men acting in concert, and parties stood condemned with other groups. It was this liberal dogma, in fact, which surely accounts for the general failure to recognize parties in public law—a failure noticeable in the history of all states free enough to have parties.[14] It was not then self-interest which was at fault, but the self-interest of the few imposed upon the credulity of the many. There is a certain parallel between the development of the respectability of individual self-interest and the eventual acceptance of party, although it is more a matter of a similar sequence of positions than of identical subject matter. The power of interest was first judged to be, in some degree, inevitable and from there it gradually came to be perceived in increasingly favourable terms. In more or less the same manner, parties were taken by some people to be an ineradicable part of certain forms of government, though not, of course, coeval with human nature. It then became a matter of making the best of a bad situation by canvassing whatever virtues could be salvaged from the presence of parties. In both cases growing approval was the eventual response to a factor which just would not go away. Some eighteenth-century writers, such as Adam Ferguson, seem to have been led to insights about party from their reading of human nature and its basic self-interest.[15] He was, however, in the minority, as wholehearted acceptance of self-interest remained quite compatible with the usual pleas to sink all differences in a common patriotism. At the same time, some perceptive early students of party, e.g., Shaftesbury, were able to see that a universal selfishness was not really its social or psychological root, that indeed the thoroughly selfish man was unlikely to respond to such demands for co-operative activity. The point, put this way, was far more effective than the popular but woolly distinction between parties "from interest" and those "from principle".

Attempts to mobilize opposition were thwarted by arguments and prejudices drawn from the above description of two different sorts of parties. Parties from interest were presumably peopled by disconsolate office-seekers, differing from the men in power, not by their desire to preserve the constitution or to check harmful policies, but only by their failure to share in the spoils of office. It was generally assumed that such an opposition would harass a ministry and prevent the management of public business; it was more difficult to make a plausible case for their being dangerous to the political system, especially since constitutional conventions gave no reason to suppose that the most ambitious party could force itself upon an unwilling sovereign. For, while there were circumstances when elements of opposition successfully "stormed the closet", making themselves indispensable to the king, he retained the constitutional right to choose whomever he wanted for his advisors. Fox, in the crisis which followed the defeat of his East-India Bill, could rightly complain that Pitt's Ministry was the first since the Revolution to be retained in the face of a hostile House of Commons. But this was more a tribute to successful management of the House than to any legal restraints on the king's power to choose ministers. Responsible government had yet to arrive, and the claim of a parliamentarian of the Augustan age that there was no necessary connexion between a new parliament and a new ministry remained formally true.[16] There were reins, then, on ambition, and politicians who merely wanted office had normally to adopt a placatory attitude. Bolingbroke and later the Rocking-hamite party had gone beyond this ambition, presuming to claim office as their right and as a body, but neither had enjoyed any remarkable success.

If opposition managed somehow to escape the charge of a trivial quest for personal honour, it courted the more serious charge of harbouring seditious designs. The problem here was that the parties lacked programmes that differed significantly on specific issues, and so "principles" tended to mean constitutional doctrines, not day-to-day policies. It became a nice point whether it was more admirable to be venal and narrowly ambitious but loyal to the constitution, or fanatically devoted to principles inimical to the present establishment. In either event, one must not attack the king personally, nor was it easy to accuse him of being misled by his ministers—kings disliked being given the title of fool almost as much as that of knave.

PARTIES IN THE BALANCED CONSTITUTION

Before tracing the emergence of some of the early stages in the respectability of party, two major factors in the eighteenth-century setting must be explored. These are the conventional perception of the constitution and the relevance of the religious issue. Although one might suppose that the first might contribute to, the second militate against, an appreciation of party conflict, the actual situation was quite the reverse of this. The constitution established by the Revolution and sanctified throughout most of the eighteenth century consisted, in essence, of the ideal mixture of the principles of monarchy, aristocracy and democracy—or so it was supposed.

While the English constitution leaned more towards monarchy than had that of republican Rome, it was thereby better able to preserve itself, since the function of the king was to prevent a direct confrontation between the nobility and the populace. The theory postulated a certain independence on the part of each of the three main organs of English government—king, lords and commons—combined with the useful characteristic of their checking one another should any one of these three estates or orders presume to overbalance the other two. Normally it was assumed that all would co-operate in order to expedite public business, without any impediment to the proper functioning of each organ.

The problem for an acceptance of party and opposition lay, of course, in grafting them on to the different scheme of a constitutional balance between the estates. For the theory of balanced government postulated a tension which had little to do with intra-estate proceedings, except for the fact that the king's ministry intruded on Parliament. Indeed some of Walpole's writers rejected calls for a general place bill precisely on the grounds that, even with the great officers of state still in Parliament, it would reduce understanding between the legislature and the executive, thus creating "a continual Opposition".[17] The use of influence within Parliament was thus defended as a means of maintaining relative harmony among the components of the balanced constitution. On the other hand, Bolingbroke's *Craftsman* called for limitations on the disposal of places in the name of the independence of the House of Commons, not as a means of bringing party competition into Parliament.

It was widely assumed, nevertheless, that mixed government somehow invited opposition and even parties. John Perceval, the future Earl of Egmont, had implied as much when, in 1743, he wrote that opposition was not unusual in systems where the people were represented in the legislature, and numerous later writers carried the point to the length of assuming that parties too were properly part of the picture. Swift, writing at the beginning of the century, and John Adams writing at the end were agreed that unless the parties in a mixed government were limited in their influence by constitutional safeguards, the state would succumb to faction. Both writers referred expressly to "parties", and both sometimes meant by the term Whigs and Tories, or their equivalent. However, their historical illustrations were full of references to the struggles of the nobles and commons in the republics of the ancient world; for it was these, and not the clash of Whig and Tory, which fitted the tradition of the balanced constitution. Swift accepted the tension between different orders of men while condemning, here and elsewhere, the parties of his day. It so happened that the social divisions of the ancient politics corresponded to those state organs between which power was divided. Swift experienced no difficulty in referring to these divisions simultaneously as powers in the state, orders of men and parties, applauding their conflict, if properly channelled, while in the same breath dismissing the parties surrounding the King.[18] Other Englishmen exaggerated the constitutional opinions of Whig and Tory, in part, because it was convenient to depict the parties as favouring different parts of the constitution. If Tories could be seen as friends to prerogative and Whigs as the guardians of popular liberties, then the parties might better be understood and accommodated within the balanced constitution.

Adams, who wrote a learned hymn of praise to the principle of balance, drew both upon classical experience and upon such works of Harrington as *Oceana* and the dialogue *Politicaster*. As a man of affairs, aware of a full century of party struggle in England, Adams was still a captive of the literary tradition of mixed government. Here, in describing the Spartan government, he approved of the taming of the contending interests of town and country by separating them in different assemblies. Turning to the Athens of Solon—the source of so much eighteenth-century rhetoric about partisanship—he discovered parties espousing different constitutional principles and divided as well by economic and regional differences.[19] He assumed that these again were different orders of men who translated their social differences into conflicting constitutional views. By contrast, Whigs and Tories were apparently only expressing differences in temperament. Adams anticipated that in any unicameral state the assembly would contain four parties—those representing the principles of monarchy, aristocracy, democracy and a mixture of the previous three. It was in this spirit that he insisted on different assemblies embodying the ambitions of the various orders, and confessed his temptation to propose a third assembly for the United States which might speak for the executive power and, presumably, the monarchical principle.[20] As always, Adams sought a fruitful tension between the parts of a constitution, not within them, and it is in this sense that one must interpret his famous admission about the inevitability of parties in all states. So strong was the association of parties in this sense with mixed government that it is sometimes difficult to know what connexion, if any, was intended with the sort of party divisions familiar to the unlearned.

Thus when Thomas Pownall, later Governor of the Massachusetts Bay Colony, declared his dislike for mixed government because it bred parties,[21] it was not entirely certain whether he was stating a causal generalization or just citing one of the properties of those government called "mixed". Since Pownall followed general practice in equally describing ancient orders and modern connexions as parties, his frequently-cited references to the case for party competition are less valuable then one might suppose. This confusion or ambiguity informs much of the political writing not narrowly partisan or closely related to current issues, such as the otherwise fascinating work of Adam Ferguson, for instance. It explains why various people in the Old Whig tradition might admire Machiavelli's thoughts on conflict and still not find any way of applying the moral to the England of their day. Although Machiavelli's account of the popular party in ancient Rome might sometimes find eighteenth-century application in support of the Country case, it was stretching a point. At times the Court journalists were led to assert that a balanced constitution required no balance between parties, for that would be to share the public power between the friends and enemies of the constitution, a point particularly stressed by William Arnall.[22] However, this involved no clear contrast between parties ancient and modern. Robert Wallace was then unusually careful when he insisted that one must not pass judgement on ancient parties as though they shared the "principles and manners" of his own enlightened age, and took Hume to task for failing to make the distinction.[23]

Classical learning might supply an appreciation of the virtues of class struggle without closing the way to a realistic assessment of eighteenth-century politics, as the work of Edward Spelman indicates. However, the more usual result of familiarity with the classical antecedents of the balanced constitution was to create expectations unfulfilled by the English political system. Nostalgia for a form of conflict quite impossible in English conditions persisted into the nineteenth century, as witnessed by the Reverend Robert Hall's lament at the party warfare of his day:

> The purest times of the Roman republic were distinguished by violent dissentions; but they consisted in the jealousy of the several *orders* of the state among each other; on the ascendence of the patricians on the one side, and the plebians on the other; a useful struggle which maintained the balance and equipoise of the constitution. In the progress of corruption things took a turn; the permanent parties which sprang from the fixed principles of government were lost, and the citizens arranged themselves under the standard of particular leaders, being banded into factions. . . .

The useful jealousy of the separate orders is extinct,
being all melted down and blended into one mass of corruption. The House of Commons looks with no jealousy
on the House of Lords, nor the House of Lords on the
House of Commons; the struggle in both is maintained
by the ambition of powerful individuals and families. . . .[24]

One might add that rarely since the days of *Ashby vs. White* in
the reign of Anne had the significant political conflicts been between the two houses. The power of the eighteenth-century House
of Lords was that of some influential individuals; it had not been
a corporate power. Until the nineteenth century, party played a
reduced role in that house, since so many peers simply supported
the government of the day.

An inherent tension between orders in the state could even be
accepted as the undisputed foundation of "political science" by
R. J. Thornton, that compiler of political wisdom, and he accepted
the institution of the opposition party. However, time was getting
the better of the balanced constitution. From the time of the "eco-
nomical" reforms of 1782-3 and the continuing constitutional discussion over "influence", it was becoming clear to an increasing
number of observers that the balance of the constitution lay in the
House of Commons with all interests having to contend for influence there. Thus the powers being balanced were focused in a
single body within which the modern opposition functioned, and
this recognition involved an enhanced understanding of British
politics embracing not only the formal relations between the parts
of the constitution but also the extra-legal groups sheltered by the
House of Commons and essential to its operation. At a time when
the balanced constitution was being deserted by men of all persuasions, Gould Francis Leckie condemned mixed government for its
vacillating counsels and party jostlings. The riposte of *The Edinburgh Review* managed to explain both how the constitution worked
without any balance of estates and why parties were a necessary
part of it.[25] The rise of the House of Commons and its recognition
as more than merely "independent" contributed mightily to the
respectability of those parties which organized its business. This
special status for the popular chamber was not the only route
through which an appreciation of party could emerge, for early
defenders of party had managed simultaneously to believe in
mixed government. But by clearing away false expectations about
a fictitious balance of orders, the theory of the constitution could
be founded on a new ideal—a balance of parties, truly parties in
the modern sense.

THE PLACE OF RELIGION

The merit of the theory of the balanced constitution was that it drew upon a long tradition of relating the formal organs of government to major groups of people in the society at large. The corresponding defect was its relegating the bulk of the population to the third estate For this obscured the nation's most important divisions which were within the commons and not between them and the peerage. It was, nevertheless, a theory of politics, however, imperfect, not just one of public law, and so it was distinct from a separation of powers, however much the two theories became intertwined. But there was another way of connecting eighteenth-century parties to forces in society without reference to any fictions derived from antiquity. One might simply indicate how various interests, other than the orders of king, nobility, clergy and people, were protected by the parties. For these purposes "Court" and Country" or the later "Government" and "Opposition" would not do, for they were functional labels, admirable for designating the pattern of conflict and the roles of participants, but incapable of supplying bases of loyalty in the same manner as Whig and Tory.

Despite the aristocratic leadership on both sides, the Whigs and the Tories did receive their support from somewhat different sectors of the community, and while their constitutional differences of emphasis were stressed long after they had ceased to be very important, contemporaries also recognized social differences between the two camps. The alliance between the City and the Whigs and the strength of the landed interest in the Tory party, in the early part of the century, have been substantiated both by modern scholarship and by the testimony of the participants. A Whig tract of 1715 assured readers that the interests of traders would not be shut out of the House of Commons simply because of the landed property qualifications introduced in 1711, for there remained an adequate supply of good Whigs who were eligible to represent the monied men and the boroughs. This writer argued that the monied interest and the Whigs had in fact "as deep a footing in the *Landed,* as their *October,* and all their Clubs put together"[26]—an observation again not grossly inconsistent with modern findings. The admitted respectability of both landed and trading interests did not suffice to entrench party as an institution, if only because the two interests were not perfectly distinct. Land and trade did clash, especially over taxation, and had done so since the naming of the two interests at the Restoration. However, throughout most of the eighteenth century it remained fashionable to regret any tension between them and to attribute it to divisions fomented by cynical statecraft.

So economic lines of cleavage did not serve to render party in any way a reflection of genuine and necessary social conflict. Religion was another matter, for unlike the case of economic categories, membership in religious confessions, despite the evasions allowed by the practice of "occasional conformity", tended to be exclusive. By contrast, the same person might be a member of both landed and trading interests. Furthermore, while the presence of different economic interests might invite the advice to pursue one's material interests to the neglect of the irrational spirit of party, this course of action was less feasible for the English Protestant Dissenters, still subject to certain civil disabilities, even after the Toleration Act of 1689. With such people it was unconvincing to urge that they sink all unique concerns in the fate of the English nation—the laws of England prevented this—making it difficult for instance for Dissenters to hold public office, although, if otherwise qualified, they could vote.

It is no accident, then, that rather a large proportion of the perceptive analyses of party policies were concerned, in some measure, with the religious question. Here were large numbers of people distinguished from the rest of the population by arrangements which required a political solution. Sometimes a sensitivity to the prevailing intolerance produced a latitudinarian perspective which stood prepared to accept, without embracing, a number of doctrines and, in politics, more than one party. Such was the author of a pamphlet at the beginning of the Hanoverian era who noted the prevailing misuse of sectarian terms of abuse, coupled with a misleading assumption that there was an orthodox and properly national position both in politics and in religion. What the term "schism" connoted in religious affairs, "faction" covered in politics, always with the assumption that factions were detrimental to the public good. Such views foundered on the fact that "everyone is orthodox to himself".[27]

This sentiment was most fully expressed by Shute Barrington, a doughty if sometimes unpopular champion of Dissent for thirty years. However, the feeling of outrage at the common practice of calling the pursuit of rights "factious" was one which characterized the public statements of many Dissenters. The fact that Dissenters were a minority not fully citizens made their plight very different from the occasional inconveniences suffered by influential economic interests. Land and trade were said to be one, and most of those involved usually accepted that assumption; but the Dissenters were noticeably set apart from the rest of the nation and so had to contemplate a political strategy for the duration of their domestic exile. The problem of an appropriate electoral strategy for a permanent minority was then a new one—such minorities had not previously been accorded an opportunity to fend for themselves within a party system. If the estates of the realm could not provide a special status for such a group, it was normally excluded from peaceful competition. The eighteenth century created new possibilities, but also problems.

Barrington, a Whig politician, advocated making every effort to bind Dissent to the cause of that party in the expectation that the reward would be the necessary remedial legislation. His numerous opponents argued against a strong political presence for Dissent, insisting that they had few interests which distinguished them from their fellows and none should be admitted in the form of an exclusive reliance upon the Whigs. When this was not an eighteenth-century version of the clash between the serpent of policy and the dove of Godliness, the alternative was the cultivation of both parties. For, while disagreement with Barrington might dictate a general distrust of parties, it might equally well suggest the conclusion that they would maximize results by playing one party off against the other. Dissenters should not deprive themselves of the benefits of being courted by both Whigs and Tories, to which end they should follow the rule of "keeping a due Balance among the other and greater Parties".[28] Contrasted with Barrington's frank partisanship, this was the equivalent to the American labour philosophy of Gompersism, or the practice of rewarding political friends and withholding support from the unco-operative. Basing their argument on Whig performance in the past, the advocates of this position pressed the point that the Whigs, with whom the Dissenters were generally associated, would lack any urgent incentive to be of assistance if it were clear that the Nonconformists had nowhere else to turn. This strategy was dependent on establishing the numerical weight of the Dissenting interest—a topic of considerable debate during the 1730s—and, of course, on there being two parties between which to choose.

Barrington's analysis of the prospects for Dissent also involved the continuation of party competition, not because he contemplated deviating from his Whig loyalties, but because he attributed the maintenance of political freedom, toleration and the balance of Europe to party conflict—a fascinating, if occasionally bewildering concatenation of factors. Basic to Barrington's argument was the eighteenth-century faith in the efficacy of balance. Not only did he apply it to the constitution and political parties, but also to the relations between various religious bodies. This was the model of toleration known to the previous century as the *concordia discors,* a system of mutual jarrings in which stability followed from the checking of any aggressive group by all the rest. While calculated to bring government to a standstill, it was an attractive scheme for religious toleration where nothing more was required than the maintenance of the *status quo.* More familiar to Dissenters than cynical strategies for balancing court parties, the *concordia discors* between groups of private men outside government surely provided Barrington with his model for the political system as a whole. Other Dissenters, lacking Barrington's sophistication, might still come at matters from the opposite direction, arguing for a balance between religious groups based on the experience of civil parties:

> the different Parties amongst us are, in the Hand of Providence, instrumental of a great deal of good. I have read of some States, where different Parties have been maintained for politic Reasons to keep a Ballance and support the publick Peace; and why it may not be something like it in the Case of Religion, I cannot see.[29]

The great push to repeal the Test and Corporation Acts petered out in 1739 and the contribution of Dissent to public awareness of the virtues of conflict ended for a time. The persistence of the Dissenting viewpoint lingered, however, in the political writings of Joseph Priestley, a member of that generation of radicals still attached to the orthodoxy of the balanced constitution. Although prone to the reigning confusion in sorting out the various balances of estates, powers of government and parties, Priestley displayed very clearly the politically sophisticated Dissenter's characteristic acceptance of party. In the course of making the case against a general system of public education, he argued that any one interest controlling the government, and hence the schools, would be in a position to impose its values on the rest of the nation. Should the commons, nobility or court be placed in this position of power, the constitution would undoubtedly come to favour that order. Similarly, he saw that balance, supposedly existing "among the several political and religious parties" as posited upon shielding education from the control of any one persuasion. Especially dangerous was control by what was ambiguously called the "Court", for it would prevent "that opposition from the country, which is . . . so essential to the liberties of England . . .".[30] The Dissenters were, in essence, a country party, but differed from the voice of the whole people by virtue of their having interests distinct from the rest of the nation. This difference made the competition between political parties an important instrument in securing their ends. Having these interests quite separate from those followed by office-seeking parties, they might still lend substance to the competition for office by injecting a specific issue into the party struggle.

Burke expressed relief that the "great parties" of the seventeenth century were no more, just as Hume had assailed the modern parties of religious principle, but religion was not therefore irrelevant to party competition or the acceptance of it. The boast that democracy and sundry good things have their origin in the travail of English Dissent is an old one, and sometimes the claim has embraced party respectability, although this has never really been explained.[31] The Dissenters' major need in the field of political argument was to establish that increasing the opportunities to express interests would not threaten the stability of the state. At a time—early in the eighteenth century—when the institution of party conflict lacked an understanding public, some Dissenters found in their own plight a basis for that understanding. This was not a revival of the old conflict feared by Burke, but a basis for the new.

THE THEORY OF OPPOSITION

The rationale for opposition which emerged in the 1730s was narrowly confined by the need to avoid the appearance of treason. In theory most government writers accepted the practice of opposing, on principle, bad measures; they differed from the opposition in denying that their measures were bad and in the fact that they added various additional qualifications regarding the manner in which this opposition should be carried on. Spokesmen for Walpole's Ministry, however autocratic, could not deny the right of resistance upon which the existing regime was founded, and it never being in the interest of a government to remind subjects too frequently of this shadowy prerogative, the sensible thing was to concede that a bad ministry would rightly have its measures opposed—but not all its measures, and not all the time, nor with a view to supplanting the men involved and not by a formed opposition, but one as much as possible speaking spontaneously for the people. Writing against Lord Bute and his unpopular accession to power, Dr. John Butler once wrote that the power of a minister should be "natural, constitutional, gently asserted, and generally admitted", if the minister were to be spared a vigorous opposition. These same criteria were applied to opposition itself, if one makes allowance for oppositions being self-appointed, but in the case of the opposition the conditions were more difficult to meet. Not that Walpole's writers were ungenerous, for excepting Whigs such as Lord Hervey, who was consistently harsh with opposition claims, the Government was surprisingly accommodating to the notion that parties were to be expected in English government.

The use of "Opposition" as a term denoting a more or less permanent body seems to have been formulated in the years following the organization of the Camarilla against Walpole in 1726. Government-subsidized newspapers made extensive use of it in the next few years, even drawing upon the astronomical origins of the word to indulge in vast cosmological generalizations about the ubiquity of opposition throughout creation.[32] Such efforts did not necessarily constitute a major concession, since anything so all-pervasive had no special status in the England of their day; however, due regard was paid to the inevitability of political conflict. The Government position is particularly interesting in that Bolingbroke was arguing at this time for opposition with a view to putting an end to party. By contrast, the Government hacks seemed to foresee a longer life for parties, and this despite the fact that it was opposition, a general principle with respectable antecendents capable of constitutional dress, that was easier to defend. Party, on the other hand, was but one possible expedient for expressing opposition, although its value in consolidating a ministry had already been shown.

The election of 1734 afforded an opportunity to define the bounds of conflict, and again the Government, without encouraging opposition, seemed to extend a generous mandate to conflict in general. A pamphlet, sometimes (but dubiously) attributed to Henry Fielding, went further than most:

> Where an unrestrain'd Freedom and Liberty is allow'd, Sectaries in Religion and Parties in Politicks, whose Interests are as opposite as their Tenets and Opinions, will abound; and thus it is impossible for any Administration whatsoever, in such a State, so to ... accommodate their Conduct, as to gain the Good-liking and Affection of all the different Parties. The utmost within the Compass of human Nature, in such a nice and ticklish Station, is so to maintain the *internal Balance* between the great Variety of Interests; as to preserve the Government stable upon the broadest Basis; to attach a Majority of the Nation's Strength to the governing Power, that the Constitution may never be liable to any destructive Changes and Revolutions.[33]

The argument is unusual in its description of an administration trying to maximize its support with all groups—an ambition only justified if all of these interests were somehow legitimate. Nonjurors, Jacobites, republicans or disappointed place-seekers had always been beyond the pale and presumably they stayed there. So the statement was an exaggeration, but still an impressive description of a pluralistic society with a highly responsive administration. Pondering the effects of tolerating a great variety of active interests, the writer concluded that it would ultimately be less disruptive than repression. At the same time he condemned, as did most social commentators during the century, any exacerbation of tensions between the landed and trading interests. Presumably with an eye on the activities of Protestant Dissenters, he equally rejected the tactics of "playing . . . one Party against another" as productive of that sort of political distemper which the age called a "national Hyppo".

The tract reflects Walpole's good-humoured acceptance of organized diversity, combined with the serene belief that only his own party could be trusted with the care of English freedom. The portait of social pluralism was drawn from the lofty vantage-point of men in office who found it convenient to mollify otherwise unruly subjects. It was not acceptable for these subjects to take advantage of divisions by flirting with a party out of power. Here then was an acceptance of parties as a normal part of the political process, which simultaneously minimized that opposition which might normally be inferred from their presence. Walpole's Whigs were themselves a party—much the best organized one—and so they had most reason to defend the institution. However, the diversity of interests and parties was usually seen as a consequence, not the cause, of that general freedom which Englishmen enjoyed, a freedom much emphasized by an administration accused of trying to establish tyranny founded on corruption, riot acts and excise bills.

The realignment of parties and the broadening of the Government which followed Walpole's resignation was the occasion for the most searching dissection of opposition that had occurred up to that time. The most significant outcome of the flood of party writings was that no major persuasion was prepared absolutely to disavow the weapon of opposition; under the appropriate circumstances, which varied according to the loyalties of the writer, opposition could be the virtuous course. The literature generated by the Pulteney-Carteret following group, now ensconced in power, was aimed at justifying their previous opposition to Walpole, while denying to others the ladder which they had successfully employed. The Government and the moderate members of the new opposition agreed on the formula "measures, not men", for no one could deny that there would at times be ministerial designs obnoxious to most of the people. This common ground had been consistently explored by Walpole's writers when they objected to the practice of forming parties in opposition "not to Things, but to Persons".[34] This was not the position of Bolingbroke. He sought to bulwark an initial assault on measures by one on the persons in power, with the eventual intention of assuming that power. A comparable view, though less subtle in its argument, was sometimes put forward by the "broad-bottom" group of discontented Whigs —those excluded from the reconstruction of the Ministry. The Tories on the other hand, the men so often libelled as Jacobites and enemies of the constitution, limited themselves to claiming a right to continued opposition—a position which fell within the tolerable limits of conduct, however much it might be condemned as a factious doctrine.

Adherence to the rule of "measures, not men", supplies a good indicator of views of party. Bolingbroke, in quest of his patriot king, and the broad-bottoms, involved in a less dignified scramble for office, were both interested in capturing power rather than with justifying the continuation of party into the foreseeable future. The Tories, on their part, joined to their reasoned treatment of the limits of justifiable opposition a number of pamphlets which broached the necessity of accepting party divisions as the only practicable alternative to an eventual extinction of such odious distinctions. Their arguments extended at times to cautious suggestions that those called Jacobites might eventually "partake of that more moderate and justifiable Party called an Opposition".[35] It was left for the broad-bottoms to regret that the party labels, such as "Tory", continued in use.[36] This group, a faction if ever there was one, described party as an evil and insisted that opposition would expire with party. While the latter lived, opposition remained on occasional and necessary corrective for the constitution, but never an indispensable part of good government.

The new Ministry, not satisfied with explaining their recent conversion to the view that opposition should be mild or negligible, also assumed a position on party. Those who had accepted offices under the Crown needed both to explain why they were acceptable and why others were not. An answer to the first might be supplied by citing the king's well-known right to choose his advisers; the second answer gained support from the unceasing barrage of pamphlets citing the dangerous principles of those out of power. The Jacobites, as one Tory wryly remarked, "are become a most necessary Generation to all Administrations".[37] In the course of resisting calls for a "national ministry", the Government writers might go a long way towards making party organization respectable on the part both of government and of opposition. The prevailing use of "influence",—largely in the form of places—by which the party in power retained its cohesion, was a subject of genuine concern to most of those who did not benefit, and a strong talking-point for every opposition. Corruption had been linked to parties before, and sometimes to the credit of party, as when *The Craftsman* declared factious disorder to be superior to settled tyranny.[38]

In the early 1740s the Government undertook to defend both influence and party. Noting the circulation of division lists and the opposition habit of recording the distribution of those places which cemented the Government majorities, an Administration writer complained that the cohesion of the Treasury Benches was exaggerated, while the ties securing the effectiveness of the Opposition were quite neglected. It should be recognized that the leaders of the malcontents employed

> that kind of Influence, which is in their power to balance
> that of the Court. Yet after all, what is this, better or
> worse, than avowing that amongst a free People, Influence
> is requisite to the Views of all Parties, and consequently
> no more Corruption in one, than in the other.

This writer scouted the practice of William III in governing by coalitions and assured the reader that such schemes would never again be tried.[39] From the broad-bottom group this provoked the retort that the Government was presuming both to unite England and to prevent the broadening of the Government—a seeming contradiction. If the Whigs in power had deigned to answer, it would have undoubtedly been to say that there was a difference between gaining singleness of purpose in the counsels of government and satisfying all dissident groups. Clearly that party wished to do only the first.

John Perceval's giant tract *Faction Detected*, the publication which more than any other had triggered the paper war, is another good index of Government attitudes towards party. In damning the current opposition as factious, Perceval tried to distinguish between those "great parties" of Whig and Tory and the two kinds of factions then known—those led by Jacobites and those led by Republicans. Occasionally lapsing into an identification of Tory and Jacobite, he still displayed some reluctance to condemn those Hanoverian Tories then in opposition. As it was, his unclear distinction between the Opposition and its leaders allowed him to maintain a useful ambiguity as to what parties were legitimate. The great debate of the 1740s ended, and there followed a period of close to twenty years during which party strife was less prominent. The controversy described had reaffirmed that opposition, as distinct from violent resistance to tyranny, did have a place in political life, while Government writers had moved opinion closer to the possibility that parties were natural, and certainly difficult to avoid, if not yet really respectable. Party and opposition had yet to meet to any considerable degree in a theory which defined an opposition as rightly mobilized as an alternative government. Bolingbroke had written of such a vision but with severe qualifications as to the nature of the party—it was to be spokesman of the nation, in a way reminiscent of older ideas of resistance to tyranny—and with a time limit on its effective life, successful patriots needing no opposition. For the most part, Walpole's successors, the Pelhams, had little to say about party. For, being comparatively unchallenged, they had few occasions to argue the point. Meanwhile the malcontents understandably laboured the merits of opposition.

One important outcome of the reconstruction period was that the acknowledged difference between "opposition" and "faction" was leading to a further distinction between "party" and "faction". These two terms remained subject to confusion even after the Rockingham party rejected the assumption that it was factious to oppose men as well as measures. However, as early as the 1740s, party was already dissociated from faction by many writers—a change in usage and in opinion that long eluded Samuel Johnson and other dictionary-makers. Faction was associated with a single-minded pursuit of office and was also applicable to men already in office, depending upon their behaviour.[40] "Party" more frequently carried the connotation of a union based on principle, although it was not yet widely appreciated that these principles might dictate striving for office.

DISSOLUTION AND REVIVAL

The years of the Pelhams and of Chatham saw party strife at a low ebb, with opposition almost nonexistent. This was especially so after the death in 1751 of Frederick, Prince of Wales, who, as usual with one of his rank, had been a focus for disaffection.[41] The calm continued until the troubled era of John Wilkes and his various causes. This temporary abatement of political conflict had an interesting theoretical by-product. Unburdened by its unlovely presence, men regretted the passing of opposition, and in some quarters party itself took on a new aura of virtue, mixed now with that tempering of abuse fitting on the occasion of a death.

James Ralph, who wrote several of the spirited, but short-lived, opposition journals, reflected the change in tone in the development from *The Remembrancer* of 1747 to his *Protester* of 1753. The latter communicates a growing alarm at that calm which could signal the triumph of corruption and a bloodless tyranny. By 1753 he had reached the stage of advocating what was then known as a "formed" opposition, disciplined, unanimous and based on party. His excuse was one which had served earlier attempts to thwart corruption: one could only prepare for bad times during those reigns sufficiently liberal that they afforded an opportunity to organize; later would be just too late. This argument, which had always been invoked in the name of place bills, was now placed at the service of a call for opposition which presumably would be permanent, and this quality of anticipation was precisely what had been lacking in the pleas for opposition to bad measures. A journalist such as Ralph was less preoccupied with the specific questions of policy, such as the "Jew Bill", which filled other journals, than with the general desirability—even necessity—of effective opposition. The very abstractness of his approach encouraged him to consider the way in which opposition might be linked to such blessings as freedom of the press. This sort of observation was rare in the writings of those chiefly interested in wresting power away from its possessors, although several other short-lived publications written against the Pelhams, and later Chatham, had the same tendency. Other men, further removed from day-to-day issues, showed the same capacity to ponder the importance of party and opposition, but Ralph's work had the virtue of being an argument more accessible to the public than, say, Spelman's essay on the Roman constitution.

The concern for an effective opposition even characterized some of the pamphlets written for Chatham while he was in power, indicating that while a holiday from party activity would not generate a great deal of overt sentiment in favour of conflict—ideas about party have always been most responsive to major tides of activity—it could occur in various quarters. Horace Walpole spoke for men of more than one persuasion when he recorded with fascinated horror the major fact of the absence of conflict. In this case he was concerned specifically with the state of Parliament in 1751 and its prostration before the Pelhams:

> Opposition, which had lasted from the days of Queen Elizabeth, and even the distinctions of parties having in a manner ceased at this period ... all the factions which had distracted King William, possessed Queen Anne, and ridiculed the House of Hanover; and the Babel of parties that had united to demolish Walpole, and separated again to pursue their private interests; all were now sunk into a dull mercenary subjection to two brothers. ...[42]

This cessation of principled and steady opposition did not, in fact, signal the onset of tyranny. Without any systematic rethinking of political ideas, the sixties would see the growth of a body of shared opinion on the respectability of party and opposition. George III and his dislike of party distinctions only encouraged sentiment favourable to them. Already in the 1750s the literature accompanying the rise of Chatham was ambivalent about political conflict. This was a time when opposition formed within ministries and the loyalties of the pamphlet-writers became difficult to identify. The prevailing opportunism contributed to a situation where the merits of conflict gained currency in political argument, although Chatham placed himself above the fray, refusing to tolerate party after the fashion of Robert Walpole. From the fall of Newcastle until 1770 there were six ministries, and opinions about the legitimacy of opposition became adaptable to circumstances. All groups could anticipate the eventual need of appealing to the rights of opposition and this included Newcastle, who, on his resignation in 1756, required instruction in the nature of the institution.[43] Understandably, none of the various connexions, including that of Rockingham, to whom Burke contributed his eloquence, was as enthusiastic about opposition when in power. If few writers were prepared to indulge in uncritical admiration, the conventional position had become that of lamenting the defects of party, emphasizing their inevitability, and cautioning that their activities must be rendered as moderate as possible. This need not involve anything more than a cynicism about politicians and parties which is probably as characteristic of our own day as it was of the eighteenth century.

Of course there was Burke, lending to the ambitions of the Marquis of Rockingham's following a dignity which far transcended the immediate issues. Certainly Burke better described the nature of parties than had most of his predecessors, many of whom accepted party as inevitable, said so in print and relied upon the contest between parties to neutralize the defects of each. Too often, from such mechanical premises it was judged unnecessary to dwell upon the nature of party—it sufficed to know that there were more than one, always allowing that there was a difference between a fronde and a constitutional opposition and that no case was made for the former. Writers who overcame conventional prejudice and swallowed the idea of party conflict were tempted to do so whole, and might then treat the contending groups as though they were weights in a balance. This dictated nothing more than the presence of two parties so that opposed forces might be roughly equal, but no qualitative considerations necessarily entered the picture. Shedding old ideas to embrace the value of conflict remained compatible

with a failure to distinguish clearly between faction and a more
respectable political union. This was the position of the many
writers who had accepted parties only with reluctance. To see
parties as antidotes to diseases for which they were, at least in
part, responsible, was no great improvement in understanding over
the opinion that they were simply poisonous.[44] Burke did more than
this.

To record that others did so as well need not reduce Burke's
stature; it would be very surprising if England had lacked any
others with both the political interests and the theoretical capacity
to make that difficult passage beyond party names and party slogans
to contemplate their functions.[45] Burke's classic defence of party
may not have changed the views of many public men immediately,
but it came to serve as a convenient point of reference for others
who wished an authority for their own acceptance of it. While one
encounters more defences of party in the years just prior to 1770
than in the early 1770s, endorsements of party competition came
thereafter with increasing frequency. Various factors are responsible
for this, including the fact that one finds both Fox and Pitt, the
Younger, accepting opposition in the form in which it then existed
—the former proclaiming in the House of Commons that he had
always been a party man, the latter more guarded, but prepared
to subsidize literature explaining and justifying the institution of
opposition. A more direct confrontation came before the fall of
Lord North when John Courtenay described "opposition of parties"
as a "Revolution principle" and was chided by Richard Brinsley
Sheridan only because he had described the Opposition as but a
useful "drag-chain".[46]

Party after Burke is the story of a journey towards enshrinement
in the formal constitution, a journey interrupted only slightly by the
strains imposed by a weak and frustrated opposition. There were,
of course, coalitions, presumably above party, but in the 1780s
such marriages of convenience were more on the defensive than
the notion of party conflict itself. The remainder of the eighteenth
century was unable to add startling new dimensions to the understanding of party, if only because political practice had not yet
evolved into the modern mass party. Eighteenth-century party was
a matter of sentiment and influence, not wholly without organization—especially after the election of 1784—but still largely dependent upon alliances between handfuls of prominent men. So the
pamphlets asked why politicians clubbed together, not how they
were organized.

The two major developments of the late eighteenth century were
the clear affirmation that parties expedited public business in Parlia-

ment—a point put very clearly, for instance, by the journalist William Combe—and some insights regarding the role of parties "without doors". Politicians in and out of power had long condemned any apparent departure from fixed principles in the interests of electoral success,[47] and so observations about the place of party in the country rarely went beyond references to providing the electorate with alternatives. The business of informing the people about current issues played quite a modest part in electoral activity, and was limited by uncontested elections, lingering reservations about the propriety of pledges and the resulting generality of election addresses. Thus even in the early nineteenth century the people's vigilance was more often seen as directed to protecting their liberties than to expressing preferences about policy. The power of public opinion was widely noted after 1790, but it was left to nineteenth-century thinkers, such as Frederick Grimke in America, to put the case for educating a mass electorate through parties.[48]

A measure of the hold that party and opposition had gained is evident in the bitter days of 1797 leading to the withdrawal of Fox's Opposition in protest at Pitt's high-handed conduct of the war. Publications supporting the Government and having no great regard for Fox, still insisted that the French should not misinterpret the tensions in Parliament and in the country. For had he been in office, Fox would have followed very much the policies of Pitt, while even faction and civil war were "temperate evils" in England.[49] One reaction to the secession from Parliament was that Fox had sullenly deserted his post and that even were a change of ministers advisable, their replacements were now nowhere to be found.[50] Fox was condemned for not playing the game, suggesting the emergence of an acknowledged game which could be played. It is more compelling evidence of the triumph of a practice to consult its natural enemies than its friends; by this standard, opposition and party would seem to have gained a firm place in the minds of government supporters—and in the midst of war. Specific oppositions and party manoeuvres would continue to be condemned. However, by the end of the century England had such a long experience with parties that it was a simpler matter to condemn a current opposition by contrast with its virtuous predecessors than to presume to challenge such long-standing institutions.

This, then, was not the end of disenchantment with conflict, because human beings will always find reasons for wishing everyone to rejoice in the success of their point of view. The twentieth century has seen more virulent anti-party feeling than anything to be encountered in the eighteenth; for in that earlier age the response by people distressed by conflict was to condemn it, at least on the part of their enemies, and to indulge in politics as usual. There is a faint analogy to the modern one-party regime in the dominance achieved by Walpole or Pitt, the Younger,[51] but neither of these ever banished the opposition. Both, in fact, defended the institution, while successfully defeating its purposes. The closest thing to a movement above party, setting aside Bolingbroke's theory as opposed to his conduct, was the populist sentiment of radicalism, well stated in 1776 by Paine. Late in the century it posed a significant challenge to the fragile consensus on political mores—a challenge which found expression in the complaint that the Opposition sought no changes inconsistent with the prevailing distribution of power and property. Despite its own attempt to organize men and opinion, duly pointed by its enemies, radicalism remained hostile to conventional party conflict.[52] Such a rejection could never be prevented by an initial establishment of legitimate party competition within any society. Party is an imperfect expedient, accepted only because superior to arrangements which are even less perfect. This rules out the finality of a conventional happy ending. It is instructive to recall that when Cecil Chesterton and Hilaire Belloc issued their manifesto against twentieth-century parties they offered, as a more meaningful system, those of the eighteenth century.

NOTES

1. The pattern of opposition in modern America is discussed in Robert A. Dahl (ed.), *Political Oppositions in Western Democracies* (New Haven and London, 1966), pp. 34-69. For example of usage closer to the British experience see Algernon Sidney [i.e. Salma Hale], *The Administration and The Opposition* (Concord, 1826).
2. John Carswell, *The Old Cause: Three Biographical Studies in Whiggism* (London, 1954), p. 20.
3. The conclusions of Robert R. Walcott, Jr. in his *English Party Politics in the Early Eighteenth Century* (Cambridge, Mass., 1956) have recently been amended in the direction of giving a larger place to party divisions. See J. H. Plumb, *The Growth of Political Stability in England, 1675-1725* (London, 1967) and Henry Horowitz, "The Structure of Parliamentary Politics" in Geoffrey Holmes (ed.), *Britain After the Glorious Revolution, 1689-1714* (London, 1969).
4. Letter of 1700, quoted in Dennis Rubini, *Court and Country 1688-1702* (London, 1968), p. 211.
5. See "The State of Parties, and of the Publick ..." (1692) in *State Tracts* (London, 1706), Vol. II, p. 209; *A Jerk for the Jacks* (London, 1696), p. 24 and *Party No Dependence* (London, 1713), p. 2.
6. By 1717 Toland's use of Solon's maxim had come to refer to the normal state of affairs with no reference to any particular crisis. See the excerpts printed below.

7. Davenant's pamphlet *The True Picture of a Modern Whig* was answered in *The Moderator: or a View of the State of the Controversie Betwixt Whigg and Tory* (London, 1702).

8. See the Whig paper *The Observator*, Vol. VIII, No. 6 (7-10 April, 1708) and a Tory tract *The Political Balance. In which the Principles and Conduct of the Two Parties are Weighed* (London, 1765), p. 8.

9. Professor Richard Hofstadter has suggested that the relationship between classical and modern parties deserves further attention. See *The Idea of a Party System: The Rise of Legitimate Opposition in the United States, 1780-1840* (Berkeley and Los Angeles, 1969), p. 51n.

10. There were periods quite late in the century when Court and Country better described the political situation than did Whig and Tory and so the former categories lingered. The English-Hanoverian distinction related to positions taken on England's commitments to wars on the Continent. See "Petronius", *Party Distinctions, The Bane and Misery of British Nation* (London, n.d. [1744]), p. 12. In the 1790s all previous divisions were described as happy and innocent ones compared to the new one of the nation into French and British. See *A Letter Upon the State of Parties...* (London, 1797), pp. 7-8.

11. Hervey, *Some Materials Towards Memoirs of the Reign of King George II*, ed. Romney Sedgwick (London, 1931), Vol. 1, p. 6.

12. See *The Danger of Faction to a Free People* (London, 1732), p. 17 and *Party Spirit in Time of Publick Danger Consider'd* (London, 1756), pp. 11-12.

13. *The Present Necessity of Distinguishing Publick Spirit from Party* (London, 1736), sig. A2.

14. On this tendency, see François Lachenal, *Le parti politique, sa fonction de droit public* (Basel, 1944), pp. 43-4 and, with some interesting qualifications to the normal judgment on individualism and parties, Mario A. Cattaneo, *Il partito politico nel pensiero dell' illuminismo e della rivolizione francese* (Milano, 1964).

15. The connexion between self-interest and party in Ferguson's work has been treated by David Thomson, *The Conception of Political Party in England in the period 1740 to 1783*, unpublished Ph.D. thesis (Cambridge, 1938), fol. 179. Ferguson also referred to that sort of sociability noted by Shaftesbury as the basis of parties, but Ferguson did not contrast it with self-interest.

16. See the speech of Archibald Hutcheson in *Parliamentary History*, Vol VII (1716), col. 364.

17. *A Letter to a Member of Parliament Concerning the Present State of Affairs at Home and Abroad*, 2nd edn. (London, 1740), p. 26.

18. Swift, *A Discourse of the Contests and Dissentions between the Nobles and Commons in Athens and Rome...* (1701), ed. F. H. Ellis (Oxford, 1967). *Cf.* [Samuel Squire], *An Historical Essay upon the Ballance of Civil Power in England... in which is introduced a new DISSERTATION UPON PARTIES* (London, 1748), where the promised dissertation on parties is lost in an account of the balance of the estates.

19. Adams, *A Defence of the Constitutions of Government of the United States of America* (London and Boston, 1788), p. 215.

20. Adams, p. 306, misnumbered 206.

21. [Pownall], *A Treatise on Government, being a Review of the Doctrine of an Original Contract* (London, 1750), pp. 19-29.

22. See *The Free Briton*, No. 128 (11 May, 1732). Arnall edited this paper

in which he defended Walpole's administration. Extracts from Arnall's other thoughts on parties are presented below.

23. [Wallace], *Characteristics of the Present Political State of Great Britain,* 2nd edn. (London, 1758), pp. 70-1.
24. Hall, *An Apology for the Freedom of the Press, and for General Liberty* (1st edn. 1793), 6th edn. (London, 1821), pp. 40-1.
25. Leckie, *Essay on the Practice of the British Government, Distinguished from the Abstract Theory on which it is Supposed to be Founded* (London, 1812), p. 95 *et seq.*, and the review in *The Edinburgh Review*, Vol. XX (1812), esp. pp. 343-5.
26. *Remarks on a Late Libel privately Dispers'd by the Tories, entitled English Advice to the Freeholders of England* (London, 1715), p. 21. This was a very sensitive point with the Whigs; see too *The Observator*, Vol. X, No. 29 (7-11 April, 1711).
27. *Reflections on the Management of Some Late Party Disputes, and the Abuse of the Words, Church, Schismatick . . .* (London, 1715), p. 42.
28. *The Interests of the Protestant Dissenters Considered*, 2nd edn. (London, 1732), p. 12. This was a time when people distinguished between "parties in religion" and those in politics. Significantly, both Government and Opposition publications accepted the Dissenters' strategy of balancing parties. See the extracts from *The London Journal*, No. 748 and *The Craftsman*, No. 379 in *The Gentleman's Magazine*, Vol. III (1733), pp. 518 and 540.
29. *Some Observations upon the Present State of the Dissenting Interest* (London, 1731), p. 25.
30. Priestley, *An Essay on the First Principles of Government . . .* (London, 1768), pp. 95-7. Priestley went further than most in treating political and religious parties together, although he did not, of course, identify the two. Lord Dupplin was probably more typical of the time in arguing that parties would always exist in a free country, but that religion had less relevance to English divisions than ever before. See *Parliamentary History*, Vol. XIV (1753). col. 1378.
31. See, for example, George H. Williams, "The Religious Background of the Idea of a Loyal Opposition" in D. B. Robertson (ed.), *Voluntary Associations: A Study of Groups in Free Societies* (Richmond Va., 1966), pp. 55-89.
32. This was true, for instance, of *The London Journal*, the major Government organ of the early 1730s.
33. *The Freeholder's Alarm to his Brethren: or, the Fate of Britain Determin'd by the Ensuing Election* (London, 1734), p. 9. The tentative attribution to Fielding is to be found in the valuable study by Caroline Robbins, "'Discordant Parties', A Study of the Acceptance of Party by Englishmen", *Political Science Quarterly*, Vol. LXXIII (1958), pp. 505-29. For another Administration tract, citing the advantages of opposition both to the government and the governed, see *An Address to the Freeholders of Great Britain in Favour of our Constitution* (London, 1734), p. 27.
34. *The Free Briton,* No 224 (14 February, 1733-4) By 1744 a newspaper could truly say that the reigning preference for measures, rather than men, had been declared a thousand times in writings on the constitution. *The Westminster Journal: or, New Weekly Miscellany*, No. 157 (1 December, 1744).
35. *The Opposition Rescued from the Insolent Attacks of Faction Detected . . .* (London, 1744), p. 7.

36. Some of these men insisted that all men in public life were "thoroughly and fiercely" Whigs. [Thomas Waller], *Public Discontent Accounted for, from the Conduct of our Ministers in the Cabinet* . . . (London, 1743), p. 8. I am much indebted to Archibald S. Foord's masterly treatment of the complex events and literature of this period in *His Majesty's Opposition, 1714-1830* (Oxford, 1964), ch. VI.

37. *Opposition not Faction: or, the Rectitude of the Present Parliamentary Opposition* . . . (London, 1743), p. 13.

38. *The Country Journal: or, The Craftsman*, No. 670 (12 May, 1739).

39. *A Compleat View of the Present Politicks of Great Britain. In a Letter from a German Nobleman to his Friend at Vienna* (London, 1743), pp. 22, 27. The broad-bottom answer was called *An Englishman's Answer to a German Nobleman* (London, 1743).

40. Government writers had long admitted that such a thing as a faction in power was quite conceivable. See "Of Faction", *The Free Briton*, No. 125 (20 April, 1732). Charles Piggott's *Political Dictionary* (London, 1795) gave the impression that faction referred exclusively to men in office. While the distinction between party and faction was widely recognized, one could honour the emerging usage without becoming favourable to party. Such was, of course, the position of Bolingbroke and, appropriately enough, of his follower, David Mallet. For the latter's views on the subject, see *Memoirs of the Life and Ministerial Conduct, with Some free Remarks on the Political Writings, of the Late Lord Visc. Bolingbroke* (London, 1752), pp. 40-2. The difficulty of framing a satisfactory distinction between party and faction still exists. See D. J. Roorda, "Party and Faction . . .", *Acta Historiae Neerlandica*, Vol. II (1967), pp. 188-221. A distinction more useful for understanding eighteenth-century politics is that between a polity in which an organized government party coexisted with fragmentary opposition groups, and a party system, with organization on both sides. See Donald E. Ginter, *Whig Organization in the General Election of 1790* (Berkeley & Los Angeles, 1967), pp. xvii-xx.

41. See Foord, p. 279.

42. Walpole, *Memoirs of the Reign of King George the Second*, ed. Lord Holland, (London, 1846), Vol. I, p. 228.

43. Correspondence quoted in J. S. Millward and H. P. Arnold-Craft (eds.), *Portraits and Documents: Eighteenth Century, 1714-1783* (London, 1962), p. 74.

44. It was not uncommon for observers to express contentment that the parties exhausted each other in meting out well-deserved punishment. See *The London Chronicle*, No. 2122 (19-21 July, 1770).

45. Harvey C. Mansfield, Jr. has argued for the presence of a "school" or party in the 1760s consisting of those influenced by Bolingbroke. *Statesmanship and Party Government* (Chicago and London, 1965), pp. 120-1. Another school, but even more difficult to define, was that of the radicals who found a publisher in John Almon. See Section VII below.

46. *Parliamentary History*, Vol. XXI (1781), cols. 1278-9; 1290.

47. *The Daily Gazetteer*, No. 1852 (25 May, 1741) used this as an argument by which to turn Opposition complaints about "influence" to the advantage of the Ministry, urging that Opposition appeals at election time constituted an undesirable influence on the electorate. For electoral practices prior to the mandate see Cecil S. Emden, *The People and the Constitution* (Oxford, 1933), pp. 182-3.

48. Grimke, *The Nature and Tendency of Free Institutions* (1848), ed. John William Ward (Cambridge, Mass., 1968), ch. VIII.
49. [Richard Bentley], *Considerations upon the State of Public Affairs at the Beginning of the Year 1796* (London, 1796), pp. 88-89.
50. Thomas Lister, B.A., *Opposition Dangerous* (London, 1798), p. 33.
51. See Hugh Douglas Price, "Rise and Decline of One-Party Systems in Anglo-American Experience" in Samuel P. Huntington and Clement H. Moore (eds.), *Authoritarian Politics in Modern Society: The Dynamics of Established One-Party Systems* (New York, 1970), pp. 75-97.
52. The radicals were accused of detesting parties, but forming political associations—a charge equally applicable to Bolingbroke. See *Sentiments of a Party Man on the State of Parties* (London, n.d. [*c.* 1812]), p. 30. Many radical writers simply ignored party. One who did not was Mrs. R. F. A. Lee, whose splendidly miscellaneous book contains a short chapter on the subject inserted between a discussion of crimes and punishments and a final call to unanimity! See *An Essay on Government* (London, 1809), pp. 330-1.

Section I

PARTY AS FACTION: THE TRADITIONAL WISDOM

"For we are brought to this unhappy Dilemma, that we must be either *Whig* or *Tory* ; ....

... plain it is that our Distinction is only ill Names misapplied, and the best Men of the Nation are abus'd by false Characters, that are fixt upon them under the Colour of *Whig* and *Tory.*"

The Political Sow-Gelder, or the Castration of Whig and Tory
(1715)

During the six decades that separated the contributions by Osborne and Tindal, men generally condemned party. In the reign of Anne, the cry was for the abolition of all party names, suggesting that the fact of party conflict was sustained only by the presence of the different labels of Whig and Tory. Although exaggerated, the assumption was not entirely unwarranted, for the raging partisanship gained fuel from the growing mythology surrounding the two foci of loyalties. Thus public figures found themselves in the absurd situation of condemning divisions, while led by their passions and ambitions to perpetuate them. It should be noted that Osborne was writing of court factions in the traditional sense, while by the time of Tindal, the parties were perceived—however incorrectly—as involving the interests of most of the nation.

1

Some Advantages may be deducible from Court-Factions

in 'A Miscellany of Sundry Essays, Paradoxes, and Problematical
Discourses, ...' (1659), in *Works* (London, 1689), pp. 620-3.

FRANCIS OSBORNE[1]

It may be thought, I hope, no less *impertinent* than what went
before, if, according to my *rambling* Method, I shall drop some
conjectures in reference to a *benefit* may redound to the *Subject*
from *Court-Factions*: All which *in conclusion* will reach the *Prince*,
who cannot be *safe* and *happy*, if his *People* live *miserably*; not
likely to be avoided, where *preferments* depend wholly upon the
mediation of a *single* and *uncontrollable party*; in which case the
oppressed have no power for the present to appeal to; the cause of
our later *Parliaments* have been pestered with *clamours* and *complaints*, seldom if ever heard of in the *golden days* of Queen
Elizabeth, and from *whose root* sprung those *branches* of *misery*,
by which the greatest *felicity* any Nation ever enjoyed is become
over-shadowed, so that the *detection* of *corruption* in *officers*, and
the *gratification* of the *malice* of some, and *ambition* of *others*, in
their expulsions and *punishments*, gave them at last the boldness to
question the *integrity* of the *Crown*.

Divers persons of *equal authority*, though *both wicked*, do in
experience *produce more justice*, than a *greater probity* in a *single
Individual* hath been (at least in these *depraved Ages*) *heard* to
pronounce: For though *Bribery* cannot be denied a *deflowerer of
Equity*, yet remaining more palpable in reference to *detection*, it
may not happly be of so bad a consequence, as the effects of the
more uneasily detected propensities, found to follow the inclinations
of *love, fear* or *hope*; as it is easily deduced from the *practice*
usual in *private Families*, where a *great advantage* accrues to the
first Delator, and *prejudice* to the *party accused*; it not lying in the
strength of Vertue, if in any *agility of defence*, to keep a person
immaculate from the blurs of *Calumny*, for want of *proof*, or an
indifferent ear, which *superlative Powers* cannot be at *leisure* to
afford: Nor is the advantage to be drawn from two equal *Cabals*,

better discerned than by comparing the tempers of K. *James* his *Parliaments* with those holden under the *Queen*; for the first, being wholly led by a *single* and *passionate affection* to one *Minion*, lived to see never a tolerable *Minister* relating to the *Crown*, or any in Authority so *resolute* as not to *prefer* the *Favourite's command* before his *Master's*, as esteeming the *frown* of the last more *deadly*. Now the *huge rate* set upon *places* of *Judicature*, taught *Judges* to sell their *Votes*, and *People* to complain; who, by *devouring* of *instruments*, came at last so well *acquainted* with their own *strength*, as not to spare the *principal* & *first cause*; one *concession* ever *crouding* room for a *greater*, if not a more *unreasonable* demand: Whereas such instruments of State as *Queen Elizabeth* had use of, being *strained* through the *double* and *contrary interests* of a *divided Party*, no *Vertue* was *excluded*, or *Vice admitted*, any way *beneficial*, or of *prejudice* to *Prince* or *People*; contrary to the custome of later Times, wherein the most *probable designs* were *pinched*, and *miscarried*, through the *smalness* of their *parts* were imployed to *keep* them on *foot*; no more *solid Reason* appearing in the advancement of the most, but *mony* or *favour*; as no question will be found instanced in a *prodigious number* of *examples*, when *time* shall have *purchased impunity* for the *manifestation of truth*, not so likely to have proved the *result* of a *divided Court*, where the *creatures* of one were the enemies of another *no less powerful*; and so they both became liable to *accusation*, or capable of *defence*. And from the sparkles of this clashing, not only persons and actions, but the *Queens Councils* came to be refined from the rust and *Cankers* that after grew through the corruption of *foreign Coin*, no less *current* at *Court* all my time than pieces of two and twenty shillings, *Jacobuses* themselves. Now though *Monarchy* may (whether out of *perfection* or *defect*, I shall not here dispute) make use of this *Recipe*, it seems *dangerous*, if not *mortal*, in reference to a *freer Government*, where the least *siding* is a *step* towards *Tyranny*; the *weakest part* being as apt to *call*, as a *potent nighbour* may be to *come* and *assist*, upon so *advantageous an errand*. All *disparities* or *contentions*, but *merely rational*, and in *reference* to an *universal welfare*, tending to *popularity* and *disunion*; wherefore above all things to be avoided. Nor is any *near dependence* upon a *foreign Prince*, more *mighty* than *themselves*, *compatible* with *Liberty*, which renders *lending* of vast sums little less dangerous than *borrowing*. And through which the *Catholick King* may one day attain *Genoa*; it being natural to all *Creditors* to favour their designs that *owe* them *money*, in hope of *payment*; and so become *Traitors* to the *generality*, out of the desire of a *particular reim-*

bursment. Such folly lies in *many Citizens*, as they prefer *destruction of gross*, before the *hazard* of their *private interests*.

But when *Power* is *monopolized* in a *single* person, *Faction* can be no more *spared* than an *eye*, or an *ear*, *Kings* for the generality, out of *ignorance* in the World, if not for *want* of Wit, or too much *Flattery*, being unable to value what they *give* or *receive*, or whether they *gratifie* or *depress Vertue* or *Vice*, especially if they have no *other* information but what is *deduced* from a *Minion*, whose *judgment* is no less clouded through *Pride*, than *his* is by *affection*, and a *supposition* of *worth* and *abilities* not really present; such *Servants* owning *contrary interests* to *their Masters*, who by *bearing the charges* of those *follies* they daily commit, do not seldom prove *Bankrupts* themselves of all [that] ought to be esteemed dear in *Sovereignty*.

2

The Mischief of Cabals: or, The Faction Expos'd[2]

(London, 1685), pp. 26-7

... Neither can the *French Papists* be offended at the Advancement of any such, when they consider 'tis but *Equity* and the *undoubted Right* of the *Subject*; because that part of *political Justice*, which is call'd *Distributive*, always makes it a *due Debt* upon the *Prince* to reward his *Subjects* according to their *Deserts*, as the *Vindicative part* does oblige him on the other side to punish *Offenders* according to their *Demerits*; with this only *Difference*, that he can with much better *Conscience forgive* the one, than *forget* the other.

Besides, when a *Prince* has several *Factions*, whether *Religious* or *Civil* in his *Dominions*, as *Protestant* and *Papist*, *Guelph* and *Gibelline*, which he cannot easily reconcile, 'tis his *Interest*, by employing them indifferently according to their *Parts* and *Loyalty*, to keep the *Ballance* in an equal *Libration*; that while they are at emnity among themselves, they shall have no *Aversion* to him, who impartially rewards them in proportion to their *Deserts*: which must needs create such an *Emulation* betwixt his Subjects, that they will strive to outdo each other to serve their *Prince*, to the great *Advantage* of the *Publick*; and every one, instead of depending on the idle Interest of his *Party*, will endeavour to lay a better and a more useful *Foundation*, that of his own *Merit*, to raise him to *Preferment*. Whereas the contrary Practice will slacken the *Hearts* and *Hands* of many an *able Subject*, who thinking themselves oblig'd in *Honour* not to quit their *Party*, and perhaps in *Conscience* also not to change their Persuasion for *Worldly Interest*; if they find they are upon that account uncapable of a due *Encouragement*, they will be *remiss* in promoting their *Princes* service: For it is always observ'd, that *Honour and Reward are the great Motives to Zeal and Diligence for the Publick*: few being now-a-days of the old *Philosophers* temper, to love *Vertue* for it self; and therefore the *Poet* was very much in the Right, when he said, *Quis enim Virtutem amplectitur ipsam, Praemia si tollas?*

3

The Character of a Trimmer

(1688), in *The Complete Works of George Savile, First Marquess of Halifax*, ed. Walter Raleigh (Oxford, 1912), pp. 63-4

MARQUIS OF HALIFAX[3]

Our Government is like our Climate, there are Winds which are sometimes loud and unquiet, and yet with all the Trouble they give us, we owe great part of our Health unto them, they clear the Air, which else would be like a standing Pool and in stead of Refreshment would be a Disease unto us.

There may be fresh Gales of asserting Liberty, without turning into such storms of Hurricane, as that the State should run any hazard of being Cast away by them; these struglings which are natural to all mixed Governments, while they are kept from growing into Convulsions, do by a mutual agitation from the several parts, rather support and strengthen, than weaken or maim the Constitution; and the whole frame, instead of being torn or disjointed, cometh to be the better and closer knit by being thus exercised; but what ever faults our Government may have, or a discerning Critick may find in it, when he looketh upon it alone, let any other be set against it, and then it sheweth its Comparative Beauty; let us look upon the most glittering outside of unbounded Authority, and upon a nearer enquiry, we shall find nothing but poor and miserable deformity within; let us imagine a Prince living in his Kingdom, as if in a great Gally, his Subjects tugging at the Oar, laden with Chains, and reduced to real Rags, that they may gain him imaginary Lawrels; let us Represent him gazing among his Flatterers, and receiving their false Worship, like a Child never Contradicted, and therefore always Cozen'd: or like a Lady complemented only to be abused, condemned never to hear Truth, and Consequently never to do Justice, wallowing in the soft Bed of wanton and unbridled Greatness, not less odious to the Instruments themselves, than to the Objects of his Tyranny; blown up into an Ambitious Dropsy, never to be satisfied by the Conquest of other People, or by the Oppression of his own; by aiming to be more than a Man, he falleth lower than the meanest of 'em, a mistaken

Creature, swelled with Panegyricks, and flattered out of his Senses, and not only an Incumbrance, but a Nuisance to Mankind, a hardened and unrelenting Soul, and like some Creatures that grow fat with Poisons, he groweth great by other Mens Miseries; an Ambitious Ape of the Divine Greatness, an unruly Gyant that would storm even Heaven it self, but that his scaling Ladders are not long enough; in short, a Wild and devouring Creature in rich Trappings, and with all his Pride, no more than a Whip in God Almighty's hand, to be thrown into the Fire when the World hath been sufficiently scourged with it: This Picture laid in right Colours would not incite Men to wish for such a Government, but rather to acknowledge the happiness of our own, under which we enjoy all the Privilege Reasonable Men can desire, and avoid all the Miseries many others are subject to; so that our *Trimmer* would keep it with all its faults, and doth as little forgive those who give the occasion of breaking it, as he doth those that take it.

4

Maxims of State[4]

(written 1693; published 1700), in *Works*, p. 182

HALIFAX

23. That *Parties* in a *State* generally, like *Freebooters*, hang out *False Colours*; the pretence is the *Publick Good*; the real *Business* is, to catch *Prizes*; like the *Tartars*, where-ever they succeed, instead of Improving their *Victory*, they presently fall upon the *Baggage*.

24. That a *Prince* may play so long between *Two Parties*, that they may in time join together, and be in earnest with him.

25. That there is more *Dignity* in open *Violence*, than in the unskilful *Cunning* of a *Prince*, who goeth about to *Impose* upon the *People*.

26. That the *People* will ever suspect the *Remedies* for the *Diseases* of the *State*, where they are wholly excluded from seeing how they are prepared.

27. That changing *Hands* without changing *Measures*, is as if a *Drunkard* in a *Dropsey* should change his *Doctors*, and not his *Dyet*.

5

Political Thoughts and Reflections

(written *c.* 1690; published 1750), in *Works*, pp. 225-7

HALIFAX

The best Party is but a kind of a Conspiracy against the rest of the Nation. They put every body else out of their Protection. Like the *Jews* to the *Gentiles*, all others are the Offscowrings of the World.

Men value themselves upon their Principles, so as to neglect Practice, Abilities, Industry, &c.

Party cutteth off one half of the World from the other, so that the mutual Improvement of Mens Understanding by conversing, &c. is lost, and Men are half undone, when they lose the advantage of knowing what their Enemies think of them.

It is like Faith without Works; They take it for a Dispensation from all other Duties, which is the worst kind of *dispensing Power*.

It groweth to be the Master Thought; the Eagerness against one another at home, being a nearer Object, extinguisheth that which we ought to have against our foreign Enemies; and few Mens Understandings can get above overvaluing the Danger that is nearest, in comparison of that more remote.

It turneth all Thought into talking instead of doing. Men get a habit of being unuseful to the Publick by turning in a Circle of Wrangling and Railing, which they cannot get out of. . . .

It maketh a Man thrust his Understanding into a Corner, and confine it till by degrees he destroys it.

Party is generally an Effect of Wantonness, Peace, and Plenty, which beget Humour, Pride, &c. and that is called Zeal and publick Spirit.

They forget insensibly that there is any body in the World but themselves, by keeping no other Company; so they miscalculate cruelly. And thus Parties mistake their Strength by the same reason that private Men overvalue themselves; for we by finding fault with others, build up a partial Esteem of ourselves upon the Foundation of their Mistakes: So Men in Parties find faults with those in the Administration, not without reason, but forget that they would be exposed to the same Objections, and perhaps greater, if it was their Adversary's turn to have the fault-finding part.

There are Men who shine in a Faction, and make a Figure by Opposition, who would stand in a worse light, if they had the Preferments they struggle for.

It looketh so like *Courage* (but nothing that is like is the same) to go to the *Extream*, that Men are carried away with it, and blown up out of their Senses by the wind of popular Applause.

That which looketh *bold* is a great Object that the People can discern; But that which is *wise* is not so easily seen: It is one part of it that it is not seen, but at the *End* of a Design. Those who are disposed to be wise too late, are apt to be valiant too early.

Most Men enter into a Party rashly, and retreat from it as shamefully. As they encourage one another at first, so they betray one another at last: And because every Qualification is capable of being corrupted by the Excess, they fall upon the extream, to fix mutual Reproaches upon one another.

Party is little less than an Inquisition, where Men are under such a Discipline in carrying on the common Cause, as leaves no Liberty of private Opinion.

It is hard to produce an Instance where a Party did ever succeed against a Government, except they had a good handle given them.

No original Party ever prevailed in a turn; it brought up *something else*, but the first Projectors were thrown off.

If there are two Parties, a Man ought to adhere to that which he disliketh least, though in the whole he doth not approve it: For whilst he doth not list himself in one or the other Party, he is looked upon as such a Straggler, that he is fallen upon by both. Therefore a Man under such a Misfortune of Singularity, is neither to provoke the World, nor disquet himself, by taking any particular Station.

It becometh him to live in the Shade, and keep his Mistakes from giving Offence; but if they are his Opinions, he cannot put them off as he doth his Cloaths. Happy those who are convinced so as to be of the general Opinions.

Ignorance maketh most Men go into a Party, and Shame keepeth them from getting out of it.

More Men hurt others they do not know why than for any reason.

If there was any Party entirely composed of honest Men, it would certainly prevail; but both the honest Men and the Knaves resolve to turn one another off when the Business is done.

They by turns defame all *England*, so nobody can be employed that hath not been branded: There are few Things so criminal as a Place.

6

Of Private Men's Duty in the Administration of Public Affairs

(1699), in *The Political and Commercial Works of that celebrated Writer Charles D'Avenant*, ed. Sir Charles Whitworth (London, 1771), Vol. II, pp. 338-40

CHARLES DAVENANT[5]

If the wealth and power of a country depend upon the good government and stability of its affairs, it must certainly import all the different ranks of men to contribute their utmost that things may be well administered: And in mixed constitutions almost every man is able in some degree to help towards this; for if the people are honest and careful in the choice of their representatives, and if those representatives perform their duty, arbitrary power can never be settled here, and no male-administration that may hereafter happen can long continue.

That we are in no danger at present, and that matters proceed well, now is allowed; but for the security of future times it may not be amiss frequently to repeat this caution, that our whole depends upon keeping one post well defended.

The public virtue which must preserve a state is "A constant and perpetual will to do our country good;" and where this principle governs, though in the minds of but a few, yet if they persevere with undaunted courage, the small number may prevail at last to defeat the malice of the corrupt part, especially when the endeavours of the few are assisted by a Prince disposed by interest and inclination to promote the common welfare.

If good men were but as active and vigilant as their opposites, it would not be so easy a matter to change the constitution of a country: When those who are concerned in honour and interest to have things well administered, do resolutely and firmly join together to oppose such as find their profit by a corrupt and loose administration, a stand may at least be made, and some stop put to the further progress of the evil.

But though Pompey, Caesar, and Crassus, composed a fatal triumvirate, and united in a strict league to subvert the liberties of

Rome, we do not read that there was the same union and good understanding between Lucullus, Cato, Cicero, and the rest, who endeavoured to save the commonwealth; for the luxury and laziness of some, the froward [*sic*] temper, or secret ambition of others, made them either neglect or obstruct the business of the public, which might be the reason that Caesar at last prevailed.

In the same manner, if hereafter a cabal of men, in order to their own greatness, should design to change this constitution, to introduce a government by the sword, and to give away all the nation's wealth; and if to these ends they should form assemblies, and there propose what they intend to consent to in another place, they will succeed, and their attempts can never be withstood, unless such as mean England well, join in as firm a league for its preservation, as they shall enter into for its destruction.

If therefore, in future times, it shall be visible that some men, to build their own fortunes, are pushing at their country's ruin, good patriots must then exert all their virtue, they must reassume the courage of their ancestors, they must lay aside their pleasures, but chiefly, they must sacrifice to the public all their ancient animosities; they must mutually forgive one another; it must be no more remembered of what party the man was, it being sufficient to enquire, whether or no he always acted upon the principles of honesty and honour. At such a time the best men of both sides, if the name of parties shall still remain, must shake hands together, with a resolution to withstand the unanimous, subtle, and diligent enemies of the King and kingdom.

In such a juncture both sides must contend, not which shall flatter highest, but which shall best contribute to the defence of their Prince's person, and to the maintenance of the established government.

If bad men shall have meetings to consult how they may destroy our civil rights, good patriots ought to meet calmly to communicate counsels which way those rights are to be preserved; for Machiavel says, "There is not a better or more secure way to suppress the insolence, or crossbite the designs of an ambitious citizen, than to take the same way to prevent, which he takes to advance them."

7

A Essay Towards the History of the Last Ministry and Parliament: Containing Seasonable Reflections on: I Favourites, II Ministers, III Parties . . .⁶

(London, 1710), pp. 8-10; 39-40

It may be said, indeed, That a Wise and Just Prince will not punish Many, for the *Errors* and *Follies* of a Few; nor make a *Thorough Change* of His Ministers, because One or Two have done Amiss. To be sure, 'tis not with out *Reluctance* that he consents to part with some Persons, whose *Wisdom, Integrity* and *Abilities* he has often Experienc'd and entirely Approves: But yet when these very Persons grow *Sullen* and *Resty,* and obstinately reject a COALITION with others, for the sake either of an *Overgrown Minister,* or an *Insolent Favourite*; in such a Case, a Prince, that hath any Spirit, will employ *another* set of Men. For he well knows, that Parts, Uprightness, Knowledge and Experience in Affairs, are not confin'd to this, or to that Party; and rightly considers, *That Ministers or Favourites, who should be able to Protect themselves by a CABALL, might first presume to think they subsist by their proper Strength, and so advance at last, either to slight, or defy his Authority.*

Moreover, it has been justly observ'd, That *Partiality, which is the Weakness of Private Men, is unbecoming the Greatness of a Sovereign, whose Favour should shine on the whole Body of his People: And therefore a Wise and Good Prince ought to make it his Principal Care, and use his Utmost Endeavours to Root out FACTION.* But if the Disease be too Inveterate to be entirely Remov'd, he must try, by turns, the Persons most Eminent for their Abilities in Both Parties, in order to beget a Virtuous Emulation which may produce good Effects: For by that means, both sides will be at strife which shall do the Prince and the Nation the most Honest, and the most Faithful Service, and with the fewest Selfish Designs.

*　　　*　　　*

These few Hints and Instances shew, at the same time, the main *Scope* of the *late Changes*: Which is not to cramp or streighten the

Government, by *Turning out* one *Party*, and *Taking in* another; but rather to strengthen it, *by enlarging its Foundation*: It being the Queen's fix'd Design and Resolution, to encourage and reward all such, who with Honest and Virtuous Principles shall embrace and promote Her Majesty's and the Nation's Service, without any regard to *invidious Distinctions. Usurpers*, or *Incroaching Favourites*, and *Ambitious Ministers* may, for a while, support themselves by a *Faction*; but our Rightful and Lawful QUEEN has nothing more at Heart, than that the Names of *Tory* and *Whig* may be buried in Oblivion; She thinks it below Her Royal Dignity, to make use of the mean Arts of Indulging any of Her Subjects in *Follies* and *Animosities* to themselves fatal, and injurious to Her Power. As She has a Right to Govern All, so She scorns to be Queen of no more than half Her People: And as She is able to Judge whose Merits are the greatest, and who are the fittest Objects to be shin'd on; so she will, for the future, impartially distribute Her Rewards, and Countenance the Best Patriots; Which cannot fail of Strengthening Her Auspicious Administration, with the Hearts and Hands of all Her Subjects.

8

The Art of Governing by Partys

(London, 1701), pp. 40-4; 176-8

[JOHN TOLAND][7]

There are great complaints now of the Immortality of the Nation,
and I wish there were not such just reasons for it: but with all our
failings it can scarce be paralel'd in History, that any People under
the like Circumstances preserv'd their Liberty. This may well be
allow'd for a miracle, tho' I must reckon it a greater that any
remains of these Animosities shou'd disturb us under the present
King, who is no way ingag'd in the treacherous designs of his
Predecessors; but on the contrary came generously to rescue us
from Popery and Slavery, and to secure us for ever hereafter from
those worst of Plagues. Yet there's but too much of these ill
humours stirring among us still. Divisions ought carefully to be
avoided in all good Governments, and a King can never lessen himself more than by heading of a Party; for thereby he becoms only
the King of a Faction, and ceases to be the common Father of his
People. If he's visibly partial to one Party, and confers on them
only all Places of Honor and Profit; he naturally makes the other
Party hate him, who, finding themselves unjustly excluded from
Confidence and Preferment, will be incessantly laboring to destroy
him as their Enemy and Oppressor. The Matter is still worse if
instead of Governing his whole Kingdom, he's actually Govern'd
himself by a Party; for they care not in what dishonorable, difficult,
or desperat attemts they involve him, to gratifie their revenge on
the other side, whom they fail not to represent as Enemies to his
Person, or Dangerous to his Government, and they are sure to be
treated acordingly. But the worst of all is, when he not only chuses
to Govern by a Party, but is given to change sides as he finds it
make for his turn, or as either of them happens to outbid the other
in executing his projects, or complying with his desires. Then all
the Administration grows unsteddy, Councils uncertain, no Union
at home, less Credit abroad, and a general slackness in Execution;
no body knowing what Party to please, or how to act with security,
since what is allow'd by those in present power, may for no other

reason be disaprov'd by the others when it coms to their turn to be
the Favorits. And such Revolutions are quickly made: for as soon
as one Party looses their Credit with the Nation, or refuses to grant
any of the Princes demands tho' never so unseasonable, they are
turn'd off without farther Ceremony, and their mortal foes advanc'd
into the Sadle. If a Man were so indifferent or hard-hearted as to
sport with our Calamitys, it were no unpleasant entertainment to
consider what miserable handles are taken somtimes when the dis-
grace of a Party is resolv'd. The Knavery, for instance, or Miscar-
riage of som few is heavily charg'd on all those of the same
denomination, and nothing less can do than wholly to change hands
for the opposite Faction; just as if there were no wiser or honester
Men among the Whigs, than those who were lately turn'd out.
But as his present Majesty dos not govern by such Arts, so these
are not produc'd for an Example; nor is there any fear of his
imploying Tories on this account. As no mortal, tho' incomparable
for virtue, or in never so exalted a station, is secure from the
censures of Jealous, Weak, and Malitious Persons; so we must not
dissemble that even King *William* was calumniated by many to
affect this method of governing by Parties, that is in Plain *English*
of governing by Tricks. The unhappy accidents that gave occasion
to this surmise are very accountable: and I question not so to
vindicat his Majesty from such an unjust Imputation, that he must
stand clear of it in the minds of all his loving Subjects. Pursuant to
his Heroic and God-like design, he resolv'd on his first coming
here to abolish our infamous distinctions both in Church and State,
and intended to receive the good Men of all Parties into equal
Favor, Protection, and Trust: not that he designed to Imploy any
who continu'd still a Tory; that is, who retain'd his old notions of
Passive Obedience, unlimited Prerogative, the divine right of
Monarchy, or who was averse to Liberty of Conscience.

*   *   *

Provided the matter has in any degree the Effects intended, I
shall be the less concern'd for any want of Art which Haste may
occasion in the performance; and if this Parlament be of that heal-
ing Disposition which all true Patriots most heartily desire, som-
thing may be offer'd that may not be altogether impracticable nor
unsatisfactory towards abolishing those fatal Distinctions of Whig
and Tory, and making us at least bear with one another in Religion
where we cannot agree. Such a piece must be without all Resentment, or shewing any more approbation of one side than another.
'Tis confest I have bin oblig'd to follow somwhat a different Conduct on the present occasion, because the Parties are not yet

calmly dispos'd to an Accommodation, but rather more violently inflam'd than for a long while past; nor wou'd it be difficult, were it as safe or seasonable, to discover by what Intriegues, and to serve what Ends their Heats are reviv'd. Tho both Factions are in several Things to be equally blam'd, yet I believe there's no Body who dos not imagin one of 'em to be more in the right than the Other: and I have not disgu'd in this whose Discourse, which of 'em has most Reason in my Opinion; tho without palliating their faults, or charging those unjustly whom I hold to be most in the wrong. Did I follow my natural Inclination I shou'd be always for a Neutrality, and I promise to be a very indifferent Judge when the critical Opportunity presents itself; but when there's a Sedition in the City, I think (with *Solon*) it ought to be capital for a Man to remain an unconcern'd Spectator, but that he shou'd be necessitated to ingage on the side he most approv'd, as the fittest means to appease the Tumult, or to keep the best Party from being overpowr'd.

9

The State-Anatomy of Great Britain

(London, 1717), sigs. A2-A4; pp. 102-3

[JOHN TOLAND]

They are neither the remotest Foreigners, nor our nearer Neighbours beyond the seas, who alone are to seek for the meaning of our Party-words and Distinctions. The Natives even of our own Islands are very often at a loss, or, which is of worse consequence, highly mistaken; as well in the nature and tendency of our several Parties, as in the names, civil or religious, by which they are commonly distinguish'd. Nor are they less frequently ignorant of our various Interests, with relation to our Adversaries or Allies, to our honour or reputation abroad: and many hearty friends to the Royal Family, are as great Strangers to its happy circumstances; as their worst enemies either or, or affect to be. A remedy in these cases became absolutely necessary. MONARCHY therefore and a COMMONWEALTH, WHIGS and TORIES, HIGH and LOW-CHURCHMEN, FORSWEARERS and NON-SWEARERS, TOLERATION, NATURALIZATION, the BALANCE OF EUROPE, the DANGER OF THE CHURCH, but (above all things) the Word CHURCH it self, with the whole train of those other heads mention'd in the TABLE, and many more there not mention'd, are so perspicuously, and, where it is necessary, so minutely deduc'd in the following MEMORIAL, that it was deem'd of publick service to have it printed. To this the Author has the more readily consented, that he's now on the spot to justify or explain what ever he has advanc'd; shou'd any Person sophistically cavil at his Expressions on the one hand, or on the other hand sincerely desire more light with regard to his Facts. He has imparted every thing to his Correspondent without favour or fear, without any gloss or reserve: and for his vouchers he's ready to produce, not the misrepresentations of Antagonists, but the books of both sides, containing the accounts they have given of themselves, tho the practices of some among 'em prove not seldom repugnant to their principles. He's so farr from presumeing to dictate to the King, those considerations he thinks self-evident to a person of less penetration and judgment than his Majesty, that he fears not being thought a false Prophet in affirming; that neither he himself, nor any of his Royal family, can hold these Realms securely, nor govern them peaceably, by any other Principles, than those by which he has acquir'd them: and therefore the only effectual way to bring the bulk of his Subjects to become insensibly of one mind as to him, is a steddy, unshaken, resolute adherence to this rule; whereby the daily and unavoidable espousing of those Principles, by men of a different cast or education, will not be any longer reckon'd deserting a Party, but wisely embracing the Publick Interest. This is the only way left for the Tories to be even with the Whigs: for the merit or demerit of Party is gone, when once all Men profess the same Political Creed. Every Division, however, is not simply pernicious: since Parties in the State, are just of the like nature with Heresies in the Church: sometimes they make it better, and sometimes they make it worse; but held within due Bounds, they always keep it from stagnation.

*　　　*　　　*

But I am weary of these tools, and afraid I have weary'd you likewise: wherefore since we were just now upon their discord, I hope to congratulate with you, for the harmony you'll find reigning among our present Ministers; as I hope the same Spirit will continue among all the other Whigs, and that they will not be foolishly drawn into any artificial cry, under the notion of a Country party, or other the like threadbare topick. They cannot but remember that the Tories cou'd never enter, but by the gaps they made for them in their own body. The king is convinc'd that Whigs and Tories are incompatible in the Ministry; that drawing two ways, is makeing no way at all; that they will be perpetually undermineing one another, and that each will be a clog or dead weight upon the other's measures. A sort of neutral Gentlemen are much commended by some, but tis by such as know no more of politicks than what's ideal: for those Neuters are real Indifferents, and a Trimmer (which is the name they affect) is like a bird of prey, hovering over two Armies, being ready to feed on the dead of either side. The whole race of Sir *William Coventry's* Trimmers is long ago extinct, if ever they had a being out of his brain; since we all now follow *Solon's* law, which made it capital not to be of some Party. Besides the King is most averse in his generous soul to that foolishly politick and ever-deceiving maxim, of *neglecting friends to gain enemies*; upon the precarious supposition that friends will continue friends still, while enemies are perhaps farr from being **gain'd.**

10

The Defection Consider'd, and The Designs of those who divided the Friends of the Government, set in a True Light

5th edn. (London, 1717), pp. 5-6, 7-10

[MATTHEW TINDAL][8]

The *Jews* cou'd not forbear their *Party-Divisions*, ev'n while their Capital was besieg'd by the *Romans*; and they fell on one another with that implacable Fury, that they hurted themselves more than the *common Enemy* was able to do; and had not *Josephus* been a *Jew*, and an Eye-witness, we cou'd never have believ'd the Account he gives of the Heights, those Quarrels were carry'd to among the beseig'd, without Regard to their common Safety; notwithstanding they were press'd to the last Degree by Famine, and the Enemy.

Nor were the Divisions at *Constantinople* between the *Greeks* and *Latines*, who resided there, less fatal, when that Place was besieg'd by the *Turks*; and 'twas no small Occasion that that famous City, and with it all the Remains of the *Greek* Empire, fell so easily into the Hands of those barbarous *Infidels*.

But what need we look Abroad, since we find by our own Historians, that we were never conquer'd by Foreign Enemies, or fell into any great Miseries, but by being unhappily divided among ourselves.

*   *   *

If, as the Gospel assures us, it holds true of a *Kingdom divided in itself*, that it *cannot stand*; 'twill, no doubt, hold as strongly of any Party in a Nation, if they chance to be at Variance among *themselves*; and constant Experience might have taught those Parties, which so unhappily divide us, this Truth; that when either of them were so impolitick, as to quarrel among *themselves*, they have been quickly forc'd to give Place to the Common Enemy; and then in the Anguish of their Souls, what *Resolutions*, what *Vows* did they not make, of never splitting upon that Rock, if ever, by the Folly of their Adversaries, they got uppermost again? and yet

almost as soon as they did, those *Resolutions* were forgot, and the
Devil of *Ambition, Envy,* and *Avarice,* setting the Top-men at
Variance, the Underlings divided of Course, and came into any
Measures, which might prejudice the opposite Leaders, without
regarding how it affected the *common Good*; and thereby they
demonstrated, that they were not govern'd by *Principles,* but by
the vilest Things they cou'd be govern'd; *viz.* the *Passions* of the
Great Ones; which cou'd have no other Effect, than ruining the
whole Party, and the Cause, for which they wou'd have the World
believe they were most zealous.

The smaller the Number of any Party is, (as that of honest Men
will never be large) the greater is the Reason for a *Strict Union*;
since by the least Division there's the utmost Danger, lest the
common Enemy, like a vast Torrent, break in, and bear down all
before them.

It's notorious, that the Party, which prevail'd in the latter End
of the Queen's Reign, have, ever since, acted after such a Manner, as
if they had a Mind to perswade the World, that the Majority of
the Nation were Fools and Mad-men; but 'twas to be hop'd, that
the other Party, opposite to them in almost ev'ry Thing else, wou'd
have been so in *This,* and warn'd by their Folly, have had so much
Regard to the Nation's Honour, and their Own, as not to give
People just Occasion to think *as vilely* of them, when they see, that
by their *intestine* Quarrels, their *King, Country, Liberties, Religion,*
and ev'ry Thing that's valuable is expos'd to the utmost Danger.

Foreigners, with Amazement, look on *these Divisions,* when they
perceive, that there's still so considerable a Party most industriously
labouring to destroy *both Sides,* weaken'd by their *Dissentions.*

Strangers think these Quarrels among Men, whose *Principles* are
the best calculated for the *Good* of *Mankind,* must have some
extraordinary Reason; they can't well imagine, that *They,* who
have caus'd *those Divisions,* have nothing to object against the
Present Administration; and that it is chiefly for the sake of a
single Person, who, not content with the most beneficial Posts,
threw up in a Pet, because he cou'd not govern ev'ry Thing; and
then confederated with such, as 'till the Moment he declar'd himself a *Country Gentleman,* he continually represented as the *Vilest*
of Men, and *Traitors* to their *King,* and *Country.*

It's a melancholy Reflection to consider, that Men of the *worst
Principles* are more steadily govern'd by them, than others by the
best: When the most Celebrated Champion of *High-Church* went
over to the other Party in the late Reign, he was not able to bring
with him one Man, and his own Side hated him as a *Renegado*;
nay, which is more remarkable, when that Minister, who, for so

long a Time, had the Disposal of ev'ry Thing, and thereby capable of obliging great Numbers, tho' he did not, contrary to the Will of the Queen, lay down, but was turn'd out; yet he cou'd not make any Party, or the least Division among the *Tories,* much less was he able to prevail on any of them, to throw up their Places, and fly in the Face of the Queen; but they all stuck to *their Principles,* and to the *Ministry* that continu'd in.

If any of their Leaders, tho' ever so much belov'd, shou'd, immediately upon Quitting his Employment, enter into a *New Alliance* with the adverse Party, and join in Voting with them, they wou'd, no Doubt, despise him as the most infamous of Mankind; and what must we think of a *Whigg,* who has acted such a Part, and of those, who have join'd with him? *Vertue* was low enough before in all Parties, but after this, what will the World say of the *greatest Pretenders* to it?

The Dispute is not only about *Places* and *Preferments,* but concerning all that can be valuable to an *English-man*: There are but *Two Grand Parties* in the Nation, and scarce a Man, or Woman, which is not of one, or t'other; and tho' there may be several Things, done by their own Side, which some may dislike, yet if they do not dislike them more than they like their Party, they will come into ev'ry Thing essential to it.

Section II

THE USES OF CONFLICT

"Can Conformity render the Dissenters more peaceable Subjects...? Will the Balance of Parties be better preserv'd, on which the Balance of Power in *England* and Europe does in a good Measure depend?"

Shute Barrington, *A Letter from a Lay-Man, in Communion With the Church of England* ... (1714)

Early eighteenth-century partisanship had its most exciting theoretical outcome in Barrington's wedding of Whiggism and Dissent. Party and the cause of religious toleration would meet in other writings of the century, but never again in such dramatic and novel fashion. Barrington's calm acceptance of party—even to the extent of using it to justify what were presumably less obvious goods, such as toleration—indicates that opinions were changing. The seemingly paradoxical conclusion that conflict could be valuable also appealed, in different ways, to Shaftesbury and Paterson, Defoe and Gordon, all of whom discussed the subject in general terms, not closely related to the urgent issues of the day. A similar distance was maintained by Rapin and Saussure, two of the few foreigners who exhibited a knowledgable interest in English parties. Resistance, even civil war, had previously been justified by republicans, such as Algeron Sydney, for the vigour thereby given to a state. Now vigour, and with it freedom, were being found in the menacing, but bloodless, contests of party.

11

The Interest of England Consider'd in Respect to Protestants Dissenting from the Establish'd Church

2nd edition (London, 1703), pp. 16-18; 21-7

[JOHN SHUTE, later VISCOUNT BARRINGTON][1]

This much therefore is plain upon the Supposition, that a Test that should bar Dissenters from Places would disoblige them, that it would *endanger the Government*. And I think it will appear yet much more plainly, that such a Test, if it should not ruin it, must necessarily *weaken it*, and subvert the Constitution. For as to the first. Will it not *rob the Government of the Service of a great Body of Men*, who are as willing and as able to serve in the *Commissions* of Taxes, Peace and Lieutenancy; in the Bench of Aldermen and Assistants; in the Courts of Judicature, and Offices of State, or in Commands at Sea or Land, as any of their Fellow-Citizens? Will it not take all Dissenters out of our Navy, and keep them from listing themselves for our Land-Service? Or is it to be expected, that any will undergo the Dangers and Fatigues of a common Souldier, or a Seaman, who knows he can never receive any greater Reward than his common Pay? No, the same Answer, upon all accounts, must be expected from a Dissenter, if he should be ask'd to enter into her Majesty's Service, that the common People of Rome made, when they were desired to give their names to the Service, after they had been ill us'd by the Patricians: "Let them fight the Battels [said they] of the Commonwealth, who share its Advantages. But since we are to have none of the Emoluments of a War, we'll have none of its Dangers."

*   *   *

Thus you'll incapacitate all Dissenters for Offices: And when you have done that, you need not do any thing more to *incapacitate them* from bearing a part in *the Legislature*. For when they shall no longer be in Commissions in the Countys, nor of the Bench in the Citys and Boroughs of England; their Interest in those, whom they are to represent, which depends in a greater measure upon their Power and Authority than their Capacity and Merit, must necessarily sink and fall. Now one must either suppose that the Dissenters are really incapable of being useful in that Honourable Body, or that the excluding them must be very prejudicial. But what Man or Party can have the impudence to deny, that the House of Commons have receiv'd the greatest Assistance from the accuracy and diligence of some Persons and Families, that dissent from the Church of England; and who are not less considerable for their Interest in their own Countys and in Parliament, than for their Capacitys of using it, to the Service of the Nation? I have known Dissenters, who in their greatest Intimacys have not only assur'd me, but given me convincing Reasons to believe, that it is no more for their Interest, than it is in their Power to subvert the Church. This Principle must keep these Men from being dangerous in that great Assembly: And would not their Interest, which is known to be so closely connected with the Libertys of England, and the Moderation of the Church, render these Men the most highly useful in an Assembly, design'd to be the Rampart of the Libertys of England, against any Encroachments of the Crown, which the Mitre has but too generally endeavour'd to support?

*   *   *

But there are yet other *ways* by which the Dissenters are of *more general Service*, and in those too this Test makes them *useless*. It cuts them off from the Body, and hinders them from performing any Ministry to the whole. For is it to be expected that they should give any Assistance to those, that they think would use it to make them more miserable? And thither all Uneasiness tends, in a greater or a less degree. I confess if the Dissenters were all of them an inconsiderable parcel of People, poor and ignorant, without Interest or Influence; Their being in the Interest of the Society, could do us no service; nor their being separated from it, any hurt. But since a great many of the Dissenters are Men of Sense and Substance, considerable by their Monys vested in Trade, and the share they have in the Lands of England; and who, with the Assistance of the Government, cou'd make a considerable Interest for its Support: It wou'd be worth the while to consider, whether any of the little Ends, that the Enemys of the Dissenters should propose by disobliging them, cou'd counterballance the loss of *their Direction and their Purse.* To make the Dissenters unconcern'd for the Commonweal, is discharging so many private Sentinels, that are generally the first that take and give the Alarm of any Dangers that threaten us; and it's a forcing them to withdraw the Supplys they used to afford.

* * *

But possibly 'twill be said that, The Effect of this Test will be only like the eating away proud Flesh, that better may come in its room. Very likely so in truth: For sober diligent conscientious Men, and who hold no Principles dangerous to the Constiution, are indeed very ill Members of a Society: And on the other hand, Non-Abdicators, Non-Associators, and Non-Jurors are much more useful Men to some certain Purposes than Non-Conformists. And when the latter must be kept out, there will be so many Vacancys, that the others must of necessity be put in, and continued to supply their place. Then the hopes of the Golden Age will begin to revive the drooping Spirits of a great many good Men, who had fainted, if they had not lived to see this fair prospect of Salvation; by seeing those Gentlemen fill the Offices of England, who never qualified themselves by Civil Tests (the very thing they unjustly blame the Dissenters for, in that of a Religious one) till Honour or Advantage, or it may be the Designs of greater Service engaged them to take their Swear, as they are pleased to phrase it: Who were against the Abdication of the late K. James, the Association to support K. William, and the Abjuration of the pretended Prince of Wales, in order to maintain her Majesty's unquestionable Right to the Throne, and the Succession in the Protestant Line.

But further: Incapacitating Dissenters, will not only weaken this happy Government, by removing a great many of its Props and Supports at the present; but *subvert the Foundation on which 'tis built*. Every one knows that the English *Constitution* consists of the Prerogatives of the Crown, and the Libertys of the People. Now 'tis certain that this Constitution can only be preserv'd by a Ballance of Power, or of Inclination. That is, to explain my self, either by a Power in the Crown, as able to maintain its Prerogative, if the People should have an Inclination to invade it; as the People have to maintain their Privileges, if the Prince should have an Inclination to retrench them: Or if the Crown has not a power to maintain its Rights, equal to the power the People have to maintain theirs; then the Prerogative of the Crown must subsist, either by taking away an Inclination from all the People of invading the Prerogative (which is hardly possible) or from such a part of them, as may oppose others that have such a Design. And the latter is all that the Crown can do here to its own preservation. For since the Queen's Lands are not considerable, nor her Tenants many; Since her Revenues are not great, nor her Domestics numerous, nor her Officers of

State independent on the People; Since she can neither raise nor borrow Mony without the Consent of Parliament: The Crown has no native or internal Power (as it has in absolute Monarchys) to preserve it self; but depends upon an Inclination in a Majority of the People (as the Crown of Israel did) to maintain it.

The People on the contrary have an internal Power by their Number, Property and ready Mony, to maintain their own Privileges against any usurpation. So that the Case of the Prince and the People are just opposite: For as the Prerogative has an inward ability to maintain it self, and depends upon a Foreign Inclination; the People have an inherent Power to maintain their Libertys; which can be injur'd by nothing but an Inclination in a part of their own Body to betray 'em, in order to enlarge those of the Crown. So then: As the Security of the Crown (as we remark'd but just now) depends upon this, that no Body of Men superior to the rest, shou'd have an Inclination to rob the Prerogative; so the Security of our Libertys depends upon this, that no Body of Men superior to the rest should have an Inclination to betray those Libertys, in order to enlarge the Prerogative of the Crown. By this time I promise my self, I have sufficiently explain'd the meaning of a *Ballance of Power*, and of *Partys or Inclination*. And I hope it will not be taken amiss: For when we know that the Sphere of our Libertys, and the Prince's Prerogative, are not preserv'd like two Globes, supported by proper Pedestals, able to bear their own weight; but rather like two of Des Cartes's Whirlpools, by having either an equal and necessary Power to preserve themselves, or an equal Power by accident to hinder mutual Destruction, we shall, it may be, take more proper Methods to preserve them.

This by the way: But to return: An Inclination to preserve the Prerogative of the Crown depends upon such Principles as these; That it is as much the lawful Right of the King, and as much for the Interest of England, for the Prince to enjoy his Privileges (which are call'd the Prerogative) as 'tis for the People to enjoy theirs. And an Inclination in the People to preserve their Rights, depends upon such Principles as these: That a King is a Minister of God, made to rule by the Consent of the People, upon condition that he shall preserve the People in their Rights and Privileges; and forfeit their Allegiance when he breaks them. On the other side, an Inclination in the People to give up their own Rights, and to enlarge the Prerogative of the Crown, depends upon such Principles as these: That Kingly Power is of Divine Right: That it can be transmitted only by a descent in the Right Line: And that when it is so transmitted, there can be no Abuse in its Exercise, for which the King can be accountable, or which the People ought not quietly to bear.

If things then be thus, we need no more, to come to a certain knowledge of what is the Ballance of England; and whether a Test which weakens the Dissenters, tends to preserve or destroy it; than to know who are the Men to whom these Principles respectively belong: And that is not hard to determine. The Whigs, of which the Dissenters have always made a considerable part (and with whom that Interest is so closely connected and interwoven, that it can't fail to share the same fate) have been the Men noted for their Popular Principles, and for having always acted sutably thereto. They have been a firm Rampart to the Libertys of the People against all the Assaults of Arbitrary Power; and have so heartily oppos'd the Designs of ill Reigns, as to get the Names of Commonwealths-men: But who to shew that they were thoro' Friends to our Constitution, and were for defending the Prerogative vested in a good Prince, who they knew would use it to their Advantage, and who deserv'd Marks of their Gratitude, for the great Deliverance he had wrought, have gone so far on the obliging side in the late Reign, as to be term'd Apostates and Courtiers, in reproach. So that to contract the whole of this matter into as narrow a compass as we can, that it may be seen at one view, you may take this Abstract of the Demonstration. If the preservation of the Ballance or Constitution of England depends upon a preservation of the Prerogative on the one hand, and the Libertys of the People on the other: If moreover the Prerogative can't be preserv'd, nor the Libertys of the People destroy'd (which are the only Alterations we can fear) but by an Inclination in the People to preserve the one, and to give up the other: If moreover these Inclinations to preserve the one and not to give up the other, depend upon Popular Principles; and the Whigs are the Men noted for those Principles; and a steddy Practice conformable thereto: And if last of all, the Dissenters are known to be the Men, with whom the Whig Interest must rise and fall: It is certain, that to weaken the Dissenters, is to destroy the Ballance of England.

Or if you will, you may view the Demonstration in this Light. No Government can be happy but by one of these three ways: Either by *Wholesom Orders, Good Men,* or *Cautious ones* Wholesom Orders make Legislators and Magistrates both Wise and Honest. Legislators and Magistrates that are both Wise and Honest, render such Orders needless by their Wisdom and Honesty. And those that are cautious, do the same thing by their Craft and Fear. Lacedemon is an instance of the first sort; who by the meer Mechanism of her Rules made it in a manner impossible for any part of the Legislative or Executive Power to do amiss. Rome in its Infancy, and under her Consuls, is an instance of the second; who without the help of good Orders, by the meer Virtue and Strength of Genius, that was so notorious in her Senators and Magistrates, rais'd her self to be the Envy of her own, and the Admiration of future times. Our own Country may serve as an Instance of the third: Where I think 'tis beyond dispute, that our Constitution does not determine the Actions of Legislators, Magistrates and Ministers, by any Mechanical Oeconomy, which can make Knaves honest, and Fools wise; but leaves room for 'em, to shew themselves in their proper Colours: And sure we cannot be so vain, as to brag of our Race at present. It must be own'd that the Heroic Virtue that might support us by its own force, and give a tincture to all that we do, has been spent some Years ago.

Since then we cannot depend upon Mens Inclinations to be honest, we must depend upon their Fear of being otherwise. That Fear is only to be rais'd and supported by the view of a Power that is able to call them to an account. But when the far greater part of the Legislature, Magistracy and Ministry, shall act by the same Notions and Inclinations, who will they then fear as their Check? And yet 'tis evident, that both the Check and all Regard to him will vanish and disappear, when either of the Partys which are now pretty even, come to be weaken'd or destroy'd. The Constitution of England consists in a Ballance of Partys, as the Libertys of Europe do in a Ballance of Powers. We find to our Cost that they are not to be maintained by meer Treatys; nor by the Honor of Sovereign Princes, and their want of Inclination to invade them: But that they are supported and preserv'd by keeping every Government in such Circumstances, as to be afraid to undermine the Libertys of Europe, or openly to attack them, lest the rest call them to account. But as when we suffer any Power in Europe to become exorbitant, and out of reach of the Rest, we destroy the Libertys of Europe: So when we allow one of the Partys in England to be above the Check of the other, we must bid farewel to its Libertys too. These are Maxims and Principles which we have had but too much occasion of late to examine, and less Reason to question, since we have examined them: So that 'tis impossible they should be forgot. I hope they will not fail to be apply'd to a Case, where they are so pertinent and useful.

And if we may be allowed to look *Abroad*, let us see what Consequences this Test must have there. We have at present a Treaty on foot for the uniting England and Scotland, and for making that but one Government, which Nature has made but one Island. The Treaty has been recommended with that earnestness from the Throne, both by her present Majesty, and her Glorious Predecessor, and has been comply'd with so readily by both Houses of Parliament, and so far proceeded in on both sides, that whatever becomes of the Success, the Design ought to appear to be serious. And sure the Honour and Dignity of the Government, and the care of a future good Understanding with that Neighbour Country, should engage us to avoid every thing (unless it were resolv'd to venture all to mortify Presbyterians) that should give the least Suspicion of such a Treaty's being ludicrous and collusive. I'm sure a Comprehension would be very consistent with the Scheme of an Union, and would convince the Scots we were in earnest. I wish the Rule of Contrarys may for once prove false; and that straitning the Sacramental Test, and cramping the Dissenters mayn't be as inconsistent with the Union, as 'tis with a Comprehension. If we travel but a little farther from home, and view the Reference of our Isle to the Continent, we shall find it has the Honour to be apply'd to, as the Head of the Confederacy, and the Protectress of the Libertys of Europe. But when she has lost her own Libertys, or endangered them, is she like to remain in the same Consideration? No, 'tis for Free Governments to become the Patrons of the Oppressed. But a Country that has lost her own Libertys, will never have the honor to restore or maintain those of her Neighbours. And her Neighbours, we may depend upon it, will be wiser, than to do her the Honor, of suing for that, which it will not be in her power to give.

*   *   *

In the mean while, all that we have said upon this Head, it appears, how such a Test as this must affect our *Credit*, *Alliances*, and the *Ballance of Europe*, as well as our own true Poize and *Constitution*. And after I have named that, 'twere a Folly to say any thing more upon the fatal Consequences of such a Test. Our *Religion* and *Liberty*; Our *Property* and *Trade*; Our *Peace* and *Credit*; The *Integrity of Our Councils*; The *Administration of Justice*, and the *Success* of Our *Arms*: And to say no more, Our *happy Establishment under a Protestant Queen, and the Succession in a Protestant Line*, are all built upon our Constitution and can't fail to share the Fate of the Foundation which supports them.

And thus I have dispatch'd the first Consideration; What is the Interest of the Government of England.

12

The Rights of Protestant Dissenters in Two Parts[2]

2nd edn. (London, 1705), Part I, pp. 71-4; Part II, pp. 40-2, 45-6

[JOHN SHUTE, later VISCOUNT BARRINGTON]

But if Schism after all consists in a Separation from the true Church of England, the Gentlemen that use this Definition shou'd tell us, which *of the Churches of England* they mean, since there are two at present which lay claim to the Name. This is the more necessary, since those who have wrote for the Occasional Conformity Bill, are most of 'em Jacobites and Nonjurors; and stile themselves High Churchmen. When these men charge the Dissenters with Schism, they mean nothing but a Separation from their separate Assemblys. But certainly no Churchman can think this any Objection to the Dissenters, or can wish that the Nonconformists wou'd quit their Meetings, where the Government is fervently pray'd for, and which are tolerated by Law, to go to the Conventicles of the Jacobites, to hear Sedition taught against our Lawful Sovereign in a Cockloft.

Thus we see the Dissenters stand acquitted from the Charge of Schism, according to what notion soever it is laid, whether of the Scripture, the Fathers, or Divines. But if it shou'd be resolv'd, notwithstanding all we have said, that they are Schismaticks, yet they think *they may be good Subjects*, and that they have not lost their Title to a Toleration. A Schismatick can be no Member of the Church, but he may be a useful one in the State. He can't indeed partake of Ecclesiastical Privileges, because he has no Communion with the Church : But why shou'd he be debar'd Civil Ones? For Schism does not necessarily make a Man a Seditious Subject : Where it does, let the Sedition be punish'd by the Magistrate. But so long as a Schismatick remains peaceable, he has a Right to a Toleration, as we have prov'd before. Sir H.M. indeed pretends that the Dissenters are dangerous to the State, I suppose because they are Schismaticks : But I shall consider that Question separately by it self in the Second Part, and so shall take no notice of it here.

This is what the Dissenters plead for their Occasional Conformity, and their stated Dissent, and the Right they have to an absolute Toleration. But they think 'tis as much the *Interest* as the Duty of the Government, to grant and maintain it.

'Tis the Interest of the Government, because 'tis its Duty. Duty and Interest, Propriety and Advantage, being as inseparably connected as Virtue and Reward, Vice and Punishment. But it will appear to be more particularly the Interest of the Government, by running over the *Disadvantages* of the contrary Course. For to deprive the Dissenters of any Privilege they now enjoy, and particularly of the Offices which any of them hold at present, or of the Capacity they have to enjoy them for the future, is to weaken the Government. For it is to disoblige and discourage sober, industrious, wealthy, frugal Men. It is to deprive the Nation of the readiness of their Loans, and the Benefit of their Informations: 'Tis to rob it of the help and assistance of their Courage in the Camp, and of their skilful experience in our Fleet. It is to sap it of the Strength it receives from Persons, who are highly serviceable in a prudent discharge of the Commissions of Taxes, Peace and Lieutenancy, in the Bench of Aldermen, Common Council Men and Assistants, in the Courts of Judicature and Offices of State: In a word, of Men who cou'd assist in the making of wise Laws in Parliament, as well as any other of their Fellow-Citizens; and in the execution of 'em out of it.

To cashier such Men as these from all publick Offices and Employments, is not only, with one hand to cut off t'other, as Maximus told Valentinian, when he had murder'd Aetius his brave and faithful General; but 'tis with one hand to provoke the other to rebel against the whole: For 'tis not only the way to weaken the Government, but to endanger it. This it has a tendency to do, by tempting Men first to be Discontented and Uneasy; then to spread those Discontents among their Fellow-Citizens; in the next place, to betray us to Foreigners, by revealing the Counsels of the Government, and retarding its Business; till at last a number of these combin'd together, enter into Conspiracys, and don't stop at open Insurrections.

And as these are the natural Tendencys of such Measures; so they wou'd be the Consequences of 'em too, were the Dissenters such Subjects as their Enemys represent. Or if breaking in upon the Toleration shou'd not carry Men to this extremity, nor bring things to an open rupture; it might yet have as much worse consequences, by undermining the very Foundation of our Constitution, as a latent Disease is more dangerous than one whose Symptoms break out, and at the same time point out the nature of the Distemper and its cure. For it will destroy the Ballance between the several Partys in England, upon which the Ballance of Power between the three Estates depends. And it is upon that Ballance of Power, that the framing of good Laws depends, and the due execution of them; as the Ballance of Power does upon that of Partys. Nay, 'tis ruining the very Constitution it self, and at once breaks in upon the Prerogative which the Sovereign has to command any ones service that is capable to serve; and upon the Liberty every Man has to serve; and the Rights the Country has to be serv'd by 'em. In a word, whenever the Power of England shall be put into the hands of one Party, all the Prerogatives of the Crown and the Libertys of the People, will be swallow'd up by that Party. The Will of that Party must be then instead of the Sovereign's Prerogative, and their Interest must come into the room of the general Good of the People.

But it will not only ruin us at home but *abroad* too. For by discovering our ill will to the Presbyterians and Occasional Conformists, it will disunite us more from the Scots, foment their Jealousys of us at present, and render an Union more impracticable for the future. And it will by the same Method beget a Distrust in those of our Allys, who are Presbyterians, of our Will; and by weakening us at home, beget an equal distrust in them of our Power to help them.

And if the *Church* shou'd promote such a Persecution, it must be at her own expence: For it must wound the State, upon whose Security her Safety depends. She must divide and weaken the Christian and the Protestant Interest by it, both at home and abroad; and ruin the Character of Veracity and Temper she has acquir'd by her Moderation, and the Credit she has gain'd, by being at present thought to deserve 'em both.

If these Reasons did not prove such a Restraint of useful Men, and such a Persecution of good Christians, against our true Interest at all times; yet certainly the present unhappy Circumstances of Affairs wou'd easily convince us 'twas *Unseasonable* at this: A time when all our danger is from a Potent Enemy abroad, who has the Treasures of the Indys to support his Tyranny, and has rob'd us of the Revenue of Trade that might help to secure us from it; whose Counsels are unanimous and secret, and who is vigorous in all his Enterprizes; whilst we are irresolute, divided, and slow in ours. Sure all Heads, all Hands, all Purses are few enough to resist this powerful Adversary. Let us learn some of the Methods by which Rome became so great: She naturaliz'd all Strangers, admitted all her Citizens to the highest Honors without distinction, and laid aside all Quarrels and Divisions in times of publick danger, to unite against the common Foe. If the Cocks of the Game will spar it out, let it be after we have secured our selves from the Kite that hovers over our Heads, and aims at destroying us both. And when the State has had the assistance of the Dissenters against France, and the Church has call'd in their help against the Atheists, Deists and Socinians, in the Controversys and Disputes depending betwixt 'em; and when she shall by their assistance, have secur'd our common Religion and Libertys from their attempts; let her then, if it must be then, bend her Forces against these Enemys of lesser Importance.

If coming at the Truth, or the Mistakes in the Cause of the Protestant Dissenters, as far as it lys in any of these Points, were the *true and sole design* of the Disputants, methinks the present Age might hope to see an end of the Contest. The ready way seems easier and shorter than it has been thought and represented. Direct Answers to the Strength of the Cause it self, rather than the Weakness of its Managers; and to the Management rather than to the Persons or the Party who undertake it, wou'd not take up large Volumes, nor require Replys, Rejoinders and Replications, infinite in Bulk and Number, and equally tedious and impertinent. When the Partys come to manage their Cause in this way, it will no longer be suspected that they serve Interest more than Truth, nor doubted on whose side the Truth lys: but if instead of Arguments we use Charges and Invectives, and instead of Replys, Recriminations, we only dwindle into Satyrists, and by addressing our selves to Mens Passions, give the Standers by too much reason to think, that either we don't know our Cause, or distrust it; and that we rather design to incense and exasperate both Partys, than to confirm or convince either.

*   *   *

Thus it appears, that the Dissenters are Friends to the Church, both in Fact and in Principle. But let us now enquire whether the admission of Dissenters to Offices wou'd be inconsistent with the Safety of the Church, upon the *Supposition* that they were its Enemys. And even upon that Supposition, it does not necessarily follow, that they ought to be depriv'd of all Power in the State, because the Power of some Enemys is useful. And if the Dissenters, tho Enemys, shou'd appear to be Enemys of that sort, the weakning 'em wou'd prove the ruin of the Church. The overthrow of Carthage, Rome's greatest Rival, was the destruction of Rome. And England and Holland smart in this Age for their ill Policy in suffering Spain their formidable Enemy to be reduc'd so low in the last. The Power the Dissenters have in England is of the same use to the Church, that the Power of Spain wou'd have been to our own Country and the

United Provinces, had we maintain'd it against France, when we saw it so far declin'd. For the Power and Interest the Dissenters have, and are capable of having in England, cements the Church and *secures it from the Attempts of worse Enemys.* For whilst the Dissenters have Power, they will curb the Designs of those who wou'd go upon the Cassandrian Principles, and revive the Project of Arch-Bishop Laud; and who in order to it, talk of deciding Controversys between Protestants and Papists, in an Universal Council of Popish and Reformed Divines; who wou'd patch up an Union with the Gallican Church, commence a Persecution upon Dissenters, and who affect an independancy of the Church of England from the Civil Power. These are the Formidable Enemys of the Church of England, who wou'd subvert her Constitution, and the Protestant Religion at the same time. But whilst the Dissenters have any Power, they will divert these men from their Attempts, or render them unsuccessful. So that since the Church is in more danger of being ruin'd by these men, who call themselves High Churchmen (but are nothing more than Ceremony-mongers) than by the Dissenters; and that the Dissenters can no longer help to ballance 'em when they are excluded from all Offices, and depriv'd of all Power; the Effect of such a Deprivation will be, that the true Church of England will find her self overballanc'd and ruin'd by them. And what mistaken Policy wou'd it be then in the Church to divest the Dissenters of all Offices, tho it did appear that they were its Enemys?

But the Power and Interest of the Dissenters is useful to the Church, by being a *Check* upon *her* own *Members,* as well as upon her Enemys. The Jealousys of the several Professors and Pretenders to Religion, has been one of the greatest means God's Providence has made use of to perpetuate the Purity of Religion in its different Dispensations from Adam down to his Posterity in all Ages. And 'tis the Fears and Jealousys which the Church has of the Dissenters, that animate its Members to unite amongst themselves, and incite 'em from a noble emulation to be more exemplary in their Lives, and to make greater advances in useful Learning. But were there no such separate Bodys, whose Reproach the Church fear'd, and whom she did not supect of any Designs to take the advantage of Indecencys and Divisions, 'tis to be fear'd, that as Rome fell into Disorders and Factions at the destruction of Carthage; and as it happens to all Assemblys and Societys, whose Unanimity depends upon the Wisdom and Authority of their own Members, rather than of their Orders and Constitution, so the Church wou'd fall into gross Ignorance, more Heresys, a greater Dissolution of Manners, remissness of Discipline, and into inumerable Partys and Divisions. If the Church therefore wou'd keep Disputes and Animosities from entring her own Doors, she must suffer 'em to live between her and the Dissenters; as the Senate of Venice does the trifling Quarrel among the common People, Which are the better men, they that live on one side a Canal, or they that live on the other, under the Factions of the 'Castellani and Nicolotti', to prevent them from falling into those, that wou'd relate to the Constitution. Since the Church, then, to sum up this head, is in infinitely greater danger of ruining her self than being ruin'd, nothing can be possibly so fatal to her, as to rob the Dissenters of that Power, the Fear whereof is the best Preventive of the Ruin which the Church ought chiefly to apprehend.

* * *

Perhaps indeed it may be said, that she wou'd secure her self against any Alterations that a majority of Dissenters in Parliament cou'd be suppos'd to make. But there is so inconsiderable a number of Dissenters among the Nobility, Gentry, or Professions, and consequently so very few that are ever likely to come into Parliament, that the danger that can be fear'd from their Parliamentary Alterations, is but barely possible, and therefore what no wise man shou'd provide against. But if there were any real danger from hence as there is in a manner none at all, yet if this were the only danger the Church was in from the Dissenters, she wou'd be in no danger of any Alterations, but *such as all Constitutions* must be in in a Free Government. And if she desires a Security against Parliamentary Alterations, she desires a greater Security than our Civil Constitution either has, or is capable of having. Our Government precludes it self from no Parliamentary Alterations, because it supposes that those Alterations will be for the good, and agreeable to the Inclinations of the People: or else that the Alterations will not continue. The Church has this Security as much as the State: And methinks 'tis unworthy of any Churchman to discover the fears of such Alterations from the Dissenters, as shall be agreeable to the majority of the Representatives, and of those they represent. But if the Church had a mind to be secur'd against Parliamentary Alterations, to exclude the Dissenters from Offices, and thereby in a good measure from Parliament, wou'd, instead of giving the Church that Security, *leave her the more expos'd*. She wou'd then lie open to all the Alterations of the High Churchmen, whereas the best Security our Constitution can possibly give her against any Alterations whatsoever, is to ballance the Power of the Dissenters and the High Flyers; and by keeping both in Offices, or at least both capable of 'em, to keep one a constant check upon the other.

13

*Remarks on the Letter to the Dissenters by a Churchman*⁵

2nd edn. (London, 1714), pp. 4-7; 20-1; 25-6

[?JOHN SHUTE, later VISCOUNT BARRINGTON]

The Writers, whom we are most troubled with, are those, who, under the Pretence of vindicating the Q—— and Ministry, who, God be thanked, do not want such Advocates, treat the best and greatest Men of the Kingdom, whole Orders and Communities, as *Factious* and *Seditious*; and confine Loyalty to a Party that have been strangers to it ever since there was any Merit in being Loyal.

Before I talk with this Writer more particularly as to the main Subject of his *Letter*, I shall beg leave to say a Word or two about the Terms *Sedition* and *Faction*, and the Conduct of the *High-Church* Faction towards Her Majesty and Her Ministry.

It is not for three or four Persons who are honour'd with the Administration of the Publick Affairs, to call themselves the *State*, any more than it was in the Time of the *Memorial*, for three or four Bishops, and a few pious and wise Members of the Lower Houses of Parliament and Convocation, to call themselves the *Church*: And yet that they did so, may be seen by that ever memorable *Romance*, where Faction and Sedition appear triumphant, and we may know who the Men are that have distinguish'd themselves by their Obedience and Respect to Her Majesty and Her Ministers.

*　　　*　　　*

These Men might as well call themselves the *Church*, as some others call themselves the State. For as the Church is not compos'd only of *Bishops*, *Deans*, and *Prebendaries*; so neither can the State be said to consist only of *Chancellors*, *Treasurers*, and *Secretaries*. The *Constitution* is really the *State*, and those that by indirect Practices, and for private Ends, make Breaches in it, weaken its Foundation, and endanger its Establishment, are truly the *Factious* and *Seditious*, however they are dignify'd and distinguish'd.

When a Nation is in full Prosperity, their Arms every where victorious, their Credit strong and flourishing, their Counsels steady and happy, what Name is there for such Men as shall confound these Counsels, destroy their Credit, and disarm those Generals that had made them so safe and so glorious by many suprizing Victories?

When a State is at the Head of a powerful Confederacy, in the Defence of the Common Liberty, when the *Destroyer* is himself on the Brink of *Destruction*, and nothing but Union is wanting to finish the Deliverance of Kingdoms and Commonwealths from a long-threatened *Tyranny*, What is it to divide the Members of so necessary an Alliance, to restore Vigour, and even Fortune, to a vanquish'd *Tyrant*, and hazard again the Freedom of the World? If there is an Instance of such Management in History, see whether every honest Reader will not cry out against it as *Factious* and *Seditious*, whatever Accidents and Circumstances may intervene to seem to justifie or authorize it. These Marks are indelible: Such bad Actions as these create Ideas, for which there are no other Words in Language, but *Sedition* and *Faction*. 'Tis in vain to cloath *fair* Actions in a *foul* Dress; the Ideas Men have of them in their Mind, are spotless and clean; and when a Man is lawfully doing his Endeavour according to his Ability and Station, to serve his Country, encrease its Wealth, and advance its Honour, whatever Success his good Endeavour may be attended with, 'twill be in vain to call it *Factious* and *Seditious*. Every one will justifie him in his own Mind, for having done his Duty, and will condemn those that hinder'd the good Effect of it, let them be never so great and so powerful.

Was there no other Reason but this, That all Parties among us have in their Turn thrown *Sedition* and *Faction* in the Teeth of their Opponants, it shou'd methinks, make some People find out other Terms to villifie those they hate. Their Lexicon abounds with Phrases of *Calumny* and *Scandal*, but then their Weapons wou'd at once lose all their Edge. 'Tis neither their Wit nor their Reasoning, which they dare trust to; 'tis their Power, their Privilege: This Bullying-Air goes through the whole Body of them. You have it, not only in their *Libels*, but in their common Discourse. I cou'd not help smiling at the *Play* the other Night, when one of the Spectators said aloud to another, speaking of the Duke of *Marlborough*, *I hope in a little while to see him in* England *again. What's that, Sir*, says a third, *do you speak Treason*? The man's Mouth was stopt presently, he had not a Word more to say for the Hero that drove the *French* to the *Somme*, and might perhaps in another *Campagne*, have hung up his new Trophies in *Notredame*.

* * *

This, Gentlemen, is the honest Man who *designs your Good*:

This is *his calm and friendly Advice.* If it is not *Sedition* to act the
Part of an *Incendiary*, and foment Discord in so villainous a manner,
What is *Sedition?* Himself owns, p. 29. *The Dissenters are a great
Body of the Nation.* As they are so, Shall they not have the Liberty
to act in *Spirituals* and *Temporals*, according to their Consciences?
What wou'd he insinuate, by *depriving them of other Liberties beside
the Toleration and Exemption*, p. 45? Is it the Liberty to buy and
sell, to eat and drink, to breathe *English* air? What can this *Mercenary* pretend by this cursed Insinuation, especially where he farther
suggests, that Her most sacred Majesty *will not be ty'd by the Letter
of Her Promises*, p. 43. Wou'd not this be almost Treason in any
of you or me? And yet has he the Forehead in the same *Invective*,
to affront the Throne with his filthy *Panegyricks.*

He very kindly tells you, that for this once, he did indeed let you
you *Vote* in *Elections* of *Parliament*, and wou'd not say a Word
against it, but at the same time gives you to understand, that if he
leaves you that *other Privilege over and above your Exemption*, he
expects you will behave your selves to his good liking at the next
Opportunity. 'Tis true, Endeavours were us'd in some Places to
take away this *Right* from some of you at the last Struggle, and
you may assure your selves, his friendly Endeavours will never be
wanting to *cut you short* in that Part of your *Birthright.* Tho' for
this time, he trys you, he says, p.47. *He did not publish his Letter,
tho' long ago written, till all your joining and voting on one side
or other, was finish'd and over.* If *Englishmen* must not *vote* as
they think fit; if they are to be charg'd with *Faction* and *Sedition*,
every time they do not *vote* as Ministers wou'd have them, of what
use to them is their *Privilege of Voting?* Happy is the Nation
where the *Administration* is always to the *Good* and Interest of the
People: But since that is rather to be despair'd of than hop'd for,
it being a Degree of Perfection of which all sublunary things are
incapable, since the greatest Stations do not defend Men from
Error, and the People sometimes are the best Judges of their own
Interest, 'tis certainly their *Right* and *Duty* to *Vote* for such Men
and such Things as they believe will contribute most to the Welfare of themselves and their Posterity, when they are legally call'd
upon to Vote, and to go about to awe them or influence them in
Voting, is *Tyranny* worse than either *Faction* or *Sedition.* Will he
call all those worthy Members of the last House of Commons,
who Voted against the Bill of *Commerce*, a *Faction?* Will he call
the *Electors* that voted for them in this Parliament, or for other
Members on that account, *Factious?* Why is he so outragious
against the *Whiggs*, for doing their utmost that the present *Parliament*, of whom such great things are expected on all Hands, shou'd

be free? And why so angry with the *Dissenters*, as *Tradesmen*, for endeavouring to give their Powers to such as were best *Judges* of *Trade*, and most concern'd in it? This is what they have most at Heart. The Law secures their Religion to them, and excludes them the Places; What need they care who are in or out? But certainly it behoves them to do what they can, in a legal way, to maintain and encrease their Property; in which no doubt, they will act according to their best Light. Property is of no side, Interest never lies, and *Whigg*-Merchants and *Tory*-Merchants are *Englishmen* alike, when their Commerce is in question, if they have no sinister Byas.

The greatest Enemies to the present Government, are certainly those that do their utmost to render the most sober, wealthy and valuable Part of the Nation odious to Her Majesty, to maintain whose Title, there is not a Man of 'em but is ready to sacrifice his *Life* and *Fortune*, not in Paper only, but in *Blood* and *Treasure*. Why then are the best half of her loving and dutiful Subjects, we will guess only by the *Capital*, and that in the late *Election*, with all its Faults and Miscarriages, why are they represented as a *discontented Rabble, a meer confused, disunited, and dispersed Mob*? But because there are some People who cannot bear to think that *growing Party* shou'd be put in the Place of *ruin'd*, and that the *Competition* is so near a Ballance, that a Feather may turn the *Scale*.

It is the common Practice of all prevailing Parties, to represent others as *undone* and *ruin'd*, as the Writer of the *Letter*, and his Brother the *Examiner*, will have it the *Whiggs* are, tho' God be thank'd, they have enough left to pay their Tax of *Two Shillings*, and, as ruin'd as they are, they would have still paid *Four* with Chearfulness. They were themselves guilty of this Weakness, when the *Memorial* quite routed their Adversaries, and left that Field clear to them which they so gloriously maintained. My Manuscript abovementioned, treats *High-Church* as the *meer Remnant or Shreds of a Faction*, but indeed they own'd themselves to be so, in that same *Manifesto* of theirs, and that the *Lords and the whole Body of the People, were against them*; yet what a Hand have they made of it, without either Friends or Money? which of it self, methinks, shou'd be sufficient to let People know what Climate they live in, where the Wind changing so often, 'twill be very hard if it never sets fair.

14

An Essay on the Freedom of Wit and Humour

(1709), in *Characteristicks of Men, Manners, and Opinions, Times*
(n.p., 1727), Vol. I, pp. 113-15

ANTHONY, LORD SHAFTESBURY

'Tis strange to imagine that *War*, which of all things appears the most savage, shou'd be the Passion of the most heroick Spirits. But 'tis in War that the Knot of *Fellowship* is closest drawn. 'Tis in War that mutual Succour is most given, mutual Danger run, and *common Affection* most exerted and employ'd. For *Heroism* and *Philanthropy* are almost one and the same. Yet by a small mis-guidance of the Affection, a Lover of Mankind becomes a Ravager: A Hero and Deliverer becomes an Oppressor and Destroyer.

Hence other Divisions amongst Men. Hence, in the way of Peace and Civil Government, that *Love of Party,* and Subdivision by *Cabal.* For Sedition is a kind of *cantonizing* already begun within the State. To *cantonize* is natural; when the Society grows vast and bulky: And powerful States have found other Advantages in sending Colonys abroad, then merely that of having Elbow-room at home, or extending their Dominion into distant Countrys. Vast Empires are in many respects unnatural: but particularly in this, That be they ever so well constituted, the Affairs of many must, in such Governments, turn upon a very few; and the Relation be less sensible, and in a manner lost, between the Magistrate and People, in a Body so unwieldy in its Limbs, and whose Members lie so remote from one another, and distant from the Head.

'Tis in such Bodys as these that strong Factions are aptest to engender. The associating Spirits, for want of Exercise, form new Movements, and seek a narrower Sphere of Activity, when they want Action in a greater. Thus we have *Wheels within Wheels.* And in some National Constitutions (notwithstanding the Absurdity in Politicks) we have *one Empire within another.* Nothing is so delightful as to incorporate. *Distinctions* of many kinds are invented. *Religious Society's* are form'd. Orders are erected; and their Interests espous'd, and serv'd, with the utmost Zeal and Passion. Founders and Patrons of this sort are never wanting. Wonders are perform'd, in this wrong social Spirit, by those Members of separate

Societys. And the *associating Genius* of Man is never better prov'd, than in those very Societys, which are form'd in opposition to the general one of Mankind, and to the real Interest of the State.

In short, the very Spirit of *Faction,* for the greatest part, seems to be no other than the Abuse of Irregularity of that *social Love,* and *common Affection,* which is natural to Mankind. For the Opposite of *Sociableness* is *Selfishness.* And of all Characters, the thorow-selfish one is the least forward in *taking Party.* The Men of this sort are, in this respect, true *Men of Moderation.* They are secure of their Temper; and possess themselves too well, to be in danger of entering warmly into any Cause, or engaging deeply with any Side or Faction.

15

An Enquiry into The State of the Union of Great Britain
... By the Wednesday's Club in Friday-street

(London, 1717), pp. 40-5

[WILLIAM PATERSON][4]

The Word *Beard* or *Beards seems* a Word good enough on such an Occasion (said Mr. *North*) especially considering as it is a Monosyllable; But I wonder what could ail the Men at the other's Beards, for, what Hurt can another's Beard do me?

It's plain that this was only the Pretext, the Cause was somewhat else; (said Mr. *May*) without looking further abroad, it's apparent from our own Histories, that whatever the Pretexts have been, our Principal Civil Disorders and Broils here in *Great Britain* have always proceeded, either from want of Government, or by a bad one, or in other Words, either where the Government it self unreasonably oppressed the People with Taxes and Impositions, or suffered others to do it, which last Case was generally not the less, but rather still the more intolerable; and further (continued he) I doubt not but upon proper Search it will plainly appear, that the People of the Nation, tho' they be but Islanders, have generally born the Neglects and Oppressions of their Government, as patiently and with as good Temper towards Redress of them as any other in like Circumstances.

Whatever other good National Qualities his People may have (said Mr. *Far*) I never heard they were famed for Temper; did not we all find them in Parties, and are not like to leave them so?

I hope so, said Mr. *Grant*.

Hope! What, hope that the People shall always be in Parties! that's a strange Hope (said Mr. *Ford*.)

Whether we hope it or not; it will be so (reply'd Mr. *Grant*.)

What then, do you think People cannot be without Party? (said Mr. *Ford*.)

Not so long as they are People, (reply'd Mr. *Grant*.)

I thought we were met here to speak against Party (said Mr. *Ford*) but now perceive it's to speak for them, yet surely it must only be for some one Party or other, and not for all of them.

After this three or four of the Modern Party Names were mention'd in the Club, and Mr. *Grant* was desired to explain himself, and say, which of them he was for.

For all of them, answer'd Mr. *Grant.*

That's monstrous (reply'd Mr. *Ford*) I dare say, Sir, you'll never be able to attain to any considerable Place or Preferment whilst in that Mind, and that the direct Road to Advancement continues to be by the way of Party.

Patience (said Mr. *Grant*) so long as they will not put me in, they cannot turn me out; but how long has Party been so much the direct Road to Preferment?

Chiefly since the Restoration in 1660 (said Mr. *Ford*) but I have heard some of the old Men in those Days say, that formerly Party was not so very much the way to Preferment.

I remember somewhat of this (said Mr. *Brooks*) and likewise that thereby, during his whole Reign King *Charles* the Second grew still the poorer, whilst his Officers grew richer, insomuch that it became at last a common Saying about Court, *That the King would never be easie 'till they gave him a Place.*

It's pity they did not provide better for him (said Mr. *Shaw*).

He was very well provided for (said Mr. *Brooks*) but his Misfortune was to have Thieves about him, who stole away his Provision from him.

No King of this island before him was half so well provided for, (said Mr. *Sands*) it was reckon'd by some, that in the 24 Years of his Reign, he exacted more Mony from the People, than some Twenty four of his Predecssors had done; yet all this was unaccountably wasted in such a Manner, that it was almost impossible to know how it went.

*　　　*　　　*

Besides all this (said Mr. *Gage*) we ought not to forget, that by these Corruptions in the Places, Grants, Pensions, and their Concomitants, the Parties, in the time of King *Charles* the Second, were at last turned into Factions, the Growth whereof made way for the happy Revolution in 1688, and I hope we all think that a good Effect.

As Good comes out of Evil (said Mr. *Brooks.*)

But seriously, do you think then (said Mr. *Bruce*) that those who had the publick Places and Benefits in that time did, by all this their

Management, or rather Mismanagement, intend the Revolution?

By no means (reply'd Mr. *Brooks*) you may venture to take it for granted, they seriously intended only their own Business.

Their own Business? What was that (said Mr. *Gage*.)

The making the best of the Publick Places and Benefits they were possess'd of, (answer'd Mr. *Brooks*.)

But were not these Grievances redressed, particularly the Places mended by the Revolution? (said Mr. *Gage*.)

They were not mended by it (said Mr. *Brooks*.)

I know not what you mean by mending (said Mr. *Gage*) but to the Point, were the Places made better by the Revolution?

They were made more and greater (answered Mr. *Brooks*) as the Nation then did, and still continues to feel.

At this rate (said Mr. *Gage*) probably we cannot expect better times, 'still the Places are mended.

Possibly there may be something in it (said Mr. *Brooks*.)

The more I think on it (said Mr. *Ford*) the more I am surpriz'd to find even Mr. *Grant* so much for Parties, and for all of them too; but possibly he thinks there can be no Nation, City, nay Family, without somewhat of Party, and if it were so, a Man at this rate can never be free of Party unless he will live alone.

Nor hardly then neither (reply'd Mr. *Grant*.)

Why so (said Mr. *Ford*?)

Because he may happen sometimes to differ with himself (answer'd Mr. *Grant*.)

I perceive your Meaning not to be quite so bad, as I at first thought (said Mr. *Ford*.)

You say, you are for Parties; Are you for Factions too?

By no means (reply'd Mr. *Grant*) these are wicked things.

A very nice Distinction (reply'd Mr. *Ford*) pray wherein do your Parties and Factions differ? Since I confess my self so wise as not to know.

The difference is manifest several ways (said Mr. *Grant*) particularly your natural Parties are things consisting only of Members without Heads, but your Factions, or in other Words provoked unnatural Parties, have Heads.

By what other Properties can we distinguish them? (said Mr. *Ford*.)

Your natural Parties are pretty tame, unless in some lucid Intervals (reply'd Mr. *Grant*) but the others are always wild and voracious; the first is capable of Good, as well as Hurt, of Love as well as Hatred, and frequently produce Emulation, a very good thing. But instead thereof, your unnatural Parties hate, but love not, are hurtful in their Nature, and chiefly produce Enmity, a dangerous Quality in Men.

What is then the best way of destroying these dangerous things with Heads, you call provok'd Parties, otherwise Factions? (said Mr. *Ford*.)

Changing or removing the Subject Matter that breeds and feeds them (answer'd Mr. *Grant*.)

16

The Conspirators, or, The Case of Cataline

Part II (London, 1721), pp. 9-12

[THOMAS GORDON][5]

Before I enter upon the Remainder of my History, I think it highly to my Purpose to make some Reflexions upon a Maxim of MACHIAVEL's, which has very much the Air and Countenance of a *Paradox,* to wit, that the *Disagreement* of the *People* and the *Senate* of *Rome* made that Commonwealth both *free* and *mighty.* For it is most evident, that the Agreement of the *Senate,* and the *Tribunes* of the *People,* in suffering *CATILINE* and his *Accomplices* to escape *publick* Punishment, was as certainly the *Ruin* of that Commonwealth: So that Concord, in this Case, produc'd Confusion, Ruin, and Disorder.

I know that some Politicians strenuously maintain, that *Rome* was a most disorderly Commonwealth, and disturb'd with so many Seditions, that if their great Virtue and military Discipline had not supply'd other Defects, it would have been inferior to any Republick now in the World. It is not to be denied, indeed, but that Virtue, good Fortune, and military Discipline, were the Causes of the *Roman* Grandeur. These naturally produce each other; where there is Virtue and good Discipline, there will be Order; and where there is Order, there is commonly good Fortune. And yet I shall not scruple to maintain, tho' it may startle some Men at first view, that all These proceeded from the *Tumults* and *Civil Broils* that arose in the City of *Rome.*

For, if we examine all the Tumults that happen'd in *Rome,* from the Death of the *Tarquins* to the Creation of the *Tribunes,* and from thence till the Days of *Marius,* and *Sylla,* and afterwards of our CATILINE, we shall find that all these Commotions were occasion'd by some *Incroachments,* which were attempted by the *Government* against the *Liberty* of the People. For it was a long Time before *Gold* had any Influence in *Rome,* to corrupt the *Virtue* of her *Patriots*: Therefore the *Tribunes* of the People, who were the Guardians of their Liberties, being Proof against all Temptation, never gave up one Title of their sacred Rights, which, to their immortal Honour, they kept for so many Ages inviolable.

The *Tribunes* thus acting up to the Duty of their Trust, and opposing the most distant Designs of the great Men against the People, were not to make publick the Transactions of the *Senate*: The People, by this Means, taking Alarm when they saw their Liberties aim'd at by some new Law, were accustom'd to run tumultuously through the Streets, to shut up their Houses, assemble in Numbers, and so resort in Bodies to the Senate-House, calling out and exclaiming against them: And tho' this Custom may seem extravagant, and a little outragious, yet it produc'd an admirable Effect: For it kept the *Great Ones* in Awe of the *People's* Resentments, and hinder'd them from proceeding in any *Arbitrary* Law.

MACHIAVEL upon this Subject observes, that every City has its peculiar Ways, and this was one peculiar to the *Romans*: It was the Method they pursued of venting their Discontents, and letting their Superiors know wherein they dislik'd their Proceedings. Let no Man therefore, *says he*, call *Rome* a disorderly Commonwealth; for good Examples proceed from good Education, good Education from good Laws, and good Laws from these Tumults which some take upon them without Judgment to condemn.

CICERO, I remember, says, that the Desires of a free People never tend to the Subversion of Liberty; and that their Discontents proceed either from actual Oppression, or from some Danger, which they foresee, of falling into it. And in Case the *People* should be *deceiv'd* in their *Opinion* of Things, there is nothing more easy than to set them right, if some *Orator* of *Honesty* and *Credit*, will but take the Pains to shew them their Errors: For the People have a Capacity of comprehending Truth, that the People are the best Guardians of Liberty; and if we look back into the *Roman* History, we shall find, that from the Expulsion of the *Tarquins*, to the Time of the *Gracchi*, which took in the Space of Three Hundred Years, the Civil Broils in *Rome* seldom caus'd *Banishment*; and much seldomer the Shedding of Blood. I say, that in all that Period of Time, their civil Discord did not occasion the Banishment of more than ten *Romans*, and very few were fatigued with pecuniary Punishments. But in the Time of CATILINE, whose History we are writing, when Gold had influenc'd the Minds and Affections of Men, and the *Tribunes* of the People so shamefully sold the Liberty of the *Romans*, there was a villanous Harmony in the Senate, the Cause of all the Murthers, Depredations, Taxes, and Innovatons of Government which follow'd.

17

On Government by Parties

Applebee's Journal (11 May, 1723), in *Daniel Defoe: His Life and Recently Discovered Writings*, ed. William Lee, reprinted (Hildesheim, 1968), Vol. II, pp. 133-6

[?DANIEL DEFOE][6]

A. J., May 11.—Sir, There was a Book published in London some Years ago by a well-known Author, the Learned (to say nothing else of him,) Mr. *Toland*. Learning, without all doubt he had, but for anything else, 'tis enough to say he is in his Grave, *de Mortuis nil nisi bonum*; I say there was a Book publish'd by him, with this subtle Title, *The Art of Governing by Parties*.

If all Mr. *Toland* advances there be true, Parties are in the main no Disadvantage to the Nation, or to the Government; only provided that the Government find themselves strong enough to govern these Parties as well as to govern by them. Governing by Parties, is call'd by the Politicians, playing the Parties one against another; by which means the Party who are OUT, are always a Curb, and a Bridle to those which are IN, and the Parties which are IN, are always a Terror and a Stirrer up to Vigilance in those which are OUT. In a Word, they are mighty useful to keep one another awake, and make one another Uneasy; and in their uneasiness, very often the easiness and safety of the whole Body may consist. All this, I say, is upon Mr. *Toland's Hypothesis*, and according to his Notions of Parties.

If I was to be asked, whether it is best for us to be divided into Parties, or no? I must answer that, *Negatively*, certainly it were best to have a Nation of one Heart, and of one Mind, as well in Political Principles, as in Religious, if that were possible. There is a great difference between there being a Set of Politick Statesmen in the World, or in a Court, who can make their Advantages of the Divisions of the Subjects, and setting one against another, form their own private Interest from the Contention and Strife of others, and the Halcyon calm Enjoyments of a Dominion entirely united; where the King and the People have not only one Interest, but one

Heart; where the King has the Hearts of all his Subjects, and the
Subjects equally enjoy the Favour and Affection of their Prince.

But as the World never was of one Mind since there was but
one Man in it, and never will be so again, so long as there are two;
and since Divisions must come, the Politick Statesmen will make
their Advantage of it, and make their Market of both. When the
subtle Angler fishes for Gudgeons, he takes a long Pole, and rum-
mages and disturbs the Gravel at the bottom of the River, makes
an Uproar in the Water, and raises the Stones and Sand; and then
the Fish come blindly together, and are caught with the more Ease.

Thus I have seen a Press Gang, when they have wanted Seamen,
set a couple of Fellows to Fight in the Street, thereby drawing a
Crowd together; and while one takes Part with JACK, and t'other
takes part with GILL, the Press Gang come upon them all, and
sweep away from both Parties the People they want.

It is true, it were to be wish'd there were no such Things as
Parties among us, *as above*, and that we were Religious without
Separation, and Loyal without Faction; but as Offences must come,
and Divisions must happen among Mankind, as above, 'tis the
wisdom of our Ministers of State to work the Safety of the Government out of the Mistakes of the People, and out of those very
Feuds by which, *if left to an ungoverned* ARISTOCRACY they would
destroy all Civil Government in the World. Thus the wise Mariners
have so improved Navigation, that those dangerous Shoals and
Sands, and those frightful Rocks, which in former Times made the
Northern Seas be the Terror of all the Navigators of the World, are
now artfully made assistant to Preserve, instead of Destroying
those that sail among them; affording them, by the help of Buoys,
and Sea-Marks, safe Harbours, good Roads, Skreening them from
the Fury of Storms, and contrary Winds, by breaking off the Sea,
and sheltering the Ships under their Lee; so that when our Ships
get in the Sands, or under such or such Rocky Headlands, they
are now Safe, even in those Places where they would, without that
Skill or Caution, have been most assuredly wrecked.

Of this, the blessed Apostle St. *Paul* set us a Wise and Politick
Example, when he was in danger of being Murthered by the Mob
in the famous Tumult at *Jerusalem*, when the enraged *Jews* threw
Dust into the Air, in taking off their Madness; and cry'd, "Away
with such a Fellow from the Earth, it is not fit that he should be
suffered to live." The blessed inspired Man, present to himself, and
with a turn of Wit, and Superiority of Genius, peculiar to himself,
knowing there were Factions and Parties among them, and that
they Hated one another, as much as they Spighted, and were Piqued
against him,—immediately turned his speech to the Point in which

they disagreed, played the *Pharisees* against the *Sadducees*, talked to them of their future State, and the Resurrection from the Dead, which the *Sadducees* deny'd, and setting the two Factions together by the Ears, made his own Safety the Effect of their Quarrel.

This is certainly a shining Example of the Art of managing Parties, and I could give you Modern Instances of the like in our own Time, of which I shall be more particular in my next.

18

Dissertation Concerning the Whigs and the Tories

(1st French and English edns., 1717), in *The Memoirs of John Ker
of Kersland in North Britain Esq.,...* (London, 1727), Vol. 3,
pp. 186-90

PAUL DE RAPIN-THOYRAS[7]

I have but one Observation more, to conclude what I have to
say of the *Whigs* and the *Tories*. It is, then when I spoke of their
different Views, of their Interests and Characters, I did by no
Means pretend to include every particular Person engaged in either
Party, but only their Heads and Leaders, with some of the most
active on both Sides. Though all the People are ranged, either by
Inclination or Interest, under these two Factions, yet it does not
follow that every one of them acts upon the Views I have ascribed
to them. It is certain that most of them suffer themselves to be led
they know not whither, without examining into the Tendency of
the Steps they are made to take; and consequently, they dive very
little into the Intrigues and Cabals wherein their Leaders are incessantly busied. A Man perhaps has drawn himself in to be a *Tory*,
by being very zealous for the Church of *England*; and in Time
(without knowing which May) this Man finds himself engaged to
maintain the Principles of the *Arbitrary Tories* and *Rigids*, though
contrary to his Inclination. It is not to be doubted but there is an
infinite Number of good *Englishmen* who groan to see their
Country thus torn and disfigured, and who would gladly embrace
all Expedients to heal her Divisions: But it is no easy Thing to be
without Ambition and without Avarice. Those that are Neuter (as
I said before) have neither Places nor Honours; because there is
always one Party uppermost, which has nothing more at Heart then
advancing its own Friends, or winning over some of the opposite
Party. Of Consequence there can be no Places left for Persons from
whom the reigning Party can hope for no Service. Besides, how
can any one stand Neuter between two Parties, each whereof
accuses his Antagonist of designing such Mischiefs as are capable
of striking Terror into the Heart of Man; namely, the Ruin of the
Established Religion, and the Dissolution of a Government, which

they think the only One under which a Subject can live happy?
He must be very insensible that is not moved at such Dangers, and
endeavours not to prevent them, after he is convinced they are
real.

We are not therefore to blame all the *English* for these Unnatural Divisions; but only those that foment them for their particular Ends. Who are those that would vest the King with *Absolute
Power*? Who are those that would deprive Free Subjects of *Liberty
of Conscience*? Who, lastly, are those that do their Endeavours to
bring in *Popery*? Can we say these are the Views of private Persons,
of all the *Tories*? No certainly: But they are those of their
Leaders, who for their own Profit seduce the poor People, and
without a Scruple, engage their Country in the Danger of a Civil
War.

It may be positively affirmed, It is not the Interest of the Kingdom that one of the Parties should become so superior as to meet
with no Contradiction. If it were the *Arbitrary Tories*, they would
bring *England* under a Despotick Government. If the *Moderate
Tories*, their Inclination to the Prerogatives of the Crown, will at
length enable the Soveraign to undertake what he pleases, and to
shake off the troublesome Yoke of Parliaments: If the *Papists*,
England will quickly lose her Religion and Liberty. On the other
hand, if the *Republican Whigs* regain the Advantage they have
lost, there will be no longer Talk of a *Kingdom*, but of the *Republick* of *England*, as in the Time of *Cromwell*. Lastly. If the *Moderate Whigs* might carry Matters how they pleased, they would take
so many Precautions against the Increase of the Royal Power, that
they would perhaps reduce the King to the Condition of a Doge of
Venice.

As for the Extreams of the two Parties in Point of *Religion*, it is
certain, that if ever the *Presbyterians* have it in their Power to act
without Opposition, they will not be satisfied till they have totally
destroyed the *Hierarchy*, and in general, the whole Church of
England. But, again, if the *Rigid Episcopalians* had no Counter-
poize to their Power, nothing less is to be expected than an open
Persecution of *Presbyterians*: And we know not whether they
would allow them so much as a bare Liberty of Conscience.

It is certain, the true Good and Advantage of the Kingdom is
not to be found in any of the Views which the Heads of the Two
Parties seem to have an eye to. The only Method that can in Time
restore Peace and Tranquility, is to let the Government remain
upon its Ancient Foundations, and the Church in the Condition
wherein the *Reformation* placed it. It is also necessary to give

Toleration to the Scruples of the *Presbyterians*, who are very numerous in that Kingdom. If this Method is not observed, it will always be safer for the State, that the Division should continue as it is at present, than that one of the Parties should enjoy a Superiority, which would be more fatal to the Publick, than the Equality their Discord keeps them in.

19

A Foreign View of England in the Reigns of George I and George II. The Letters of Monsieur César de Saussure and his Family

(written *c*. 1729; published 1755), ed. Mme van Muyden (London, 1902), pp. 347-51

CÉSAR DE SAUSSURE

You have, I am sure, heard of the appellations "Tories" and "Whigs" as being nicknames given to the two principal parties in England; I should be much embarrassed were you to ask me to give you the etymology of these names, but I believe the two parties first appeared under the reign of Charles II., and that these names were given them satirically and opprobriously, but this is no longer so. The Tories uphold all the prerogatives of the Sovereign, and declare that his or her subjects must submit without resistance, even though his or her power be arbitrary. The opposite party, or Whigs, accuse their opponents of wishing to upset the recognized form of government and the liberties of the nation by endeavouring to establish despotism, thus making the King a tyrant and his subjects slaves, and they, moreover, consider that respect and obedience are owed to the King only so long as the latter maintains the conditions under which supreme power has been given him, but were he to attempt to govern the consciences, lives, and possessions of his subjects, and thus violate the fundamental laws of the State, the latter should not only refuse him obedience, but also take the necessary measures to be governed according to the established laws of the country. The Tories reproach the Whigs with these principles, and declare that they are real republicans, desirous of taking all authority and power from the Sovereign, leaving him no more rights than are allowed to a Doge of Venice.

These two parties are so opposed to each other that nothing but a real miracle could cause them to become united. Many causes contribute to this animosity, and none more than the antipathy that exists between the Anglicans and the Presbyterians, together with other Nonconformists. The latter are Whigs, and so great is their fear lest a Roman Catholic monarch powerful enough to annihilate the tolerance recognized by the laws should ascend the throne, that they uphold the Whigs with all their might. Zealous Anglicans, on the other hand, are Tories, and look upon the laws of toleration as a means by which the Presbyterians are so strengthened as possibly at some future date to place the established religion and rites in danger. The numerous pamphlets that appear every day for and against these two political parties is certainly a means of maintaining and augmenting animosity between them, and another is the interests of certain individuals who become either zealous Tories or ardent Whigs, according to whether their hopes of power lie in the one or the other of these parties. The Anglican clergy of inferior rank are accused of being exaggerated Tories, and of writing the greater number of violent pamphlets in the hope of attracting the favour of the King, who disposes of the bishoprics and of many important benefices. All Anglicans are not Tories; many of them, on the contrary, are Whigs, and they try to please the people in order to strengthen their own power. You would naturally suppose that the party at Court always upholds the Tories, but it is not so; this party sometimes has reasons for raising the Whigs to power. King William III, owed his throne to this party, and always upheld and favoured its politics.

The Jacobites are entirely in favour of the Pretender. They declare that the nation has no right to exclude the legitimate sovereign from the throne simply because of his being a Roman Catholic, and they maintain that the law made under William III was not a just one, as it was voted by a parliament in rebellion against its legitimate sovereign, and therefore the law of a usurper. Almost all Jacobites are Roman Catholics; the few Protestants that follow this party do so from personal inclination or zeal for the Stuarts. Fifteen or sixteen years ago the Jacobite party was far more considerable than it is now, and it tends to diminish every day, either by the death of the Pretender's partisans or because their children favour the House of Hanover, and little hope now exists of the Pretender's ever recovering the lost throne of his fathers.

Though many people look on these different parties which divide England as a misfortune, others, on the contrary, think that they contribute to the maintenance of the liberties and privileges of the people. For, say they, were there in the country neither Whigs nor Tories, the tendencies of the Court would be blindly followed, and the fundamental laws of the State would suffer seriously by this state of things. Despotism would soon be established in England as it is in France. On the other hand, if the Tories did not uphold the King's authority and power, and if everyone followed the principles of the Whigs, the country would very soon be in a state of anarchy, as was the case in the time of Charles I and of Cromwell. Numbers of prudent politicians, who are not blinded by foolish prejudices or by their own particular interests, are convinced that this form of government is the happiest in the world, and they sometimes side purposely with the weakest party, so as to preserve to the country a wholesome equilibrium.

Section III

OPPOSITION TO WALPOLE

The *Whig-Principle* being more for the Interest and Rights of the *People*, hath made it much more easy to betray us. This sufficiently shows the Errors of *both Sides*, and the Necessity of uniting in *one national Party* against any *ministerial Party*, by what Name soever call'd, ...

"HAMPDEN"

The Country Journal: or, The Craftsman, No. 671 (19 May, 1739)

Throughout Walpole's years in office he was opposed by malcontents who equally styled themselves Whigs. The old party names were still heard, but Court and Country better described the ins and outs, especially as defections from the Ministry grew. Dominated by Bolingbroke's rejection of party as a permanent instrument, the literature of the Opposition contributed little to an understanding of party conflict. Lyttleton had something of significance to say on this theme, as had *The Craftsman*, following Bolingbroke's withdrawal to France, but most Opposition writers confined themselves to pleas for a national opposition against the party of the Ministry.

20

The Country Journal: or The Craftsman

No. 230 (28 November, 1730)

It is well known that the *Passions, Vanities,* and even *Vices* of Mankind often prove of Service to *Society,* which avails itself of the good Acts They produce, and is not in the least affected with the *bad Motives,* from whence They may proceed....

And here it may not be improper to observe that a Spirit of *Liberty* and *Opposition to Men in Power,* from whatever *Motives* it may proceed, hath often produced very good Effects, and proved of signal Advantage to the Publick; for as *Power* is a Thing of most intoxicating Nature, it ought always to have some Checks upon it; and it hath often been observ'd, that *Ministers,* who are narrowly watched and vigorously oppos'd, upon proper Occasions, will not venture upon many Things which they would not scruple to do if they were left without any Controul. On the other hand ... as *Men out of Power* are under no Influence or Temptation to act contrary to the Interest of their Country, so They often propose *good* and *wholesome Laws,* which perhaps they might not be inclin'd, or even at Liberty to do, if they were in Power....

21

A Dissertation Upon Parties

(1735); 10th edn. (London, 1775), pp. 121-2; 137-40

HENRY ST. JOHN, VISCOUNT BOLINGBROKE[1]

But whatever the state of parties was at the revolution, and for some time afterwards, the settlement made at that time having continued, that state of parties hath changed gradually, tho' slowly, and hath received at length, according to the necessary course of things, a total alteration. This alteration would have been sooner wrought, if the attempt I have mention'd, to defend principles no longer defensible, had not furnish'd the occasion and pretence to keep up the appearances of a tory, and a whig party. Some of those, who had been call'd tories, furnish'd this pretence. They who had been call'd whigs, seized and improved it. The advantages to one side, the disadvantages to the other, the mischiefs to the whole, which have ensued, I need not deduce. It shall suffice to observe, that these appearances were the more easy to be kept up, because several men, who had stood conspicuous in opposition to one another before the revolution, continued an opposition, tho' not the same, afterwards. Fresh provocations were daily given, and fresh pretences for division daily taken. These contests were present; they recalled those, that had past in the time of king CHARLES the second; and both sides forgot that union, which their common danger and their common interests had form'd at the revolution. Old reproaches were renew'd, new ones invented, against the party call'd whigs, when they were as complaisant to a court as ever the tories had been; against the party call'd tories, when they were as jealous of public liberty, and as frugal of public money, as ever the whigs had been.

*   *   *

Now, that we may see the better how to proceed in the cause of liberty, to compleat the freedom, and to secure the duration of our present constitution; it will be of use, I think, to consider what obstacles lie, or may hereafter lie, in our way, and of what nature that opposition is, or may hereafter be, which we may expect to meet. In order to this, let us once more analyse our political divisions; those, which may possibly exist now, or hereafter, as we did those, which were form'd at the revolution.

ONE possible division then is that of men angry with the government, and yet resolved to maintain the constitution. This may be the case at any time; under the present, wise, virtuous, and triumphant administration; and therefore to be sure at any other.

A SECOND possible division is that of men averse to the government, because they are so to the constitution, which I think can never be the case of many; or averse to the constitution, because they are so to the government, which I think may be the case of more. Both of these tend to the same point. One would subvert the government, that they might change the constitution. The other would sacrifice the constitution, that they might subvert the government.

A THIRD possible division, and I seek no more, is that of men attach'd to the government; or, to speak more properly, to the persons of those, who govern; or, to speak more properly still, to the power, profit, or protection they acquire by the favour of these persons; but enemies to the constitution.

Now, as to the first and second of these possible divisions, if there be any such among us, I do not apprehend that we are at present or can be hereafter, in much danger; or that the cause of liberty can meet with much opposition from them; though the second have certainly views, more likely to bring slavery upon us, than to promote liberty; and though prudence requires that we should be upon our guard against both. The first, indeed, might hope to unite even the bulk of the nation to them, in a weak and oppressive reign. If grievances should grow intolerable under some prince as yet unborn; if redress should become absolutely desperate; if liberty itself should be in immediate peril; the nature of our constitution would justify the resistance, that we ought to believe well enough of posterity to persuade ourselves would be made in such an exigency. But without such an exigency, particular men would flatter themselves extremely, if they hoped to make the nation angry, because they were so. Private motives can never influence numbers. When a nation revolts, the injury is national. This case therefore is remote, improbable, nay impossible, under the lenity, justice and heroical spirit of the present government; and if I mention'd such an imaginary party, it was only done that I might omit none, which can be supposed. The projects of the second division, stated in the same hypothetical manner, are surely too extravagant, and their designs too wicked to be dangerous. Disputes may arise hereafter in some distant time, about ministers, perhaps about kings; but I persuade myself that this constitution will be, as it ought to be always, distinguish'd from, and preferr'd to both, by the British nation. Reasons must arise in process of time, from the very nature of man, to oppose ministers and kings too; but none can arise, in the nature of things, to oppose such a constitution as ours. Better ministers better kings, may be hereafter often wanted, and sometimes found; but a better constituted government never can. Should there be therefore still any such men, as we here suppose among us, they cannot expect, if they are in their senses, a national concurrence; and surely a little reflection will serve to shew them, that the same reasons, which make them weaker now than they were some years ago, must make them weaker some years hence then they are now.

As to the third division, if any such there be, it is in that our greatest and almost our whole danger centers. The others cannot overthrow, but these may undermine our liberty. Capable of being admitted into power, in all courts, and more likely than other men to be so in every court, except the present (whose approved penetration and spotless innocence give a certain exclusion to them) they may prevent any farther securities from being procured to liberty, till those already establish'd are dissolv'd, or perverted. Since then our principal danger must arise from those, who belong to this division, it is necessary to show, before we conclude these discourses, by what means such men may carry on their pernicious designs with effect, and by what means they may be defeated. These considerations will lead us to fix that point, wherein men of all denominations ought to unite, and do unite, and to state the sole distinction of parties, which can be made with truth, at this time, amongst us.

22

Letters on the Spirit of Patriotism ...

written 1736; (London, 1749), pp. 58-60; 61-2

HENRY ST. JOHN, VISCOUNT BOLINGBROKE

They who affect to head an opposition, or to make any considerable figure in it, must be equal at least to those whom they oppose;
I do not say in parts only, but in application and industry, and the
fruits of both, information, knowledge, and a certain constant pre-
paredness for all the events that may arise. Every administration
is a system of conduct: opposition therefore, should be a system of
conduct likewise; an opposite, but not a dependent system. I shall
explain myself better by an example. When two armies take the
field, the generals on both sides have their different plans for the
campaign, either of defence or of offence; and as the former does
not suspend his measures till he is attacked, but takes them before-
hand on every probable contingency, so the latter does not suspend
his, till the opportunity of attacking presents itself, but is alert and
constantly ready to seize it whenever it happens; and in the mean
time is busy to improve all the advantages of skill, of force, or of
any other kind that he has, or that he can acquire, independently
of the plan and of the motions of his enemy.

*   *   *

It were easy to demonstrate what I have asserted concerning the
duty of an opposing party: and I presume there is no need of
labouring to prove, that a party who opposed, systematically, a
wise to a silly, an honest to an iniquitous, scheme of government,
would acquire greater reputation and strength, and arrive more
surely at their end, than a party who opposed occasionally, as it
were, without any common system, without any general concert,
with little uniformity, little preparation, little perseverance, and as
little knowledge or political capacity. But it is time to leave this
invidious subject, and to hasten to the conclusion of my letter before
it grows into a book.

23

Letters from a Persian in England to his Friend at Ispahan

(1735), in *The Works of George Lord Lyttleton* ... 3rd edn. (London, 1776), Vol. I, pp. 303-5

GEORGE, LORD LYTTLETON[2]

On the third day our travels were at an end, and I arrived at my friend's house with all the pleasure that we receive from retirement and repose, after a life of tumult and fatigue. I was as weary of elections, as if I had been a candidate myself; and could not help expressing my surprize, that the general disorder on these occasions had not brought some fatal mischief upon the nation. That we are not undone by it, replied my friend, is entirely owing to the happy circumstance of our being an island. Were we seated on the continent, every election of a new parliament would infallibly draw on an invasion. It is not only from enemies abroad that you are in danger, answered I: one would think that the violence of domestick feuds should of itself overturn your constitution, as it has so many others; and how you have been able to escape so long, is the wonder of all who have been bred up under absolute monarchies: for they are taught, that the superior advantage of their form of government consists in the strength of union; and that in other states, where power is more divided, a pernicious confusion must ensue. They argue rightly enough, said the gentleman who came along with me; but they carry the argument too far. No doubt, factions are the natural inconveniences of all free governments, as oppression is too apt to attend on arbitrary power. But the difference lies here, that in an absolute monarchy, a tyrant has nothing to restrain him; whereas parties are not only a controul on those that govern, but on each other; nay, they are even a controul *upon themselves*, as the leaders of them dare not give a loose to their own particular passions and designs, for fear of hurting their credit with those whom it is their interest to manage and please: besides that it is easier to infect a prince with a spirit of tyranny, than a nation with a spirit of faction; and where the discontent is not general, the mischief will be light. To engage a whole people in a revolt, the highest provocations must be given; in such a case, the disorder is not chargeable on those that defend their liberties, but on the aggressor that invades them. Parties in society are like tempests in the natural world: they cause indeed a very great disturbance, and, when violent, tear up every thing that opposes them; but then they purge away many noxious qualities, and prevent a stagnation which would be fatal: all nations that live in a quiet slavery, may be properly said to stagnate; and happy would it be for them if they were rouzed and put in motion by that spirit of faction they dread so much; for, let the consequences of resistance be what they would, they can produce nothing worse than a confirmed and established servitude: but generally such a ferment in a nation throws off what is most oppressive to it, and settles by degrees into a better and more eligible state. Of this we have received abundant proof; for there is hardly a privilege belonging to us, which has not been gained by popular discontent, and preserved by frequent opposition. I may add, that we have known many instances, where parties, though ever so inflamed against each other, have united, from a sense of common danger, and joined in securing their common happiness. And this is more easily done, when the points that were once the great subjects of heat and division are either worn out by time, or changed by the clearer and more temperate medium through which they are seen: for in that case, parties, which thought that they stood at a very great distance from one another, may find themselves brought very near; and the only *separation* remaining would be the *essential* and *everlasting* one, between *honest men* and *knaves*, *wise men* and *fools*. That this may happen, experience shews; and this, I think, ought to free us from the reproach of sacrificing our country to our divisions; and make those despair of success, that *hope by dividing to destroy us*.

24

The Country Journal: or The Craftsman[3]

No. 674 (9 June, 1739)

The words PARTY and FACTION, by being often us'd as synonimous Terms, the Ideas properly annex'd to each of them have been so confounded, that it becomes necessary to explain them.

By *Party*, as I understand the sense of the Word, and think I could prove it from the *English* History, was always meant a national Division of Opinions, concerning the *Form* and *Methods of Government*, for the benefit of the *whole Community*, according to the different Judgments of Men; that their Conformity to *those Principles*, as the Motive of their respective Actions, distinguish'd the *Party*; and that *by the Fruit we* might know the Tree; that from the Moment the Contention for the real Service of their Country was given up by Men invested with *Power*, and a *Corrupt Influence* [established], upon which They united, They became a *Faction*; for I conceive a *Faction* to be a Set of Men arm'd with Power, and acting upon no one Principle of *Party*, or any Notion of *Publick Good*, but to preserve and share the Spoils amongst *Themselves*, as their only Cement; that They may be able to do every Thing contrary to the Interest of the Nation, and the Bent of the *whole People*—This is properly a Faction; . . . .

What hath been already said is sufficient to point out this Distinction between *Party* and *Faction*; but more especially between a *national Party*, and being servile Followers of *one Man*, who can therefore be intitled, at most, to the Denomination of the ministerial Party. . . .

"Hampden"

25

The Sentiments of a Tory in Respect to a Late Important Transaction and in Regard to the Present Situation of Affairs[4]

(n.p. 1741), pp. 4-9; 16-19; 23-4; 57-8

We may certainly stifle Heats and Animosities, tho' we may not be able to eradicate Distinctions. Nothing is more certain, than that the honest Men of all Parties mean their Country well, though they may differ about the Means of serving it; but, at the same Time, if these Differences rise so high as to take away all Regard to Justice and Decency, it is evident, that however private Men may serve themselves, the Publick will run the Hazard of not being served at all. A Proposition, which, whoever will grant, let him be of what Party he will, he cannot be displeased with the following Pages.

*   *   *

When private Men have any particular Purposes to carry in Virtue of Pretences to serve the Publick, they have always Recourse to plausible Discourses, and pretend to act from Principles widely different from their real Motives. This seems to have given Birth to the modern Doctrine of abolishing, or, which is the same Thing, uniting all Parties; a Kind of Methodism in Politicks, whereby a Pretence is made to a higher degree of State-Purity, than can be reasonably expected amongst *Englishmen*. That it would be really a very happy Thing, if there were no Parties, no Distinctions, no Separation of Interests among us, is, I presume, what no Man in his Wits would dispute; but that ever we shall be in this State, that Patriotism shall perform more than Religion ever could, that is, make us all of one Mind, is, I likewise presume, what no Man in his Senses will believe. In short, in my Judgment, a Coalition of Parties is as chimerical a Notion, as the Kingdom of Saints, or the fifth Monarchy.

It was originally broached by the *Shaftsbury* of the present Age, a Man, to be sure, well versed in the History and Interest of Parties, since, in the Course of his Life, he has been of all, and,

I believe I may say, at the Head of all the capital Parties in these Kingdoms, I mean *Whigs, Tories* and *Jacobites,* and therefore no man fitter to form this Project of a Coalition, which was, in short, a Project for the putting himself at the Head of them again all at once. I do not say this out of any Picque to this refined States-man, but I saw it out of Regard to Truth, out of Respect to my Country, and for the Sake of that Body of Men with whom I always have, and, I believe, always shall, concur.

The Reason why he proposed this extraordinary Scheme, and took so much Pains to reduce his Notions in Politicks into a System grounded thereon, was plainly this, that the Bulk of those who were to form the Party he was to use, might not perceive how small the Number of those Men were, who, in case of Success, were to reap the Benefit of their Labours. For this End, the Project was very ingeniously contrived, and if it's Author will be content with a reasonable Share of Applause, it cannot be denied him, on Account of the Address, and even Success, with which, for a long Time, he managed it. But if he, or any of his Disciples, are so sanguine as to imagine, that a certain Body of Men, who have always distinguished themselves by a steady Adherence to Church and Crown, were the Dupes of this chimerical Notion, and resolved to maintain it at the Expence of their old established Principles, they are mistaken, grossly mistaken; for these Men are alike incapable of being awed by Men in Power, or of being wrought upon to do unreasonable Things in order to serve such of their Friends as aim at Power.

Since it is impossible for us to make Mankind what we would have them, the wisest Thing we can do is to take them as they are. Instead therefore of pretending to extirpate Parties, a Work that no *Hercules* in Policy will ever be able to perform, let us be content to expect that each Party should act upon it's avowed Principles, and, perhaps, this may conduct us to the fame or to a better End. *Tory* and *Whig* are Terms that have now a settled Meaning, and the moderate Men of both Parties, I mean such as consult their Reason and the Constitution, will always acquiesce in such Mea-sures as have an evident Tendency to the publick Good. As for the Zealots on both Sides they may attempt unreasonable Things, and shew their good Will to reduce us to Extremities, but they will never be able to effect their foolish Purposes, or embroil the Nation, as it has been heretofore embroiled, by the Madness of both Parties.

In the Case of the pretended Coalition, a Spirit of Dissimulation must reign throughout all Parties, which could not long answer the Purposes of any, and must, by Degrees, disgust all. There is something extremely odd, to say nothing more harsh, in seeing a Man, who for twenty or thirty Years has professed himself a *Tory*, harranguing in a publick Assembly on *Whig* Principles, and urging, with the greatest Vehemency, what himself had as vehemently heretofore opposed and condemned. It must appear as whimsical for one known to be a thorough *Whig*, to personate a Character I shall not mention, and to throw out such Insinuations as cannot, in Reason, be supposed to give his Foes any true Umbrage, or to give any real Satisfaction to such as, for a Time, he thinks fit to call his Friends. This acting in Masquerade is so uneasy, I had like to have said so unnatural, to Men of Sense and Spirit, that they cannot persist in it long, and therefore one would think it by no Means advisable that they should be put upon playing these Parts at all.

While People profess their real Principles, while *Tories* act like *Tories*, and *Whigs* like *Whigs*, we know what we are doing, and we know the Issue of our Doings; but when once it comes to be laid down for a Maxim, that on certain Occasions Men are to forego their own Sentiments in publick Affairs, in order to carry favourite Points, why then this is a direct Declaration for illegal Influence, and it signifies not a Straw as to the Rectitude of the Measure, whether it be for or against a Court. At least, this is my Judgment, and the Judgment of many of my Acquaintance.

*   *   *

In the first Place it is said, that it is not reconcileable to Reason, for Men to scruple any Sort of Censure on the Author of Measures, which they have declared to be Wrong. The *Tories*, say their Accusers, have voted for many Years against the keeping up so large a Number of regular Troops, against the Payment of large Sums abroad for the Hire of foreign Forces, against many Articles of the Expences of the Government at home, against the Excise-Scheme, against several Penal Laws, against several Steps taken in respect to foreign Affairs, particularly against the Convention, and many other Things. After all this, say they, what Reason, what Argument can be offered, why they should not have concurred, to their utmost, in procuring a Parliamentary Censure of a Person, who promoted all these Measures, who spoke for them, who voted for them, and who laboured all he could to procure them those Sanctions from the Legislature, which were necessary to carry them into Execution?

Those who talk in this Stile do not seem to consider what, at other Times, they have advanced with great Boldness, and maintained with the greatest Warmth, *viz.* that a Spirit of Opposition is agreeable and even essential to our Constitution. This, I must own,

is a Doctrine which sometimes, I think, has been carried too far;
and yet while it is taken in a modest and moderate Sense, I confess,
I think it true. There ought to be, especially in Parliament, a Spirit
of Enquiry; or, if you will, a Spirit of Jealousy. Power is a dangerous and intoxicating Thing, and those who are possessed of it are
but too apt to carry it a little farther than they ought, let them be
of what Party they will. For this Reason there hath been, and, I
hope, there always will be, a Party willing to inspect the Actions,
and ready to controul the Councils, of every Adminstration. But
this is far from doing any Hurt to the People in general, to the
Parliament in particular, or to the Administration itself, which it
opposes. On the contrary, it does good to all, it encourages the
People not to submit tamely to any Grievances, it keeps up that
Life and Freedom which ought to appear in Parliamentary Debates,
and it serves to restrain Men in Power from the vain Imagination,
that either they may do what they will, or that it is in their Power.
Besides, it procures the Examination of whatever Points are proposed, it creates Circumspection in all who have any Thing to do
with publick Affairs, it excites, by Controversy, the Delivery of
various Councils, whereby Ministers often reap great Advantages,
even from those who mean them no Good. From all this it follows,
that Men of the strictest Honour, Men of the greatest Loyalty to
their Prince, Men who have the utmost Zeal for the Constitution,
may engage in such an Opposition with a View only of coming at
Truth, of serving their Constituents as they ought, and of promoting the true Interest of their Country, without any selfish Views of
Profit, or personal Prejudges against those whom they oppose.

One must easily perceive, that the Burthen of rendering this
good Office to the State, must naturally fall upon such as have no
Share in the Administration, or, at least, chiefly upon them. Because, having less Knowledge of the Springs of Action, they are
the more ready to entertain Jealousies, even of just and reasonable
Measures; which however begets no Inconvenience, since, from
their being opposed and examined, they come to appear just and
reasonable, which otherwise they would not have been so thoroughly known to be. Because such as have no Connection with the
Administration, have less Opportunities of knowing their Capacities
and Zeal for the publick Service, and, consequently, are by no
means inclined to take any Thing they offer upon Trust; which, tho'
it may be sometimes inconvenient for them, yet is very rarely
detrimental to the State. Because such independent Persons are
usually applied to by the People, and by such as have, or think they
have, as great Knowledge in Matters of publick Concern, as those

who manage them; of which Sort of Folks there will never be any
Dearth in a free Nation.

*   *   *

But the great Point in Debate is, how far these People might be
governed by Principle; and therefore my Business is to shew, that
such of the *Tories* as have been accused, acted exactly conformable
to their Principles; which, if I can do, they ought surely to be
acquitted. It is necessary here, however, to take Notice of the
Difference between a Party and a Faction, for want of attending to
which many People, and even some political Writers, have run into
great Mistakes. A Party is the same Thing, with respect to Civil
Affairs, as a Sect with Regard to Religion, they act from the
Dictates of their Conscience; and conformable to a certain System
of Opinions, which they take to be right. A Faction again, is a
Body of Men acting upon no scruples, but from a selfish Scheme of
Interest, which allows them to go any Length with any Party,
provided they may thereby serve themselves. For Example, those
who opposed the Court in 1641 were a Party, but those who, leaving the House of Commons, fled to the Army, and afterwards sitting
under an armed Force, in order to give, as far as they were able,
the Colour of Law to the most illegal Acts, these, I saw, were a
Faction.

*   *   *

While such excessive Pains are taken by Men, of all Parties, to
prepossess the Minds of the Electors in favour of themselves and
their Designs, while such as pretend to the highest Degree of Purity
in their Intentions, openly avow their taking certain Measures, with
a View to influence Elections; such a Gap is made in our Constitution, as seems not only to allow, but to invite all kinds of Influence
whatever. It has been already observed, that the general Out-cry of
Parties against each other, whatever those who compose them
imagine, does, in Reality, prove nothing, or rather proves too much,
by proving that they are all in the Wrong. This being the Case,
Sollicitations on one Side warrant Sollicitations on the other, and
those who exclaim against undue Influence, actually provoke and
induce it, by attempting to influence themselves. If all Parties
appeal to the People, then all Parties ought to forbear influencing
the People; but if after so solemn an Appeal, any Party begins to
exert its Interest amongst them by caressing and cajoling, this
opens the Way to all the rest, and Men of honest and disinterested
Principles lose all their Hopes at once. For where all kinds of
Application are made, where the Influence of all the Parties
amongst us are exerted, how can we call such a Choice free?

Section IV

WHIGS IN POWER

"... the *Folly* and *Madness* of Party will never be cured till human Nature is cured; and, perhaps, 'tis better for the interests of *Liberty* they never should be cured: ..."

"OSBORNE"

The London Journal, no. 760 (19 January, 1733-4)

Walpole's writers were far more partial to party than was the "patriot coalition" in opposition. The Government's propaganda had an odd tendency (though understandable in the circumstances) to praise party in the same breath as it damned opposition. Now an opposition above party was quite conceivable, but party without an opposition or any contest for power was difficult to defend. Thus, while Arnall might attempt to justify the use of "influence" by the party in power and simultaneously denigrate the Opposition, a more sensible course was taken by the author of *A Second Letter*, who accepted party in and out of power. From this point of view, influence and opposition balanced one another, and the presence of one made the other legitimate. The most consistent defender of party in the 1730s was James Pitt, "Osborne" of *The London Journal*, and this accounts for the prominence given here to the writings of an obscure man.

The London Journal [1]

No. 547 (24 January, 1729-30)

In all *free Countries*, where the People have Liberty to examine and discuss *Publick Affairs*, there ever were and ever will be *Parties*: He who wishes them at an End, wishes all that's valuable, and worth contending for upon Earth, at an End too. The different Passions and Ways of Reasoning, the different Interests, Views and Circumstances of Men; their different Acquaintances and various Means of coming at Knowledge; naturally produce different Opinions and Inclinations: and those particular Opinions and Inclinations produce *Parties*. And there is no help for this: No Remedy but what's infinitely worse than the Disease. Look into the *absolute Monarchies* and States Abroad, and you'll find no Parties indeed, but the Reason is, because *there's no Liberty*. France, which is the best of all the absolute Governments, has some *Liberty*, and is therefore subject to *Party Divisions*; we have 'em in the highest Degree and God be thanked for the *Cause of 'em*. Courts will, as long as Liberty lasts, be guarded against, and Power suspected; the Conduct of Ministers will be critically examined, and their public Actions narrowly inspected, and so *they ought to be*. None but *little Minds and half-Thinkers*, count these Divisions an Evil; they are good as they are the Source and Spring of the greatest Good in the World, and absolutely necessary to preserve and secure that Good.

"Anglicanus"

The London Journal

No. 658 (5 February, 1731-2)

Thirdly, the Governors of a *Free Kingdom* should weigh and consider the *State of Parties* in that Kingdom: for 'tho 'tis true, that a *wise*, *just*, and *steady Management* will, in a Course of Time, abate the *Violence* of Parties, yet they will subsist, as long as Liberty subsists; and great Regard is to be had to Them: All of them should meet with *equal Protection*, tho' not with *equal Favour*: That Party.

in a *Free State*, which appears by its *Principles and Actions* to be most in the *Interest of Liberty*, ought to be most *favour'd*; and the great Posts of *Trust and Power* reposited in their Hands. . . .

"F. Osborne"

The London Journal

No. 665 (25 March, 1732)

Arbitrary Government without Faction, and Legal Governments with Faction, Compared . . .

It has been the business of *Slaves and Cowards*, of *designing* Knaves and *believing* Fools, to *magnify* the Good and *lessen* the Evil of *Arbitrary* Governments, and to *aggrevate* the *Evil* and extenuate the Good of *legal* Governments. . . . These *Advocates for* Power tell us, That in *Arbitrary* Governments there are no *Factions*, all Men are quiet and submissive; or as our poet has it,

All Things are hush'd, as Nature's Self seem'd dead: There is but *one Will* and *one Power*, as there is but *one Faith* and *one Church*. Blessed Unity and Uniformity! But in Free Governments there are *Factions* of all Sorts: *Factions* in the Church and *Factions* in the State.

Let it be; while we examine the Truth of these Notions, lay before the Publick a faithful Account of *Arbitrary* and *Legal Governments*, and shew that the *Good* of being without Faction is not so great as is imagin'd, or rather is *no Good* at all; and that the Evil of *Faction* in a *legal* Government is not so great as is imagined, or, at least, is *productive* of much greater Good than Evil; that 'tis impossible we should have so much *Good* as results from *Free Goverments,* without the *Evil* of Faction, and, that the *Good of Free Governments with Faction* is infinitely greater than the *Good of Arbitrary Government without Faction.*

. . . In *Free* States, 'tis true, there are *Factions;* tho' *all Opposition* is not Faction, any more than all *Killing* is *Murder*: *Opposition* when *ill Measures* are carrying on, is so far from being *Faction*, that 'tis a Duty, and a *moral Virtue.* Faction is an *unreasonable* Opposition; and this indeed, is sometimes carried to that Height, thro' *Passion* and *private Views*, as to become *an Evil* to the Publick: But then, if the *Good* of Free Governments be consider'd; as, the *absolute* Security of Person and Property; *full Liberty* of examining all Doctrines and Opinions; and that the *Liberty* of examining is the *Root and Source* of all *Virtue and Happiness*; This small *Evil of Faction,* will be like a Spot in the Sun, not easily discerned, or rather lost in the *Glory* which surrounds it.

"F. Osborne"

The London Journal

No. 686 (19 August, 1732)

A DISSERTATION on the USE of FACTION;

... Mr. D'Anvers having lately pleased the Town with a Dissertation on the Good of *Ill Ministers*, or the *Use* which *Bad Ministers* are to the Publick; we shall in this Paper shew the *Good* of *Ill Writers:* and that even *Factious* and *Seditious* Pens are of great Service to Mankind.

It is the unalterable Nature of Things in the World, that Good and Ill should be ever blended together. There is no *Good* without some *Ill,* nor any Ill without some Good. The World subsists by *Opposition*: The *natural World,* by the continual *Strife* and *Contention* of the several *Elements;* the *moral* or *rational World,* by the *Opposition* of Passions, and *Counter-Interests* of particular Men; and the political World, by the *never-ceasing Struggle* of Parties. Laws and Liberties are preserved by *Opposition*; and in those Counries where there is no Opposition, there is a Death of *Liberty* and *publick Virtue.*

"F. Osborne"

The London Journal

No. 786 (20 July, 1734)

Some Writers on Politicks have affirmed that no Country in the World was so much interested with *Parties and Oppositions* as *England.* I shall not enter into a particular Examination of the truth of this, (tho' I think that *all free Countries* will always have *Parties;*) but if true, 'tis so far from being a Reproach, that 'tis an Honour to us; that we have a Sense of Liberty and Publick Virtue: for *all Power* is subject to Abuse; and *all Men in Power,* even the best, if not check'd and controul'd will be apt to leap the Bounds of Law and Reason, so that Parties and Oppositions are often useful to the Publick. ...

The *Tory-Opposition* is not worth our considering; because *They* always opposed, either to bring about a *Restoration,* or else to get themselves into Power, on purpose to induce the King to act, as they always *encouraged* and *assisted* the *Stuarts* to do. . . .

The Opposition of the *Whigs*, indeed since the Revolution, is of another Nature, and arises from another Fountain; their *Views* and *Designs* have been very different from the *Tories*: But Truth obliges me to say, they were *seldom National*, and too often terminated *solely in themselves*. The *Whigs in Power* have generally acted better. . . .

"F. Osborne"

27

The Case of Opposition Between the Craftsmen and the People

(London, 1731), pp. 12-14

[WILLIAM ARNALL][2]

The Struggle between the *Whig* and *Tory* Parties for the Succession to the Throne, ended in the Victory gained by the *Whigs*, who fixed that Prince, and that Family on the Throne, whom they had always wished to see there. The Motives of Prudence and Gratitude induced the late King to chuse those Men for his Servants, who had been his Friends; and to look upon those as his *natural Support*, who had been his *constant Adherents*. The *Whigs* being thus admitted into Trust, and the *Tories* excluded, the latter became Mutineers against the Government, because they had no share in the Government; but their Designs were not concealed, they complained of their Exclusion from Power as their capital Grievance. And having nothing more alarming than this, the People at length saw the Folly of the Clamour, and in the end grew unconcerned at those Complaints, which wholly arose from *private Interests*.

The *Tory Faction* thus declining in Credit, and grown unformidable in their Opposition, the *Whigs* had all the Power and Favour of the Crown to share among themselves; nay, there is a Time still recent in memory, I mean when *Layer's Plot* came before the *British Parliament*, at which time there was not a *Whig* in the House of Commons dissenting from the *Body of the Party*.

The *Tory Interest* grew weak, and the *Whigs* powerful by the Disposition of Favours and Employments. For if the Profit of serving the Publick in Places be computed at any Sum, and this be raised equally upon the People, that Party which is admitted into Trust will have more than a Retribution, whilst the other Party is like a Scale, continually losing Weight, without any new Accession to maintain the Balance; so that in a certain Process of Time the losing Party must quite dwindle to nothing, and the prevailing Party, by continuing in Employments of Profit, must become able to purchase all the Lands in the Kingdom.

This had an undoubted Tendency to secure the present Establishment on the most lasting Foundation, as it would most effectually have given the Weight of the *Landed Interest* entirely on the Side of the Government, and have lodged the *natural Power* of the State with those who were *natural Friends* to the present Establishment.

28

The Landed Interest Consider'd:
Being Serious Advice to Gentlemen, Yeomen, Farmers and Others, Concerned in the Ensuing Election
By a Yeoman of Kent[3]

(London, 1733), pp. 8-9, 12-13

It has been an Observation long made, and may be a very true one, that it will always be to the advantage of a Kingdom to have one Party a *Watch* upon another; and thereby a Check may be put to exorbitant Proceedings.—But then, if the Love of Empire and Dominion be so impetuous and headstrong, that they'll stick at nothing, how unreasonable and mischievous it be to others, so they can but gain their own Point; that they'll throw down every thing that is in their Way, and break in pieces all Orders and good Government, unless *they* can have the Management of it—then they act beyond their Province, and, instead of Friends, are to be look'd on as formidable Enemies. These Men's Violence cannot be controuled; they fret, and foam, and spread Sedition in every Breath; their Ambition drives their Malice beyond all *Reason*.

*　　*　　*

There must be something of a very binding Nature, that holds these Malecontents together.—Strange, that they should have their Heads so moulded, and their Judgments so exactly formed, that the *same* Bills should please or displease them *all*! Stranger still, that disgusted Persons that go over to them, should be so steady in their Judgment, as to go on regularly with the old habituated *Gainsayers*!—What a wonderful Illumination falls upon their Minds at once! For the Truth of this, I appeal to the *Votes* in one House, and the *Protests* in the other. Now I mention this, I cannot forbear expressing my Dislike of the Privilege that the *Protesting Few* have over a *Majority* in that House, in being allowed to publish their Reasons; which the other, by the Constitution, are debarred from; confiding in this, that the Honour and Honesty of the Votes in that august House is *Sanction enough.* Nay, it is more to be lamented, when these very *Protests* are drawn up in such a manner, as not so much to *instruct*, as to *inflame* the People; when a *Caleb D'Anvers*, or any *Grubstreet* Author, shall lend, not to say dictate, smart Sentences, to be dispersed under that right honourable Name.

What the Cement is that holds this discontented Party so closely together, is pretty well known—and what mean and base Ways do they take to increase and strengthen their own Side? They vastly applaud themselves for setting on foot the Repeal of the Sacramental Test, thinking themselves sure of Success one way or the other— either to gain Churchmen or Dissenters to their Party.—But sure both will be cautious how they are drawn in by them, as knowing that they would only make use of them as *Tools* to serve their own Turn; to effect which they would give up what ought to be most dear and valuable to us all.

Of the very same sort is their voting against the *Excise Bill*, in order to bring over to themselves the *trading* and flourishing Part of the Nation.—If their *Petitions* had been more unreasonable, they would scarce have met with a Denial, whilst they could have so fair a Prospect that this would turn to their own Advantage.—If the *Bill* had been opposed by the *Ministry*, it is my Opinion that a great many of these *Gentlemen* would have been for it, to try if they could add to their Number the *Landed* Men:—And then how would they have cried up themselves as Friends to their Country, who would not suffer it to continue oppressed under a heavy Load?—To what a Height does Party Zeal, and Party Views, carry Men! What Frauds, what Villanies, will it not protect and applaud!

The Conduct of the Opposition and the Tendency of Modern Patriotism

(London, 1734), pp. 57-8

[JOHN, LORD HERVEY][4]

I have but one Question to put to the Defenders of the Craftsman's Honesty, and his Followers' Loyalty, and that is, whether the new Distinction he has coin'd at the end of his *metaphysical Dissertation upon Parties*, of some People being Friends to the Government but Enemies to the Constitution; and others Enemies to the Government but Friends to the Constitution, will bear out any other Interpretation, than that he means to insinuate, that the Followers of the *Pretender* are Friends to the Constitution, and the Followers of King *George* its Enemies.

Opposition no Proof of Patriotism; with some Observations and Advice Concerning Party-Writings[5]

(London, 1735), pp. 6-8; 11

[WILLIAM ARNALL]

Many People think that there is an inherent Virtue in Opposition, nay, a Sort of Divinity in it; and are apt to treat such as are violent in it as something more than Men, without ever distinguishing between Opposition to unjust Measures, and Opposition to just as well as unjust. Can there be a more unjust Thing than opposing Measures necessary to the Support and Being of a State? And is not such Opposition destructive of Patriotism?

I will be bold to say, that if the Opposition in King *William's* Reign had succeeded, instead of Liberty and the Revolution, we should have had King *James* and Popery again. I will be bold to say, that if all the Oppositions in the late Reigns had succeeded, instead of the present Illustrious *Protestant* House, we should have had the *Pretender* and his *Popish* Priests. I will be bold to say, that if the present Opposition had succeeded, at least universally, we should have been at the Mercy of a neighbouring Power, which has effectually shewn to all the World how ready it is to take Advantage of the Weakness of its Neighbours. This seems to me so plain, and I dare say appears so plain to some in the Opposition, (such is the good Opinion I have of them) that in Spight of all their Anger and overt Declarations, they are heartily glad that their Opposition has not succeeded, at least in every Instance. Sure I am, that in the above Instances, *Patriotism* was on the Side of the Government, and the *Opposition* repugnant to *Patriotism*.

It is ridiculous as well as dangerous to estimate the Virtue of Men by their Vigour or Eagerness in opposing a Ministry. The *best Ministers* have been often opposed by the *worst Men*; even bad Ministers have been opposed by Men as bad as themselves; and the worst Men have always cloathed their Opposition with the Cloak of publick Good, with Tenderness and Compassion to the People, and a Zeal for relieving them by abolishing Taxes, and for securing and increasing their Privileges. But Ambition, which rarely owns its true Name, generally chuses that of *Patriotism*.

*   *   *

What follows then? Is all Opposition to be discouraged and abolished? God forbid. Let Oppression and Oppressors, and every unjust Administration be for ever opposed. But where the Laws rule, where Liberty flourishes, and where a legal Administration prevails, *General Opposition* ought to be out of Countenance and cease. When under such a Situation, the Opposition continues constant and furious, all good, all calm and disinterested Men will condemn it; even the Vulgar will at last cease to mind it, and they who are the Authors of it will make but an ill Figure with Posterity. It may flourish amongst the Multitude for a while, but in Time it will lose its Force, and at last grow contemtible, or be forgot.

31

Proceedings of a Political Club[6]

in *London Magazine*, Vol. 7 (May, 1738), p. 242

[?THOMAS GORDON]

Whilst you continued to publish *a Journal of the Debates and Proceedings in Parliament* we thought it would be unnecessary and even impertinent, to publish an Account of any Thing that passed in our Club; but as we suppose a Stop is now put to your publishing any *such Journal* for the future, we flatter ourselves that an Account of some of the Debates that have happened, or that shall thereafter happen, in our Club, may not only be agreeable but useful, and even necessary to some of your Readers; for to make a proper Enquiry, and to form a right judgement upon every dispute of a publick Nature, is, we think, a Duty incumbent not only upon every Man who has a Vote in our Legislature, but upon every Man who can, by his Vote at an election, contribute towards making one Man rather than another a Member of our Legislature.

The Election of Members of Parliament is the only *legal* Method our People have for vindicating or affecting their just Liberties and Privileges; and no Man can judge how to behave upon any such Occasion, without having examined the late publick Transactions: For as this Country has always been, and from the Nature of our Constitution must always be, divided into the *Court* and the *Country* Party; it is impossible for an Elector to judge whether he ought to vote for the *Court* or the *Country* Candidate, without having examined the Schemes and Measures for some Time before being pursued by each Party. These two are the only two Parties that can naturally spring up in this Kingdom, and these two, I hope, will always subsist; because, while they do, the one will be a proper Check upon the other; and by this Check, our Constitution will be secured against the Incroachments of either. They may sometimes be called by other Names, they may be called *Whig* or *Tory*, high Church and *low*, or what else People please to call them; but whatever Names they pass by, the proper distinction between the two is, That one of them generally approves of the measures pursued by the *Court* and the other as generally disapproves and opposes. The only Support the Court can have by our Constitution, ought to depend upon the Wisdom and Justice of its Measures; and no Elector can pretend to judge fairly of this Wisdom and Justice, without a free Enquiry into every particular Measure pursued.

It is therefore the Duty of every Elector, to examine narrowly into all the Contests that happen between these two Parties, in order to form a Judgment of the Views of each, and to vote accordingly at every Election. When he finds the Court Party are really prosecting any wicked Schemes, or have guilty of weak and ridiculous Measures, with respect either to the domestick or foreign Affairs of the Nation, no Man ought to vote at an Election for any Candidate, who has contributed, or who, he thinks, will contribute, towards the Support of such an Administration, or towards their Continuance in Power. On the other hand, if the Opposition preceeds from nothing but Faction, Envy, or Malice, without any just cause of Discontent, no Elector who thinks so, can, in Justice to his Country, give his vote at an Election for any Man who has countenanced, or who, he thinks, will countenance, such a factious and causeless Opposition.

A Word to the Good People of England upon the Present Posture of Affairs[7]

(London, 1739), pp. 5-6

There have, for some Years past, appeared in *England*, a Sett of Gentlemen who publickly avowing the Spirit of Party, have employ'd all their Pens to shew, that contrary to the Wisdom of all former Ages and Nations, the Preservation of States, and the Strength of Kingdoms, depended, not upon Unanimity, and the Co-operation of all the Members in the Service of the Whole, as the old obsolete Maxims of Government would have it; *but upon the happy Influence of intestine divisions and Party Rage,* which by perpetually drawing different ways, must therefore support the Orb of Government, like the Carthesian World firm upon its own Center.

It is really true, that these Gentlemen, by a labour'd Search into Antiquity, have produced some Instances, wherein, Rebellion and civil Discord have happily check'd the growing Greatness of one particular Part of a Government, and by forcing back Matters to their first Establishment, have brought the State to its original Beauty and Order; and this, no doubt, has convinced many unthinking Gentlemen that they were under a sort of Obligation, to enter into this *excellent Scheme of Faction*. . . .

Speech on the Place Bill of 1740

Parliamentary History, Vol. XI, cols. 363-6

SIR ROBERT WALPOLE[8]

In all questions, Sir, which do not admit of demonstration; there must be a variety of opinions; and as questions of a political nature are less capable of demonstration than any other, it is natural to see a difference of sentiments in every country like this, where the people have not only a power to judge, but a liberty to talk and write against the measures pursued by the government: this is natural, and even necessary, in every country where the people are free; and as every man is fond of his own opinion, and fully convinced of his having reason on his side, he is apt to imagine, that those who differ from him, must be governed by some prejudice, or by some selfish consideration. From hence it is, that all those who disapprove of the measures of the government conclude, that the approbation of those that differ from them, proceeds from the influence of some lucrative post they are in possession or expectation of; and on the other hand, those that approve of, and support the measures pursued by the government, are apt to conclude, that the opposition is entirely owing to party-prejudice, or to malice and resentment. For my part, I shall always endeavour to keep in the middle course, and to believe that both are in the wrong; and therefore, I shall always be against any alteration in our constitution, when I think, that the alteration proposed is founded upon one or other of these mistakes. I should be as much against restraining the liberties of the people, in order to prevent that influence which is supposed to proceed from party-prejudice, malice and resentment, as I shall be against restraining the power of free choice of the crown, in order to prevent that influence which is supposed to proceed from the disposal of places and preferments. There may, perhaps, I believe there always will, be a little of each in the nation; but neither can ever be of any dangerous consequence to our constitution: on the contrary, they serve as a balance to each other; so that by removing either, without removing the other at the same time, the constitution will run a great risk of being overturned.

There are many causes, Sir, which naturally raise a party against the wisest administration. In this life, it is impossible for us to be completely happy. All men feel some wants, pressures, or misfortunes; and very few are willing to impute them to their own folly, or to any mistake in their own conduct. To such men, the administration is in politics, what the devil is in religion; it is the author of all their misdeeds, and the cause of all their sufferings: this naturally breeds in them a bad opinion of the administration, and then, of course, they not only condemn, but oppose all its measures. This must raise a great many enemies to the administration in every country, and their number will be considerably increased by those that are disappointed of the honours or preferments they expected, and justly, as they thought, deserved; as well as by those that wish for a change in the administration, for no other reason but because they hope for a share in the next. In all countries it is honourable to have a share in the government of one's country: in rich countries it is profitable as well as honourable; and as there are but a very few in any country that can have a share of the government, and still fewer that can have such a share as, they think, they deserve, there must be many candidates for every title of honour, or post of profit, that is to be disposed of. Of these candidates, one only can be chosen, and all the rest will, of course, think they have had injustice done them; for few men are so modest as to think such a disappointment owing to their own want of merit, or to the superior merit of their rival; and from thence they will begin to entertain a secret animosity, nay, perhaps, they will declare an open enmity to those at the head of the administration.

By these two sorts of men united together, there will always be a considerable party in every country, ready to condemn and vilify the wisest measures that can be pursued by the administration; and, as in every free country there are different parties, as in this country there are at present, and, I believe, always will be different parties, the parties that are by their profession and principles opposite to the party in power, will be ready to find fault with every thing done by the administration. In this country, I say, Sir, there are, and, I believe, always will be different parties: there are at present, and will be as long as our present happy establishment endures, three different parties in this kingdom: The jacobites of one side, the republicans of the other, which I may call the two extremes; and the party for supporting our present happy establishment, which may be justly called the proper mean between these two extremes.

Thus, Sir, we may see what a numerous party our administration must always have to struggle with. All these sorts of men, the discontented, the disappointed, the jacobites, and the republicans, will always be ready to condemn and oppose the measures of the administration, let them be never so wise, let them be never so just; and by their arguments they will often be able to prevail with some well-meaning and unthinking men, or at least to stagger them in their opinions. With regard to parliaments, and the choice of members of parliament, our administration has no defence against this formidable union of parties, but by the wisdom of their measures to engage most gentlemen of credit and fortune in their interest. Whilst the administration pursues right measures, such gentlemen will be ready to join with them, and by this means the administration will always have a prevailing influence, both in parliament, and at elections; for when a majority of those who have the best fortunes, and greatest interest in their respective countries, are friends to the administration, it is not at all surprising, that an administration, by means of such friends, should have a prevailing influence at elections, as well as in parliament. But such friends, or at least a great number of such friends, or at least a great number of such, no administration can have, that pursues measures inconsistent with the good of the community in general.

I shall grant, Sir, that a title of honour, or a lucrative post or employment, may be of some service in prevailing with a gentleman to judge favourably of the government's measures, in all cases where he is wavering in his opinion; but a bad government can never, by this way, gain many friends; even a good government can never gain near so many friends, as it will lose by causeless discontents and just disappointments; and if you should take away from the crown the chief advantage it can reap by the disposal of posts and employments, not only a good administration, but even the crown itself, may sink under the weight of party-prejudice, supported by causeless discontent, and just disappointment; therefore, to support the crown against the disadvantages and opposition which the wisest and best administration must always have to struggle with, I think, you ought to leave it in the power of the crown to dispose of all posts and employments, in the same manner they have been hitherto, without any bad effect, disposed of.

If you should, by the Bill now proposed, exclude all gentlemen in any place or office under the crown, from having seats in this House, you would, in my opinion, Sir, bring the constitution into much greater danger, than it can ever be brought into, by any number of placemen and officers that can be in this House; for the crown would, in that case, be laid under a necessity to employ none but men of low fortunes and no interest; because, if the places and offices under the crown should be given to gentlemen of character and distinction in their respective countries, and they thereby excluded from having seats in this House, the chief friends of the government being thus rendered incapable of standing candidates at elections, the disaffected, or discontented interest would prevail in every part of the kingdom; and in that case, this House would soon be filled with such as were declared enemies to the administration. To prevent this consequence, the administration would, therefore, be obliged to employ none in any post or office under the crown, but such as had neither fortune nor interest in their country, in order that their friends might be in a condition to get themselves chosen members of this House, for, I believe, it will be granted, that no administration could support itself, or answer any of the ends of government, if the majority of this House consisted of such as were its declared enemies.

34

A Second Letter to a Member of Parliament Concerning the Present State of Affairs[9]

(London, 1741), pp. 57-61

We are never to expect Perfection in any human Contrivance; and therefore, all that can be hoped for in a political Constitution, is this; that it should appear excellent in the Eyes of the wisest, and be allowed practicable by all; which Character is certainly due to our Constitution as it stands at present. This, however, does not hinder many different Opinions in relation thereto, nor will any Alteration we can possibly make, bring us to Unanimity in our Sentiments about it. Our Patriots themselves own, that there ever will be an Opposition; nay, they go farther, they affirm, there ever must, and ought to be one. Hence it follows, that if the Nation must be always split into two Parties, the People ought to take care to keep them as equal as possible, since which ever conquers, they must most certainly be Slaves. When I say this, I mean an absolute Conquest, for one will be always the prevailing Party; that is to say, while the Administration adheres to the Principles of natural Justice, and to the Rules prescribed by the Constitution, the Court will have the Ascendant; but whenever Ministers deviate from such a Conduct, though they may maintain themselves for some small Time, yet at last the Scale of the Opposition will prevail, till new Weights are thrown into the other. Now each of these Parties makes use of all such Ways and Means, as the Constitution will allow for its Support. These Methods, the Party using them, stile *Interest*, and by the other Party they are called *Influence*. Consider, dear Sir, with yourself, how your Friends and Acquaintance act with respect to the People in general, and to their Electors in particular: Do they rely altogether on their known Character for Wisdom, Virtue, Disinterestedness Loyalty and Publick Spirit? or, do they not condescend to mix with these, Applications of a somewhat different Nature? Do they not address themselves to the Passions of some Men, to the Prejudices of others? Do they not constrain their own Humours, and go out of their own Way, that by obliging Numbers they may become popular? I say nothing of Arts of another Nature, such as giving Hopes of extraordinary Munificence to a decayed Corporation, making use of the necessary Dependance of Tenants, and exerting the united Force of family Engagements. Add to all this, the Intrigues and Cabals of a Faction thoroughly formed, or as the *all-accomplished Viscount* phrases it, a well-conducted Opposition; and I conceive you will have a pretty just Idea of the Nature and Weight of what is called the *Country Interest*.

If, therefore one should incline to allow what the Speakers and Scribes of your Parliament so violently contend for, that an Opposition is everlastingly necessary to preserve our Liberties; you, on the other Hand, must allow, that the Government must subsist; for otherwise, I think our Liberties would be hardly worth preserving. If you will admit this, you must allow them the Means of subsisting; and these are no other, than such an Interest among the People as may, in some Measure, balance the Power of a continual Opposition; but you will immediately cry out, this is pleading for bare-faced Corruption: No, Sir, it is pleading for the Consequences of the Revolution, which have reduced the Crown, instead of depending on it's high Prerogatives, to stoop so low as to depend upon the People: That is to say, to depend on their Kindness, Affection, and Good-will; whence the Necessity arises of giving Places to such as have large Properties; and give me leave to say, Sir, that this is the strongest Security, which in the Nature of Things the People can have, for the perpetual Preservation of their Freedom. While the Crown cannot be without Parliaments, the Administration, in whatever Hands it is, must have a strong Dependance upon the Commons, and must cultivate a good Understanding with them, by the best Methods they can devise, and the most suitable to the Nature of our Constitution, and the Circumstances of the Times. They must cherish Principles of Liberty, they must Maintain the People in the Possession of it, they must have a due Regard to the Trade of the Nation at home, and to it's political Interests abroad. In fine, they must do their Duty in a great Measure; for otherwise the Passions of a free People are not to be restrained. Great Misfortunes, real Poverty, manifest Oppressions, are Things that the *British* People will not endure, they are apt to fire at the very Sound of them; but I believe, they are seldom apt to stir, or to hazard the great Goods that they possess, till they feel the Evils complained of. Whatever Ways, whatever Arts, whatever Means, such as are in the Administration, and their Friends use, to maintain this Interest in the Commons, and thereby to keep the Government in a steady, settled Course, the Sum of them is what you and your Friends affect to call Ministerial Influence; though in fact, it is Ministerial Dependance, the Chain by which they are bound to the People.

Section V

PARTY RECONSTRUCTION

"A Certain Progression of Power ... is natural ..., and may some-times be quicken'd by Party-Struggles, without any great Detriment; but when through the Force of Faction this Motion is increas'd to such a degree of Rapidity, the Machine of Government is no longer able to subsist, ...

An Enquiry into the Present State of our Domestick Affairs.
Shewing the Danger of a New Opposition (1742)

The rise of the Pelhams was accompanied by widespread accept-ance of opposition and party, usually qualified in various ways according to the loyalties of the writer. The above quotation is from a Government pamphlet and so reflects the same sympathies as Per-ceval's *Faction Detected*, the most successful and notorious pole-mical work of the period. The Tory contribution (extract 36) displayed the most developed doctrine of party as a permanent institution, while the broad-bottom case introduced the public to the able pen of James Ralph. Hume and Spelman were private scholars commenting on a subject usually reserved for literary mercenaries.

35

Of Parties in General

in 'Essays, Moral, Political, Literary' (1st published 1741), *Hume, Theory of Politics*, ed. Frederick Watkins (Toronto, 1951), pp. 171-3

DAVID HUME[1]

Nothing is more usual than to see parties which have begun upon a real difference continue even after that difference is lost. When men are once enlisted on opposite sides, they contract an affection to the persons with whom they are united, and an animosity against their antagonists; and these passions they often transmit to their posterity. The real difference between *Guelf* and *Ghibelline* was long lost in Italy before these factions were extinguished. The *Guelfs* adhered to the pope, the *Ghibellines* to the emperor; yet the family of Sforza, who were in alliance with the emperor, though they were *Guelfs*, being expelled Milan by the king of France, assisted by Jacomo Trivulzio and the *Ghibellines*, the pope concurred with the latter, and they formed leagues with the pope against the emperor.

The civil war which arose some few years ago in Morocco, between the *blacks* and *whites*, merely on account of their complexion, are founded on a pleasant difference. We laugh at them; but I believe, were things rightly examined, we afford much more occasion of ridicule to the Moors. For what are all the wars of religion which have prevailed in this polite and knowing part of the world? They are certainly more absurd than the Moorish civil wars. The difference of complexion is a sensible and a real difference; but the controversy about an article of faith which is utterly absurd and unintelligible is not a difference in sentiment, but in a few phrases and expressions, which one party accepts of without understanding them, and the other refuses in the same manner.

Real factions may be divided into those from *interest*, from *principle*, and from *affection*. Of all factions, the first are the most reasonable, and the most excusable. Where two orders of men, such as the nobles and the people, have a distinct authority in a government not very accurately balanced and modelled, they naturally follow a distinct interest; nor can we reasonably expect a different conduct, considering that degree of selfishness implanted in human nature. It requires great skill in a legislator to prevent such parties; and many philosophers are of opinion that this secret, like the *grand elixir*, or *perpetual motion*, may amuse men in theory but can never possibly be reduced to practice. In despotic governments, indeed, factions often do not appear; but they are not the less real, or rather they are more real and more pernicious upon that very account. The distinct orders of men, nobles and people, soldiers and merchants, have all a distinct interest; but the more powerful oppresses the weaker with impunity, and without resistance, which begets a seeming tranquillity in such governments.

There has been an attempt in England to divide the *landed* and *trading* part of the nation, but without success. The interests of these two bodies are not really distinct, and never will be so, till our public debts increase to such a degree as to become altogether oppressive and intolerable.

Parties from *principle*, especially abstract speculative principle, are known only to modern times, and are, perhaps, the most extraordinary and unaccountable phenomenon that has yet appeared in human affairs. Where different principles beget a contrariety of conduct, which is the case with all different political principles, the matter may be more easily explained. A man who esteems the true right of government to lie in one man or one family cannot easily agree with his fellow-citizen who thinks that another man or family is possessed of this right. Each naturally wishes that right may take place, according to his own notions of it. But where the difference of principle it attended with no contrariety of action, but every one may follow his own way without interfering with his neighbour, as happens in all religious controversies, what madness, what fury can beget such unhappy and such fatal divisions?

36

The Case of the Opposition Impartially Stated by a Gentleman of the *Middle Temple*

(London, n.d. [1742]), pp. 2-4; 6-7

[JOHN CAMPBELL][2]

It is now somewhat more than twenty Years, that a certain Party hath subsisted amongst us, under the Title of *the Opposition*; they have at certain Times been composed of very different People, and consequently have been considered in different Lights; but the proper Characteristic of the Party, and that from which it derives it's Name, is the *Opposing* of *Power*, or endeavouring to circumscribe in Parliament the Grants of Money and Extention of Authority, which have from Time to Time been demanded by several Administrations. Now, if this Scheme of Opposition has been right with Regard to the Interest of the Nation, that is to say, if the People of *Great-Britain* would have been Gainers, by putting into Practice what the Persons from Time to Time concerned in this Opposition propos'd, then, without Question, the Design of the Opposition is *right* upon the whole, though at particular Times, and by particular Persons, it might be prosecuted on *wrong Motives*.

It is necessary to make this Distinction between the Scheme supported by the Party, who have formed the Opposition for so many Years, and the Private Views of particular Persons, who have at certain Times engaged therein, because the common Topick of Reproach into which the Writers on the Side of Power unanimously run, is this; that Men have often contradicted themselves, and notwithstanding the Language they have made Use of when *out*, have avowed quite opposite Doctrines when *in*. Now the plain meaning of this, is no more than that particular Persons have had great Failings, and have in *different Scituations*, contended with equal Vehemence for *different Things*. That this may, and ought to affect *them* I do not deny; but certainly their Behaviour could no way affect *Things* themselves. If the Demands of the Administration for so many Years past, were just and reasonable, then all *Opposition* was *unjust* and *unreasonable* from whatever Quarter it came; and

on the other Hand, if the proposing a strict Examination into publick Affairs, a narrow Inspection of all the Pretences on which either
Money or Power were demanded by Men at the Helm, was with
respect to the Interest of this Nation *fit* and *right*, then the *Opposition* was always a *good Thing*, though possibly all who were concerned in it might not be *good Men*.

Such as have endeavoured to set the Conduct of those in the
Opposition constantly in a *bad Light*, have found themselves under
a Necessity of *misrepresenting* the Thing, and therefore the first
Step to be taken in order to give such as are impartial a just insight
into this Matter, is to render these Misrepresentations *manifest*,
which is the Design of this Paper. *Opposition* in the Stile of some
People, is a Term Synonimous with *Disaffection*, and great Pains has
been taken to make the World believe, that none ever *oppose* a
Government, who *wish well* to it. But this is certainly begging the
Question, and by proving *too much*, proves *nothing*. If we consider
the Reason of the Thing, and take for our Guide a Maxim in which
all Parties at present agree, *viz. That the* End *of* Government *is
the Good of the* Subject, then it will appear very possible for such
as *mean* the Government *well*, to *oppose* such as are in the *Administration* of it, unless it can be shewn, that Men vested with Power,
have never aimed at *violating* their *Trust*, or that according to the
Principles of our Constitution, *such* as have the *executive Part* of
the Government in their *Hands*, are the *only fit Judges* how they
ought to use it. But as these are Notions absolutely repugnant to
Liberty and Common Sense, so they have been long ago exploded;
and therefore as I said before, all Circumstances taken in, it must be
allowed that *Opposition* is not *malum in se*, or a direct and conclusive Proof of *Disaffection*, but quite the contrary.

*   *   *

In Queen *ANNE*'s Time, there were several *Oppositions*, and
these carried on with great Heat and Passion; and yet such as were
concerned in them, insisted, and many of them I believe with Justice,
that none *wished better* to the Queen and her Government, than
they did. In short, if we should pretend to take it for granted, that
all such as have opposed the Administration were at least *concealed
Enemies* to the *Government* under which they lived, we must run
into a very gross Mistake, since none shewed greater Fidelity to the
Crown at that Time, than such as acted against its *Ministers*. To
sum up all, as no set of Men amongst us have scrupled to oppose
at some time or other the Administrations under which they lived;
this is a convincing Argument, that all Parties have thought it lawful,
just, and expedient, no way derogatory to their Duty, no sort of

Blemish to their Loyalty, and therefore we ought in this Respect, to prefer their concurring Testimonies to the warm Declamations of prejudic'd Persons, who would have us believe, that *Spite* appears in no Dress, more commonly than in that of *publick Spirit*. If therefore we must condemn *all Parties*, if we condemn *Opposition* in general, it is better to acquit *all*, and to confess that *Opposition*, as well as *Attachment*, is govern'd by Circumstances, and that as it is not impossible Men may *betray* a Government they *serve*, so on the other Hand, it is not improbable that *Zeal* for the *publick Service* may induce Men to oppose the Measures of such as are intrusted with the *Management* of *publick Affairs*.

37

Faction Detected
by the Evidence of Facts

1st edn. 1743; 7th edn. (London, 1744), pp. 5-9; 168-9

[JOHN PERCEVAL, later EARL OF EGMONT][3]

Opposition to the Measures of Government, whether good or bad, is no new thing in this or any other Country, where the People have any Share in the Legislature. For wherever that Circumstance is found, Materials for the Advancement of private Views abundantly occur: And in proportion to the Importance of such a Country, Subjects ambitious of Preferment have more Incentives to urge them on to Pursuits of this Nature, more Instruments to assist them in their Undertaking, and more Pretexts to delude and to impose upon the Multitude. The Emploments in such a Country must of Necessity be numerous and lucrative, the Engagements of the Publick frequent and expensive, the Dangers from its Neighbours greater, their Jealousy and Ill-will more to be apprehended, and consequently with more Privacy and Caution counteracted. This enables artful Men to raise Murmurs against the most necessary Charges of the State, and to quarrel with the best Means of Publick Security with a manifest Advantage, because it is easy to dispute the Wisdom of Measures, which can never be intirely disclosed, till they are fully executed, and the Poison infused into the People has performed its Operation before the Nature of the thing can possibly admit a Detection of the Falsities and Misrepresentations employed against them; while the Publick, already prejudiced, never give themselves the Trouble to examine what is past; either taking more Delight in the Discovery of Error, than in the Pursuit of Truth; or not having the Means furnished with equal Industry, or being diverted by some fresh Objection, started to some new Conduct.

In proportion to the Riches of any Country, Poverty becomes more pressing upon many by a natural Contrast. In all such Countries the Wretched are certainly more wretched than in others which flourish less; because the Necessaries of Life are dear, and not to be had without that Industry, which Numbers will be found to want,

in all Places, however opportune the Means of Employment may be;
and Men of this kind may be industrious in a Faction, which is carried on by Noise, Drunkenness and Riot, when they can be so in
nothing else. In all Trading Countries the Prospect of Gain allures
many to adventurous Undertakings above their abilities, by which
some must be undone, and these never fail to attribute to Mis-
managements of Government, those Evils which arise from their
own Sloth, Incapacity or Avarice—again, in such Countries, the
Luxury of some induces others to follow them in the same Expence,
to the Ruin of themselves and of their Families, and the Generality
of these unite in Views of a like Nature.—As in all populous Countries, from a Variety of Distress, such Objects must be very
numerous; so from the very Numbers of a People alone, Faction
always derives a great Advantage, since from the Difference of
Dispositions, with which Men are born into the World, some will
infallibly arise from time to time, framed by Nature itself of a rest-
less and discontented Temper; form'd, whether they have Cause for
it or not, to be as well a Torment to themselves, as a Plague to the
Society in which they live.—Nor can Opposition, right or wrong,
want even Property to gild it over and to grace it; for Men arising
from the lowest Level of the People, and advancing into considerable
and easy Fortunes, are by a natural Consequence, too often led to
conspire against that very Felicity, Peace, Quiet and Prosperity, to
which alone they have owed their Existence.—Arrogance and Pride,
without a more than common Share of Understanding, are the
universal Product of all hasty Advancement. These Men repine at
at what they never before had Leisure to consider; that there is
still a certain Difference between their Condition and that of another
Rank, which they cannot remedy by all their Efforts to exceed
them in Expence.—This something, which they find still wanting,
sours them with their own State, and inclines them to fall in with
any popular Discontent; partly, to gratify their Vanity in insulting
those above them; and partly, to create a Chaos, out of which they
hope to emerge upon a Level with those they envy.—From whence
the Observation holds most true, That all Nations, in proportion to
their Increase, grow turbulent and factious, and from this Quarter
arise those levelling Schemes, in the Contention for which, sooner
or later, Anarchy ensues; and in process of time, the Loss of that
real Liberty, whose sacred name is so often speciously prophaned
by Malice and Ambition. Even Liberty itself, the more perfect it
is, produces these Effects more strongly; for Wantonness and Licentiousness, which are its evil Genii, tempt all depraved Tempers to
abuse it, and expose many to the Lash of the Laws, and to the just
Indignation of Power; which none, who feel, forgive, however they

deserve it. At the same time, the natural Tendency in all Mankind
to expect more Favour than they merit, provokes unjust Resentments against Government, and a certain Infirmity (of which we all
in some Degree partake) to be uneasy with what we have, and to
endeavour after more, inclines Multitudes, either out of Views of
private Benefit to themselves, or general Views of Encrease of
Privilege to the Order in which they Stand, to follow any Set of Men,
who take the Lead in Opposition of any kind.—All these move
by a secret Principle to that Quarter where it erects its Standard, be
it just or unjust, be it to save or to destroy their Country.

It is obvious from hence, and it is a Truth that cannot be disputed,
however it may effect the Credit of many pretended Patriots, that
the *discontented* Party of all Denominations consist *in general* of
Men of no Principle, and of very unworthy Character. Its Root
always the same;—but indeed its Effects are very different. It becomes in some Conjectures of very beneficial Consequence, when it
is led by Men of honest Views; and equally pernicious in others,
when conducted by Men of a different Character.—In the first Case,
it is an *Opposition*; in the second it is a *Faction*.

Faction is of two kinds in this Country.—*Opposition led by
Republicans*; and *Opposition led by Jacobites.*—Of the two great
Parties into which this Nation has long been divided—the *Whigs*
(though not *Republicans*) have formerly joined the first—the *Tories*
(thought not *Jacobites*) do constantly abet the last.—They who know
the Nature of this Country, who are acquainted with our History,
need no Definition or Description of these two Parties, and all who
are capable of Observation and Reflection can easily trace the
Reasons of their respective Conduct. It is therefore sufficient for
us in this Place, that this is a Fact, which cannot be denied; and
without a zealous Attachment of one or other of these two Parties,
Faction is incapable of doing much Prejudice to *Britain*.

A Faction of the former kind once destroyed the Liberties and
Constitution of this Nation. It grew up unobserved with the great
Improvements of its Commerce, and was nourished in the uncommon Measure of Prosperity, which arose from a long Tranquillity,
and a wonderful Encrease of Wealth after the Discovery of the
West-Indies, which diffused itself through the *Commons*, and gave
them Ability to contend with a *Prince*, who, ignorant of this new
acquired Vigour of the People, and vainly fond of Power, provoked
it by avowed Attempts to introduce an absolute Authority.

This Faction, by the Imprudence of that Prince, appeared at first
no more than an honest Opposition. But abetted at length by the
Majority of the Nation, (who neither perceived how dangerous it
was, nor could well have avoided joining with it, if they had, to

preserve themselves against the violent Attack then made upon their Freedom,) grew too strong both for the Prince and for the Laws. The miserable Consequences that it brought upon us are related at large in the Histories of *England* from 1642 to 1660.

These Evils of Faction in a Republican Form, prevented its Revival again in the same Shape.—The People of *England* had (since the Union of the two Houses of *York* and *Lancaster*) never seen it in another.—They therefore feared it in no other. This gave it Opportunity to shew itself in a new Form, and Opposition became again a Faction in the Reign of the late King *William*, and a Faction of a much more dangerous Nature than the first.

For whereas the Republicans, who are the Leaders of the first Faction, are in this Country little more than Whigs overheated by Oppression, and an extravagant Abuse of Power; as in reality there is very little of that Principle existing among Men of Property and Fortune, and as it is chiefly confined to men of an inferior Class; they may be easily brought to moderate their Views by what it is in the Power of every honest Government to apply: But the Leaders of the second Faction set out with Expectations, that no Government, without being *felo de se*, can gratify. For they set out upon the View of changing the Prince upon the Throne, and in necessary Consequence to transform the Constitution and Religion of the Kingdom.

In a word; a Jacobite Faction assumed the Shape of Opposition in that Reign; that is, the People under the Circumstances I have mentioned, and the Discontended of all Denominations acted in a Party, directed either secretly or openly by Leaders, whose Views intended the Restoration of King *James* II. or of his Family.

Now that this Faction was more dangerous than that which had appeared before, is farther manifest from hence. That the *Republicans professed a Principle*, and of a kind, which led them to do very great and glorious things. Their Zeal was indeed mistaken, but it clashed in its Pursuit, neither with the Honour nor the Independency of their Country, and the Strength of this Party lay in the Accession of those who had the greatest share of Sense and Honesty.—They were therefore steady in every Conjecture to defend the Nation against its Enemies abroad, and particularly against its most dangerous Enemy of all the *French*; and unless in Times of extream and rare Necessity, were deserted constantly by their *Auxiliaries the Whigs*, before they could bring their Scheme to any mature Effect.

But the *Jacobite Faction professed no Principle at all*, or such as deserves the Name of none. They had indeed a View, but it was private Title, the Interest of one Man, and of one Family. An

Object in itself unworthy of any Party, and criminal too in the highest Degree, in this Instance, because it was the private Title, and the Interest of a Man and Family, who by their Education and Religion were nourished in a fatal Enmity to their Country.—These Men therefore, from the indispensible Nature of this their first View, could be animated with no good Sentiment for the Publick, and from the Circumstances of their Case, were obliged to assist the Ambition, support the Power, and abet the Views of *France,* by whose Force alone they could hope to bring their Point to bear. Their Opposition therefore tended in every Step to destroy the Honour and Independency of their own Country. The Strength of their Party lay in the Accession of those who were the weakest and most dishonest Men; for who else could join in such a View as this; and therefore as all who furnished them Assistance must be either tainted in their Principles to their Country, or wrong in their Heads before they could engage with them their Conduct was constant, or wilful Error; and thus their *Auxiliaries the Tories,* if ever they separated from their Faction, never did it till it was almost too late, and never saw that they were deceived, or that they blindly concurred to the Ruin of their Country, till that Ruin was at the very Gate.

It is visible from hence, that there is much less danger from a *Republican* than from a *Jacobite,* or in softer Terms, from a *Whig* than from a *Tory Opposition.* A Whig Opposition is therefore that alone with which the People for many Years have ventured to concur, and the only one with which they can *for a Moment* concur safely.

*   *   *

Let the *Tories* in particular (I speak not to those *Jacobites* who assume the Name, but to those who are really no more than honest and well-meaning Men, and such in general they are, who have inherited that Appellation, because their Parents were such, or because of their Interests in their Corporations, or the Company they keep) let these, I say, consider, whether they ever got any Thing by joining with a *Jacobite Faction,* but Misery to their Country, and Shame to themselves? Whether they were ever led by a *Jacobite Faction,* but that they became their Dupes? Whether they were ever engaged with a *Jacobite Faction,* but they were brought to repent, and forced to recant at least? Whether they ever knew their Men, or saw their Danger, till it was almost too late to repent, and useless to recant? Whether they have not ever been carried away by *Names* instead of *Things*? And whether the Cry about *Hanover* now, is not what the Cry about the *Church* was formerly, raised and fomented with as little Reason, and for the same vile Purpose? Whether they have not too much Honesty to support an Alliance with a *Jacobite Faction*, to its End and Issue? Let them reflect, whether by acting as they now do, they put it not out of the Power of their best intentioned Friends to abolish those unhappy Party-Distinctions, which every well-meaning Man sincerely wishes to destroy? and which he will sincerely labour to destroy (whenever their Moderation can make it safe or possible) by a just and equal Advancement of Merit, where-ever it is found in *Individu*als among them? But let them consider fairly, how apt they have been on all Occasions to associate with, and to be guided by Men of worse Principles, and for this Reason, whether they can expect it, while they continue to unite with these Men, and while they claim it *as a Party,* which is their present Case.

38

The Detector Detected:
or, the Danger to which our Constitution now lies
exposed, set in a True and Manifest Light[A]

(London, 1743), pp. 58-60

I shall conclude with explaining the Difference between *Party* and *Faction*, which this *shallow-pated Politician* does not seem to understand, though he pretends to be a *Detector of Faction*. *A Party* is, when a great Number of Men join together in *professing a Principle, or Set of Principles*, which they take to be for the *publick Good*, and therefore endeavour to have them established and universally professed among their Countrymen. *Faction* again is, when a Number of Men unite together *for their own private Advantage*, in order to force themselves into Power, or to continue themselves in Power after they have once got in. From hence one may see, that *a Set of Ministers, or a Prime Minister and his Tools,* may be a *Faction*; I believe they generally are so, and I appeal to the Reader if *such a Faction* is not more likely to be made up of such Men as this Author describes in his second page, than *any Opposition* whatever; because the former can give *present Rewards*, the latter nothing but *distant Hopes*; and every Rogue knows, that *a Bird in Hand is worth two in the Bush.*

We may likewise from these Definitions see, that a Partyman, properly so called, may be a very honest Man, and a good Countryman, tho' mistaken in his Principle; whereas a factious Man can never be an honest Man, or a good Countryman; but as factious Men would certainly lose *their End* if they declared *their Motive*, they therefore always rank themselves under the Banner of some Party, and consequently it is very difficult to determine; at the very Time of Action it is, indeed, impossible to determine, whether a Man be a Partyman, or a factious Man; but by the whole Tenor of a Man's Conduct, it may be with great Certainty determined; for a Partyman never deserts his *Principle* as long as he thinks it for the *publick Good*, but immediately does, as soon as by Experience he finds it to be destructive of the *publick Good*: Whereas a factious Man will pursue the *Principle he has professed* to the *Destruction*

of his Country, if he finds he can no other Way arrive at, or retain
Power; but when he finds he can attain either of these Ends, by
deserting the *Principle he before professed,* he does it without Ceremony, and very often declares himself openly of a *contrary Principle
or Party.*

The high Pretences to Prerogative set up by King *James the First,*
formd those two Parties, which were in the next Reign distinguished
by the Names of *Roundhead* and *Cavalier,* and in the following
Reign by the Names of *Whig* and *Tory:* These two Parties had each
a *plausible Principle,* as the Foundation and Criterion of their Party:
The *Whigs* professed *Liberty,* the *Tories Loyalty,* without considering that these two Principles are very consistent; Nay, a late Author
has undertaken to shew, that neither can subsist without the other:
The two Parties having thus set up distinct Banners, factious Men
have ever since ranged themselves under one or other of these two
Banners; and therefore neither Party is answerable for what is done
by the factious Men amongst them. The factious Men among the
Whigs overturned our Constitution in the Reign of King *Charles
the First,* and were therefore deserted by all true *Roundheads,* or
Whigs, who joined in calling home King *Charles the Second.* The
factious Men among the Tories had very near done the same in
the Reign of *James the Second,* and were therefore deserted by all
true *Tories,* who joined in calling over the Prince of *Orange.* For
this Reason, both Parties ought to be jealous of their Leaders, and
take Care, that they do not lead them into Extremes; for factious
Men, let them profess what they please, will always be for ingrossing
Power, and *Whig-Leaders* have once already, under the Pretence
of *Liberty,* introduced *Slavery.* Therefore, the *Whigs* in particular
ought to be jealous of their Leaders, especially after they have got
Possession of Power; for ever since these two Parties began to be
distinguished, our Histories will inform us, that those in Power will
be for preserving and even extending it, and that *Whigs,* when they
become Ministers, have always been for preserving, and even extending the Power of the Crown; which may convince us, *that our
Liberties are not a Bit the more secure, because those who formerly
called themselves* Whigs *are employed in the Administration.*

I shall not pretend to vindicate the Conduct of either of these
two Parties, because they, or at least the factious Men among them,
have been both in their Turns to blame, and as it happens in all
Contentions, by their mutual Violence they have often drove each
other to Extremes, for their Principles may be easily reconciled.

39

A Defence of the People:
or, Full Confutation of the Pretended Facts, Advanc'd in a late Huge, Angry Pamphlet; Call'd Faction Detected

(London, 1743), pp. 8-9; 13-15; 97-8

[JAMES RALPH][5]

It is most fatally true, that Opposition hath been of long standing in this Kingdom: but then it is equally true, that it hath always been authoriz'd by the iniquitous Conduct of those in Power, and the real Grievances of the People: I make no Distinction of *Whig* or *Tory*-Administration: All have made themselves justly obnoxious, and therefore all have been justly oppos'd.

It is true, likewise, that factious and designing Men have taken Advantage of the Oppressions committed on one Hand, and the Complaints utter'd on the other, to espouse the Cause of the Public, in order to make lucrative Bargains for themselves; have first taken the People by the Hand, and then trampled upon their Necks: Our Histories are full of such corrupt and infamous Examples: But we need not have Recourse to them; our own Times have furnish'd us with those that are infinitely more strong and conclusive. Our own Eyes have beheld Faction and Opposition united: And, in the very Moment of Projection, we saw the First fly off, and the Last remain.

That Crisis is indeed the fiery Trial of a Patriot, when the Court bids for him against the People: Till then Counters may and will be current Coin: But when that Test hath discover'd the Fraud, when the Gilding vanishes, and palpable Brass stares us in the Face, we should be mad to suffer it to pass any longer for Sterling.

In plain *English*, when it appears that any Set of Men, of whatever Denomination, have bellow'd for their Country, only to find a Market for themselves, it must be allow'd the Plague of Faction is visibly among them, the Tokens are manifest, and it becomes the first Duty of all honest Men to separate themselves from their pestilent Society.

It is not, therefore, the *Whig* or *Tory, Jacobite*, or *Republican* Leaven that makes the Faction; but the Leaven of Hypocrisy and Venality; the proclaiming Redress of public Grievances, and meaning their own private Emolument. If I am to be fold, I care not by whom: If I am to wear a Yoke, I am indifferent whether it is the Manufacture, or after the Mode, of *Hanover* or *Rome*.

* * *

Or if these Particulars, however extraordinary, had escaped you, possibly forget the joint Labours of so many Men of Genius, to prove, that a solid, well-understood, and well-cemented COALITION had actually taken place; the *Whig* and *Tory* were no more, and that *Court* and *Country* were, for the future, to distinguish the Friends and Enemies of the People?

But I beg your Pardon. These plausible Stories of a *Coalition*, were, it seems, only one of those allowable, politic Frauds, which Party-Leaders press into their Service to make their Strength appear greater than it is, to render themselves more formidable to the Minister, to be held of more Importance to the People, &c. For in *P*. 16 after your frank Manner of *unmasking*, you roundly assure us: 'That the *Whigs*, tho' they could not refuse the Concurrence of their (the *Tories*) Votes, and their Assistance to swell the Number of Opponents, never *pretended*, or had any real Friendship with them.'

Indeed, you have here overshot yourself, for if they, the *Deserters*, have prov'd by their *Actions*, that they had no *Friendship* for the *Tories*, I have already prov'd by their *Words*, that they *pretended* it.

If, therefore, in this one Instance, it can be suppos'd that these Idols of yours deviated into Truth, it is yet farther apparent, that the Dust you raise about *Whig* and *Tory* is only to blind us, that you conjure up the Ghosts of these Factions, when the Life is departed; and that the present Opposition is no ways different from the Last, except, as observ'd before, that the Dross is purg'd off, and only the Gold remains.

Let me inform you farther, that the Craft of branding an Opposition by the odious Name of *Faction*, hath been put in Practice so often, and generally with such ill Success, that it ceases to be Craft, and deserves rather to be call'd Folly.

When several successive *Whig*-Parliaments, in the Reign of King *Charles* II made such noble Stands against the Oppressions and Corruptions of his scandalous Court, they were call'd a *Faction*; when all Parties, nay, the whole Nation, declar'd against the Violence and Tyranny of *James* II the Reproach of Faction was fasten'd upon the whole Nation; nay, under our great DELIVERER, who ow'd the Crown he wore to a successful Opposition, all who are steddy to their Principles, who continued to oppose whatever they could not approve, underwent the same Scandal; were upbraided in the same Terms, as if King *James* was still upon the Throne, and the *Revolution* no better than a Name.

*   *   *

But, whether of the *Whig* or *Tory*-Kind, or Both, you tell us the new Opposition is a Faction; and archly add, it was *form'd under the Title of the* BROAD-BOTTOM: *A Cant-Word, which corresponding equally with the personal Figure of some of their Leaders, and the Nature of their Pretensions, was understood to imply, a Party united to force the* Tories *into the Administration.*

What a broad Inconsistency here stares us in the Face? Why Man! the Union of Factions is the Death of Faction. This Union is here confess'd; nay, you insinuate, that one of these Factions acted so disinterested a Part, as to give up all its own Pretensions, in order to *force* the other into the *Administration.*

But it is necessary to set the *Broad-Bottom,* on its own proper Base: Which is, in plain Terms, an Association of all honest Men to abolish all Party-Distinctions, to embrace the common Interest of the Commonwealth, to free it from every Yoke, to disencumber it of every load, to labour jointly, one and all, whether in Power, or out, to restore the broken Constitution of old *England,* and, with the Blessing of Divine Providence, render it unchangeable and immortal.

40

A Parallel between the Roman and British Constitutions Comprehending Polibius' Curious Discoveries of the Roman Senate; with a copious preface, wherein his Principles are applied to our Government

2nd edn. (London, 1747), pp. v-x

[EDWARD SPELMAN][6]

In all free Governments there ever were, and ever will be Parties: We find that Sparta, Rome, Athens, and all the Greek Colonies in Asia Minor had their Aristocratical, and Democratical Parties; while the only Contest among the Subjects of the Kings of Persia was, who should be the greatest Slaves. The Truth is, different Understandings, different Educations, and different Attachments must necessarily produce different Ways of thinking every where; but these will show themselves in free Governments only, because there only they can shew themselves with Impunity. However, it was not the Existence of the two Parties I have mentioned, that destroyed the Liberties of any of those Cities, but the occasional Extinction of one of them, by the Superiority the other had gained over it; And, if ever we should be so unhappy as to have the Ballance between the three Orders destroyed; and that any one of the Three should utterly extinguish the other Two, the Name of a Party would, from that Moment, be unknown in England, and we should unanimously agree in being Slaves to the Conqueror.

Parties, therefore, are not only the Effect, but the Support of Liberty: I do not at all wonder that they are perpetually exclaimed at by Those in Power: They may have, sometimes, Reason to be disatisfied with the Parties themselves, but have much more to be so with the Heads of them; for These properly their Rivals: the Bulk of the Party aims, generally, at no more than a Reformation of what they think an Abuse of Power; the others, as the Power it self, without considering the Abuse, unless it be to continue it: the Party quarrels with Things, and the Leaders with Persons; consequently, a Change of Measures may appease the first; but nothing less than a Change of Ministers can satisfy the last. However, in one Respect, these Leaders often give Ease to Ministers without designing it; for, as they generally attack them upon Personal, rather than National Points, their Followers are unconcerned in the Contest; and, considering themselves as Spectators, rather than Parties, do not think it incumbent on them to go great Lengths for the Choice of Ministers; especially, since by the Indifference their Leaders shew for National Points, when they are aiming at Power (which is the Season for giving Hopes, as the gaining it is for disappointing them) their Followers have but little Reason to expect they will shew a greater Warmth for them, when they have attained the Possession of it.

But, whatever may be the Success of the Opposers, the Publick reaps great Benefit from the Opposition; since This keeps Ministers upon their Guard, and, often, prevents them from pursuing bold Measures, which an uncontrolled Power might, otherwise, tempt them to engage in: They must act with Caution, as well as Fidelity, when they consider the whole Nation is attentive to every Step they take, and that the Errors, they may commit, will not only be exposed, but aggravated: In the mean Time, Thirst of Power, irritated by Disappointment, animates the Application of the Opposers to publick Affairs, infinitely more than the languid Impulse of National Considerations: By this Means, they grow able Statesmen, and, when they come to be Ministers, are not only capable of defending bad Schemes, but, when they please, of forming good ones.

Another great Advantage, that accrues to the People from this Opposition, is that each Party, by appealing to them upon all Occasions, constitutes them Judges of every Contest; and, indeed, to whom should they appeal, but to those, whose Welfare is the Design, or Pretence, of every Measure? and for whose Happiness the Majesty of Kings, the Dignity of Peers, and the Power of the Commons, were finally instituted. This is, undoubtedly, the End of their Institution, and this End it is their Glory, as well as Duty, to accomplish; for, what greater Honour can be done to the three Orders, of which our Government is so happily composed, than to look upon them as they really are, that is, as the Channels, through which Ease, Plenty and Security are derived to millions of People?

I would not willingly do Injustice to Persons so useful, at all Times, to the Publick, whatever they may be to themselves, as the Head of an opposing Party; but shall mention one Point, to which I will appeal, as to a Touchstone of their Conduct, and, by which, it will evidently appear whether it is influenced by personal, or National Considerations; it is This:

There is not, I believe, in Great Britain, a Man, who is not convinced, nor a Man, not actually in the Administration, or, not expecting one Day to be in it, who will not own, that annual Parliaments are an effectual Cure for all the Evils, that are felt, feared, or complained of: If this is so evident a Truth, how comes it to pass that, for this last Century, that is, ever since an Opposition to a Ministry was made the Road to a Succession in it, that so National a Point has been neglected?

Section VI

THE QUIET YEARS

"In the mean time, let us not forget the Necessity that has been evidently deduced from the Nature of Things, for the uninterrupted Exertion of a *consitutional Opposition*; for when the Frailities of Men (to say no worse) have no certain known Intervals, such an Opposition can never sleep long with Safety."

Old England: or, The National Gazette, No. 32 (9 November, 1751)

The weak Opposition in the 1750s had no Bolingbroke, but various groups managed to publish able defences of the perpetual need for opposition to government. A number of the periodicals containing such arguments were edited or written by James Ralph, always ready to enlist on the side of the disaffected—for a price. There was no strong Government press, as had supported Walpole, although in 1762 *The Briton* and *The Auditor* made brief and ineffective forays against particularly bold attacks on George III and his favourite, Lord Bute. In the absence of commanding figures, or, until the coming of Bute, major issues, one must go to obscure sources for ideas on party. This explains the presence here of figures such as Harman and Brett and extracts from the pamphlet-like papers which flourished, unaccountably, only in the years 1755-7. The final extract—that from a pamphlet by Horace Walpole—reflects the beginning of a new era in English politics.

41

A Letter to Thomas Randolph, A Doctor of Oxford: Occasioned by his Discourse intitled Party-Zeal Censured

(London, 1752), pp. 5; 6-8; 9-10; 11-12

EPHRAIM HARMAN[1]

Thous sayest, page 5, *There are Cases, in which a zealous Contention may be very commendable, and even Strife and Division may become* LAWFUL *and* NECESSARY: And then thou dost proceed to enumerate those several Cases. And yet, page 7, thou dost affirm, *That* ALL *Divisions are indeed in* THEMSELVES *wrong: and* WHENEVER *they arise, there must be a Fault on one Side or other*; &c. Now if there are any Cases, in which DIVISIONS may be LAWFUL and NECESSARY, it follows, that all DIVISIONS are not WRONG: Or, if all DIVISIONS are WRONG, it must be allow'd, that there cannot be any Case, in which DIVISIONS may become LAWFUL and NECESSARY.

*   *   *

The next Objection, I take the Liberty to make, is to the following Paragraph, page 6, which is one of the Cases or Exceptions thou hast made to thy general Doctrine. *If our temporal Governors shall attempt to stretch their Authority beyond its lawful Bounds, if their Proceedings are arbitrary and oppressive, or their Measures weak and destructive, it may be reasonable, as far as our Station admits of, and the Bounds of our Duty will allow, zealously to oppose such Measures and Proceedings, provided it be done with that Temper and Prudence, with that Moderation and Meekness, which becomes a Disciple of* Jesus Christ.

Here, THOMAS, supposing our Governors to become Tyrants, thou declarest it to be thy Opinion, that we *zealously oppose them, as far as our Station admits of, and the Bounds of our duty will allow.* How far will that be THOMAS? Or, what dost thou mean by our *Station* and *Duty*? Here thou prescribest to us certain Measures of Opposition, but thou dost not explain what those

Measures are. And indeed in the Proviso, thou hast added, that
zealous Opposition, which thou thinkest to be so reasonable, and
which thou hast so earnestly recommended to us, seems to dwindle
into no Opposition at all, or just as much as may be sufficient to
hang the Man who makes it. Suppose, THOMAS, thou wert a
Subject of the *Czarina's*, and observing, that some of her Measures
were destructive and oppressive, thou shouldest think it thy Duty
to oppose them, but with all the *Moderation* and *Meekness* in the
World, or, if thou pleasest, *as becomes a Disciple of Christ*; shall
I tell thee what would be thy Fate? Thou wouldest first be *knuted*,
and afterwards lose thy Head on a Scaffold.

*   *   *

In the third Place, I find great fault with an Observation thou
hast made Page 11 and 12. *A melancholy, but a common, Sight it is
to see worthy and good Men,* EQUALLY DESIGNING *the publick
Good, yet engaged in opposite Parties, and hating and opposing
each other with the bitterest Rancour,* &c. *They draw contrary Ways*
(without doubt they do, if they oppose one another with the bitterest
Rancour) *and destroy each others Force, while* &c. *the publick
Good is the LAST Thing thought of.* I intreat thee to tell me, if
thou wast ever acquainted with any worthy and good Men, who at
the same time were full of Envy, Hatred and Malice. For so they must
be, if they oppose one another *with the bitterest Rancour*. If I were
to describe a very bad Man, I could not make use of more proper
or more apposite Terms, than those, which thou hast applied to thy
worthy and good Man. Indeed the Man, who opposes or pursues
his Neighbour *with the bitterest Rancour*, must be of a diabolical
Temper, and I do not think we could say any Thing more severe of
our grand Enemy the Devil himself. Thou sayest moreover in the
Beginning of this Observation, that these *good Men*, who are so *full
of Rancour and Malice*, intend the *publick Good*, and thou con-
cludest with saying, that the *publick Good is the last Thing*, which
they think of. Surely, THOMAS, thou art an impetuous Writer, and
never givest thyself the Trouble to revise thy Sheets, otherwise
how couldest thou possibly fall into such egregious Mistakes!

*   *   *

Thou sayest, Page 12. *On the other hand the weaker Party will
aim only at distressing those in Power, and will oppose and* DIS-
APPOINT *all Measures, which they may possibly enter into for
the publick Good.* Now, THOMAS, it must be owned, that we have
read in Histories, which have given us the Relations of Battles, that
the weaker Army hath often defeated the stronger, and we are told

in Scripture, that a very little Man was once able to conquer a Giant, though the Giant was covered over with Brass. But I think, there is not one Instance to be produced in all the Histories now extant, where the weaker among civil Parties (for 'tis such thou only talkest of here) hath ever conquer'd or *disappointed* the Measures of the stronger. We have in our H—— of C——— a very strong Party and a very weak Party, and whenever the weak Party shall be able to *disappoint* the measures of the stronger, I will venture to promise thee, that I will found a College for decayed Wits, and at the same time that thou shalt be deemed the greater Orator in *England*. Indeed, THOMAS, these Paragraphs seem to be big with Absurdities. For in the first thou supposest, that the Men in Power will TAKE NO MEASURES FOR THE PUBLICK GOOD, but will make every Thing subservient to their own Utility. In the second thou supposest, that the weaker Party, or the Men out of Power, will disappoint all the Measures, which the Men in Power SHALL TAKE FOR THE PUBLICK GOOD.

*A Free and Candid Inquiry humbly
addressed to the Representatives of the several
Counties and Boroughs in this Kingdom:
. . . In a letter to a person of distinction in the
North from a gentleman in town*

(Dublin, 1753), pp. 8-11

[?JOHN BRETT][2]

Another late ingenious writer seems to be of Opinion, that Parties will ever subsist among us, as long as we are governed by a mixed Monarchy, and yet admits a Principle that in Speculation at least contradicts his Assertion, "that before any Party be formed there must be some Source of Division in Principle or Interest."

There is one Source of Party which the forecited Author [Hume] or even the great Party-Builder Bolingbroke have taken no Notice of, from whence undoubtedly Parties may arise, and all the Plagues and Evils of Party endlessly issue, and which perhaps no Writer on the Subject hath ever specified, because it admits of no political Remedy, and which I confess might account for the Thing if it were our Case, that is Wantonness, the Consequence of Excessive Opulence. When in any Nation Trade hath been carried to the highest Extent, and Wealth hath flowed in greater Abundance than the Necessities of any People can demand: Such as possess large shares of it will be hot, tumultuous and unruly. . . .

That from this Source Factions in *Britain* have proceeded, is evident, if not to every Reader of its History, yet to every one who who has studied it. And my Reason for mentioning it is, not that I suppose the Party now budded and sprouting into Faction here, hath any such real Source, but only to shew, that the Thing is possible; that a Party may at least be in ESSE, without any Source of Principle or Interest to connect or bring them together.

Political Pastime;
or, Faction Displayed. In a Letter
to the Author of the Candid Inquiry[3]

(Dublin, 1753), pp. 39-40

[?JOHN BRETT]

What remains is only to consider your Notion of Faction, with which you and your Masters have branded us.

The Word, you know, is of equivocal Meaning, and wrested by all Parties to load and impeach one another: The Compilers of Dictionaries (not always the most clear-headed or sagacious Politicians) have defined it a Conspiracy or Combination of bad Men; which might do tolerably well, but that there is an Ambiguity even in the Word *bad*. You and I would differ in our Sense in the present Case who were bad, and who were good. I do not remember ever to have met with the Word in *Cicero*, if I had, to humour you, so fond of Quotations from antique Authors, I should not let it pass without the Pains of transcribing and perhaps a critical Remark, nor in any *Latin* Author except *Suetonius*, where it is used in a Sense that has no Connexion with our present Controversy. My Lord *Bacon* has an Essay upon Faction, but in him it stands indiscriminately as a Name for all Parties in a State; and indeed it is only among Moderns that I can ever find it used as a Term of Reproach: Which Observation, if we were not in haste, would afford us Ground for some very curious Remarks. My Lord *Bolinbroke*, whom you speak of as the great Party-builder, where ever there is a Court and a Country Party, fastens the Imputation upon the former; and if we suppose with him, that all Court Measures proceed upon one uniform Plan, to destroy Liberty, what he says is certainly right; but this, as it would be opening the way to a new Controversy, I will not for the present affirm: At the Time he wrote his *Dissertation upon Parties*, it was absolutely necessary to be maintained, to give some Plausibility to the Principles upon which he attacked the Administration.

Mr. *Gordon*, another great modern Politician, is not very clear, tho' so very copious on the Subject: As far as I understand him he seems to think all Parties factious, tho' at different Periods of his Life to have had different Sentiments; insomuch that I do not think the Translator of *Tacitus* and *Sallust* the same Man, at least according to Dr. *Berkley*'s Notion of Personal Identity.

44

The Protester, on Behalf of the People[4]

No. 1 (2 June, 1753)

ISSACHAR BAREBONE [i.e. James Ralph]

It is an old Observation on the political Conduct of the People of *England*, That They are apt to run into Extremes: And it is the frequent Saying of a certain eminent Modern to the same Effect, That They chuse to live either in the *Garret* or *Cellar* of their Understandings: In the *Garret*, we must suppose, then They will hear of nothing but *Opposition*, right or wrong, to Those in Power: In the *Cellar*, when *They* bow their Necks to any Yoke, and their Backs to any Load, with as much Tameness and Insensibility, as if born only to be Beasts of Burden.

The Protester,

No. 3 (16 June, 1753)

But, nevertheless, as the *Disuse* of a *Right*, has a natural Tendency to extinguish the *Claim*; and as, in Process of Time, it may be urg'd, That the People may *abdicate* their Rights, in like Manner as a Prince may *abdicate* his Throne; that, after such *Abdication*, all their said *Rights* become *Derelicts*, which lapse immediately to the Crown, and can never be *resum'd*, except by the *Grace* of the Sovereign, I could wish They would be prevail'd upon to *interpose*, now and then, in the Manner their Forefathers did, if it were only to keep up their *Pretensions* and hinder a *Foreclosure*.

Such Ministers are the most likely to behave well as are the most liable to be call'd to an Account; And a *Spirit* of *Opposition* has been the *Guardian Spirit* of our *Constitution* from the first Hour of its Establishment.

The Protester,

No. 16 (15 Sept., 1753)

I am not altogether so absurd, or so vain, as he who wish'd the whole World was of *one Mind*, provided it was his *own Mind*.

On the contrary, I know a Diversity of Humours and Situations must beget a Diversity of Opinions and Habits; and that Life may seem the less tedious and irksome, I know it is necessary it should be so.

But, how much soever this Diversity may contribute to Speculation, Amusement, and those little Agitations which serve to distinguish one Hour and one Day, as well as one Character from another, Unanimity and Perseverance are the only Principles which, in Action or Business, are of any Use or Efficacy.

In Oppositions more especially, where all are Volunteers, one Mind, one Will, one Direction, are Indispensables: And These should be the Result of Reason and Conviction, rather than of Prejudice or Passion: For tho' the Latter have the most violent, They have also, the most uncertain, Operation; and when the Fever has burnt itself out, a Lethargy always takes its Place.

The Protester,

No. 19 (6 Oct., 1753)

It cannot be denied, that over-zealous Party-Men often do by the Points they handle as the Tyrant *Procrustes* did by his Guests; That is to say, *stretch* some, and *lop* others, according to the Purpose they are to fit.

But from thence it would not be right to infer, That no Point They handle is worth attending to: For, according to that Image of *Drydens* after *Chaucer*,

> *I cannot* bolt *this Matter to the* Bran,
> *As* Bradwardin *and holy* Austin *can.*

Controversy is the very *Bolting-Mill* of *Truth*, and what the Writer does not separate, the Reader may: And it is a Remark, I think of *Seldens*, That, how much soever some People may affect to slight even *Songs* and *Ballads*, They serve to discover the Bent and Humor of the Times, better than more serious Incidents; as a Straw thrown up into the Air, indicates which Way the Wind is, better than a Stone.

But it is, in a more especial Manner, incumbent on him who writes in the Name of the Public, not to take the Name of the Public in Vain, I mean, Not to trifle with it, nor impose upon it: The Principles he advances must be sound, the Facts true; and he must not be void of Candor, tho' he may not always be sufficiently *Master* of himself to have the full Use of it.

On the other Hand, the Public ought to be sensible, That, to a certain Degree, *Parties* are as necessary to the Health of a free State, as Winds to That of the Universe: And that when there is no Principle to agitate Mens Minds, Stagnation and Corruption must inevitably follow: For tho' the Operation of Parties has of late been rather malevolent than otherwise, it has not been always so: On the contrary, if we are as happy as some People tell us we are, we owe all that Happiness to the *Party-Struggles* of *former* Times; and if we are *not*, we owe *more* of what is *amiss*, to our *own Self-Desertion*, than to the *worst* of those *Perfidies* or *Weaknesses*, which we have so long complained of like *Women*, instead of rectifying or avenging like *Men*.

What is still more remarkable, even that Diversity of Complaint, which the People have been reproached with, from Time to Time, is, in reality, no more a Reproach to them, than it is to complain of excessive Heat in Summer, and of excessive Cold in Winter. If the Pressure varies the Complaint must do so too: And then only we are inconsistent, when we suffer Grievance to be heaped on Grievance, without complaining at all.

The Protester,

No. 24 (10 Nov., 1753)

In short; of the various Points, which have been agitated for some Years passed, only the *French* Players and the *Jews-Act*, have made any manifest Impression on the Minds of the People. Whether from the Depth or Shallowness of their Understandings who shall say? They may have a common Sense, for aught I can tell, which may exceed all the Refinements of the Wise, and which, arising from Instinct, may even partake of Infallibility—They may satisfy themselves with what They see, and reconcile themselves to what they feel, under a Persuasion, That, being in general free and unmolested. They need not ruffle the Current, by nice Disquisitions, and fruitless Cavillings: And that what is in general amiss, flows rather from the unavoidable Perversions of Time and the Depravity of Men, than any settled Purpose of Heart, to injure or impair them ... And They may apprehend worse Consequences from a crude and feeble Opposition, than from the worst Effects of Power in its present Course of Administration. ... I say, These may be the Considerations, which have determin'd their Conduct; and not mere Supineness, Levity or Abjection, But whether They are or are not, the Motive makes no Difference in the Consequence. ... When the People are once put in Motion, there is nothing so light, or so heavy that the Tide they raise will not carry along with it ... But when *They* are not to be moved, *nothing* can be moved with any Vigor or to any Purpose.

* * *

Paper-Batteries, I am as well acquainted with the Use of, perhaps, as most of my Cotemporaries; but how clamorous and troublesome soever They have sometimes proved, They are of themselves and by themselves of no more Efficacy to reduce an *Administration*, than a Battery of *Pot-Guns* to reduce the strongest Fortification in *Flanders*.

Opposition implies Action: And Action requires Heads, Hearts, and Hands, Connection, Confidence, Subordination, and all the several Species of Abilities which are fit to govern the World. But all the Opposition of our Time has, on the contrary, evaporated in *Words*. And He that *talks* or *writes* of it best, has thought himself the greatest Proficient in it.

In plain *English*, Opposition might once have been called, with Propriety enough, the Virility, or Manhood of the Nation: It was then seldom if ever exerted but on great Occasions, and according to the Occasion, was exerted greatly: So long, therefore, it was the Idol of the Times: But when it sunk from Action to Declamation, from Purpose to Profession: When it grew wordy, interested and impotent, its Credit faded with its Vigor, in Virtue and its Use.

In any noble and righteous Cause, avowed as such by the People, and under a suitable Direction, my Abilities such as They are, and the Remainder of my Health (for much has already been consum'd in a Course of unprofitable Labours) should have been gladly employed: But in the present fritter'd State of Parties, merely to furnish Matter from Week to Week, for Discontent and Disaffection to feed upon, without any Possibility of performing the least Public Service, is alike abhorent to my Palate and my Purposes.

45

The Opposition
To be published occasionally[5]

(London, 1755), pp. 3-10; 12-13

If there ever was any one governing Principle in the Affairs of this great Universe, I think, we may pronounce, it is the Spirit of Opposition. The Astronomer has found it in the stronger Influences of the heavenly Bodies; the Philosopher acknowledges it in all his elemental Systems. Scholars find it among the Arts and Sciences; the Painter calls it Contraste, the Poet Antithesis, and the Churchman Infidelity. The Moralist ranks it among the Virtues by the Name of Emulation; and with Heroes, the Motto of this Paper is the very Motto of Heroism.

But in the World of Politics its Influence is universal. It actuates the whole System, and through all its Parts. For Instance, what do we mean by the Balance of Power in Europe, but a nice Opposition of all its political Interests? An Opposition wisely maintained by Queen ELISABETH; betrayed by the Pusillanimity of her Successor; ill exchanged by the first CHARLES for an unhappy one with his People; lavished away by his Son upon his Mistresses and Favourites; sacrificed by CROMWELL to the Vanity of insulting Spain; fooled away by JAMES to the Nonsense of his Religion; recovered by the Revolution, and fixed, for the Period of a few Years, by Queen ANNE.

But this Principle, so powerful upon the Interests of Europe in general, what Influence has it upon particular States? For Instance, upon the Happiness and Prosperity of Great Britain? We Answer, That to the well-balanced Opposition of her three Estates, she owes the very Being of her Constitution; her Freedom at home, her Weight and Influence abroad, to which in some measure Europe owes its Independence. Even to that Opposition between the Leaders of Parties within our Government, we are indebted for a Spirit of Jealousy, which is ever watchful over the Conduct of our Administration, either to prevent its Errors, or, if committed, to correct them. This kind of Opposition, by whatever Motives inspired, is the alone Foundation upon which a great Empire can be raised. This alone gives Laws and Statutes for the Preservation of domestic Liberty; this alone gives Strength and Spirit for foreign Conquests.

Such is the Language of Machiavel, when he treats of the Dissensions in the Roman Republic between her Patricians and Plebeians. He asserts; he proves, with his own peculiar Force of Reasoning, that whoever could have taken this Spirit of Opposition out of her Constitution, would have taken away all Possibility of her future Greatness; that, under any other Form of Government, she must have been contented with her own little Territories, or having ambitiously attempted to extend them, must have been ruined, like Venice or Sparta, by the Loss of a single Battle. In proof of this Reasoning, let us recollect, that whenever her Neighbours designed to take Advantage of her domestic Quarrels, they always found her stronger in proportion to the Violence of those Quarrels. Conquest abroad was the certain Effect of her Disensions at home.

Assuredly, there cannot in a free State be a more threatening Symptom of approaching Dissolution, than a languid Union of political Sentiments among her Citizens. Liberty is in its own Nature ardent and active; so fond of Opposition, that when there are neither any real Dangers, or imaginary Oppressions to oppose, it amuses and keeps alive its natural Disposition, by every other kind of Dissension. The Theatre and Opera; their Singers, Dancers, Fidlers and Harlequins, call forth her native Spirit; and while these unimportant Disputes maintain our Critics in their theatrical Rights, they evince the Certainty of our national Liberty. In the French Theatres, a Mousquetaire quells all this gallant Spirit, by a Whisper, or a Tap on the Shoulder.

In this kind of Reasoning, I have often, not without Wonder, heard our Members of P— open their Speeches, with wishing for the unanimous Consent of the House to the Bill they proposed; and for this Reason, that all Europe might be convinced how united they were in their Resolutions. But if Europe be well acquainted with our Constitution, or can judge of the Principles upon which the Liberty and Greatness of a free State are founded, what must they really think of such an Union? If France will believe her *Montesquieu*, she will believe, that the Spirit which hath for Ages animated Great Britain to preserve her own Freedom, and to vindicate that of others, is lost in Cowardice, Indolence, or Despair; she will believe, that Corruption or Tyranny have impressed such an Union of Sentiments upon our Politics, as Ignorance or Persecution only can ever establish in our Religion.

Let the French, therefore, at this very critical Conjuncture, be well informed, that we have a Party in our H—e of C—s, determined to oppose the Administration: A Party, not inconsiderable in their Numbers, nor lightly esteemed for their Abilities; of Sagacity to detect the Errors of the Minister, and of Power to awe him from executing any Project for betraying the Interests, or violating the Liberty of his Country; of Eloquence to plead her Cause, and Courage to defend it. Let this be reported to the French, and let us wish they may believe it. Yet, to confess my own Apprehensions, I greatly fear the Account will not prove so strictly true as Britain, either in Interest or Honour, might desire.

When I reflect, that a political Opposition is a principal Fountain of Oratory; when I remember the flourishing State of Eloquence during Sir *Robert Walpole's* Administration, I can hardly account for that Feebleness of Spirit with which our present Patriot forms his Opposition to the Measures of the Court. All the *technical Terms* of Bribery and Corruption, Subsidies, National Debts, Places, Pensions, and Standing Armies, are still remaining in our Language. Have they lost their original Meaning? or are they fairly worn out, (the common Fate of other Words), by being used upon every too light and trivial Occasion? Or have they lost their Importance and Dignity, by being prostituted to serve the bad Purposes of personal Resentment, Envy, or Ambition? Why does our Orator in vain pronounce them with his usual declamatory Tone? Why is the solemn Asseveration no longer believed? why the Vehemence of his Action no longer alarming? The Pressure of the oratorial Hand upon the Breast—why hath it lost its Pathetic? Why are the Swellings of his Periods grown languid, his Figures inanimate, and his Passions lifeless? Why is all this? Because he hath departed from that Plan of Opposition to which he was indebted for his Importance. We have heard him defend that very Administration he had for Years opposed.

*   *   *

But from frequent Examples of this kind, we may be most apprehensive, that the Opposition for which we contend, and which we hope will for ever maintain its due Influence in our Councils, may become odious or contemptible. It is confessed, that disapponted Ambition, a fancied Superiority of Parts, a sanguine Spirit of pronouncing, that all who differ from us in Opinion, want common Sense and common Virtue—it is confessed, that these, and the Passions in general, are very good Speakers, though certainly very Bad Reasoners. But when they can so far indulge their natural Impetuosity, as to stop the Business of the Nation in a most important Debate, at a Season most critical, for the sake of gratifying their personal Resentments, what Regard can they may be supposed to have for its Welfare and Honour? What Consequences may we not with Reason dread, if ever the Conduct of our Affairs be committed to their Intemperance?

46

*The Con-Test*⁶

No. 4 (14 December, 1756), pp. 20-2

No nation was ever more distracted by the commotions of private cabals, or *oligarchies,* than ours; and while these unnatural feuds subsist, corruption will spread its golden net, and entangle faction within the toils of venality. A coalition of parties for the common interest, is the only means to destroy this pernicious monster, whose fatal profusion nourishes and pampers its voluptuous prey, with all the poisonous delicacies of high fed luxury, till they grow big and saturate to their own destruction, and the ruin of their country.

The mischievous effects of political divisions are more severely felt among us, because their influence is not confined within doors; if the slaves of party, are baffled in their attempts to impede patriot operations, instantly, *ad populum provocant*: immediately the press groans with defamation. The spotless paper, is stained with the black dies of perfidious obloquy, envenomed malice, polemical equivocations, and malignant falsehoods. *Literary prostitutes,* are retained in the service of an iniquitous faction.—These ruffians in the republic of letters, who are bribed to assassinate truth and innocence—These profligates, who are too low to feel shame, and too desperate to dread punishment—*They* become the adjutants of *party* opposition.

But their abandoned use of mental endowments, is more infamous—Yes, we will hazard the assertion—more infamous, than pathetic prostitution. The mind, that *divinae particulam aurae,* which breaths after something more excellent, than it is capable of attaining; the mind, whose unbounded conception mocks its limited execution, undoubtedly claims a superiority over gross matter: And consequently it is more vile, and far more detestable, to prostitute the intellectual faculties, than the bodily organs.

In the common acceptation of mankind, PARTIES are generally considered *in pejorem sensum,* as formed by a coalition of factious men, rather than by a union of patriot principles. In this sense, they are always dangerous and destructive to the order of government, and the general interest of the community. But all united oppositions, are not to be confounded under this odious distinction, and condemned as factious: On the contrary, when a number of individuals, actuated by a laudable spirit, and guided by the sole influence of their own reason, confederate in order to support a good administration, or subvert a bad one, their labours, however unsuccessful, merit present applause, and will command future admiration.

It is the duty of every man, when he perceives that *M - - - l* treachery, or incapacity, endangers the labefaction of the fundamentals of our constitution, to exert his vigour, and form a connection with such as have segacity to discover the common danger, and virtue to assist him in sustaining tottering fabrick.—Nay more, it is the duty of every man, who feels the inward impulse of excelling capacity and conscious integrity, to undertake, nay to solicit, a share in the management of the state.

Such a desire of power, proceeds from a glorious magnanimity; and they who appear to despise it, are guilty of a mean affectation. Their contempt of grandeur, does not arise from a commendable moderation of mind, but rather from a timid inertness of soul, which makes them dread the fatigues, repulses, and contumelies, which an ardent emulation is ever exposed to, from candidates of *inferior* merit. CICERO, in his first book of offices, says, *Qui despicere se dicant ea, quae plerique mirentur, imperia & magistratus, iis non modo non laudi, verum etiam vitio dandum puto.*

Such insensible inanimate dastards, are unsusceptible of the delicate sensations of *real* glory; they are strangers to the luxury of patriot pride, which indulges in the exquisite delight of diffusive beneficence; which can calmly stand the TEST of the most invidious scrutiny, made by the collected malice of industrious animosity; which exalted in its superior worth, smiles at the low attacks of pusillanimous envy, which impotently throws its pointless shafts, against the impenetrable shield of virtue.

All party connections, under a general division, may be reduced to such, as are formed through the laudable influence of virtuous principles; or such, as are entered into from the ignoble motives of self-interest.

With regard to parties from principle—It may be meritorious to unite with those, who from a parity of sentiments are disposed to promote a particular plan of action, which our judgment approves, and our zeal applauds. But at length we may contract such a partiality for their characters, that though they may have imperceptibly wandered from their original conduct, which first engaged our confidence, yet we may still blindly follow them through the intricate paths of error, and the mazy windings of artful, treacherous deviation.

Though the calamitous sufferings of the nation, are so many fatal evidences of their perfidy, or inability; though the unanimous voice of *the people* proclaims them unskilful or criminal, yet our partial attachment will disculpate the delinquents, and fix the blame on fortune. Then our adherence to party, however originally cemented by virtue, becomes ingloriously maintained by weakness; and it is evidently absurd and unnatural, that they, who are representatives of thousands, should be governed by authority, instead of reason: For if they have not spirit and capacity, to think and judge for themselves, they cannot be qualified to determine, and act for others.

With respect to those, who form themselves into parties with base interested principles, they cannot be sufficiently despised, nor too severely persecuted.

The Con-Test

No. 12 (5 February, 1757)

The best writers have been of the opinion that factions, unless they are too violent, serve to poise and balance each other, and like discordant humours in the natural body, produce real good to the constitution. But all agree that corruption is an inveterate cancer, which gradually operates to the inevitable dissolution of the body politick.

47

The Constitution. With a Letter to the Author[7]

(London, 1757), No. 2, pp. 5-7; 18-19

Some of these Sentiments I may possibly have expressed with a little too much Earnestness in my former Paper; but I will not make an Apology for that Emotion, with which I mentioned an ambitious Attempt to enter into the Administration, by Methods unknown, I dare repeat it, unknown to our Constitution. Though we have often seen our Princes insulted by the humble Insolence of Resigning, and in this manner obliged to employ the Persons they disliked; yet never before this Instance was Majesty compelled to suffer the Aspect of a Servant, who had violently forced himself into his Presence. Yet, I frankly confess, I was rather surprised than alarmed at the first appearance of this impetuous Ambition. I was not without Hopes, that the precipitate Spirit of it would disappoint its own Projects: Neither was I much amazed, that the People, for it may not be thought decent to say the Populace, admired the Boldness of this Ambition. I knew the Depth of their Understanding, and the Extent of their Sagacity. But when I saw, not the Sovereign only, not the Administration alone, but the Constitution abandoned to an intemperate Demand of ministerial Despotism, I confess, I was both amazed and alarmed. Although I have little Concernment about Persons and Parties, yet I think Oppositions are in general of Advantage to Liberty; for I esteem it as a Maxim, that in every free State, when Men of Fortune and Abilities give up their personal Interests, and their Ambition, to such an Impetuosity, the Liberties of that State are much in Danger. The Contentions of the Great, says an Athenian Writer, for Honours and Employments, guard the Liberties of the People; let them possess those Honours and Employments unenvied, but let them leave to us our Freedom unviolated.

*   *   *

Such are the Principles, upon which this Paper would deserve the Approbation of the Poblic [sic]. Or, if Faction and Party and personal Resentments, can be supposed to profess such Sentiments as these, it is our Interest to encourage them to speak a Language, which those Sentiments alone should naturally inspire. For Instance, let it be granted that the late Lord Bolingbroke was actuated only by the Rage and Despair of disappointed Ambition, or the distempered Spirit of the Times, when he wrote his Dissertation upon Parties, yet the Work itself must be for ever esteemed as an Honour to human Reason in general, and a powerful Support to the Liberty and Constitution of his Country. Let me then wish to imitate this noble Author and let Calumny or Mistake pronounce, as they please, upon the motives of my writing.

48

*The Opposition to the Late Minister Vindicated
From the Aspersions of a Pamphlet, intitled
Considerations on the Present Dangerous Crisis*

(London, 1763), pp. 16-17; 39-41; 44-5

[HORACE WALPOLE][8]

When the Opposition was made in Parliament, there being no
Pretence for imputing it to Motives of immediate Interest, other
Motives equally dishonourable were assigned, lest the Nation should
form the obvious Judgment, that Men of the first Rank, of the
greatest Understanding, of independent Wealth, and of known
Attachment to the Family on the Throne, as well as to the Interest
of their Country, opposed the Peace upon right Motives.

They were called a FACTION, and the Word has been trumpeted
about the Kingdom. But mere Words are a feeble Support to a
public Cause; and Invectives are, in this Case, the most impotent
of all Words; If an Association of *wise* and *disinterested* Men, for
the Purpose of delivering the King and Constitution from the
dangerous Ambition of a Fellow-Subject, be a Faction, then the
Opposers of the late Minister deserve that Name, and will be proud
of it. But if a Party, composed of Men of different Views and
Principles, united by manifest Motives of Interest, and conspiring
to aggrandize one Man, against the known Interest of the King, at
the Hazard of the Constitution, and at the Expence of public
Tranquility, be a FACTION, the Name will return naturally to its
original Proprietors, notwithstanding the Virulence with which they
cast it from themselves upon other Men.

*   *   *

It is no wonder, that a Writer, who urges a Precedent of Severity
from the Reign of *James the Second*, should be out of Humour with
Party Distinctions. If that be a Reign of Authority with him, he
may well be disgusted at the Existence of a WHIG. Party Distinctions, which have no other Object, than to raise or inflame public
Disturbances, are odious at all Times, whatever the Names of the

Parties may be. But the Name of a WHIG has Objects so much more honourable and worthy of a *British* Subject, that there is not perhaps a Man in the united Kingdom, who bears that Name, and is ashamed of it; and the most suspicious Evidence an Administration can give of evil Designs, is that of treating a Name with Contempt, to which a Signification, so important to Liberty, has been annexed for near a Century past.

If any eminent WHIGS have been too conscious of their Rank and their Services, and too much influenced by their Party Principles, to take the Oaths to the Earl of *Bute*, instead of the King, what Offence have they given to that noble Lord's Successors, unless it be an Aggravation of their Guilt, that they are as little disposed to take the Oaths to them?

Our Author prescribes to his Majesty the Expedient of discountenancing both Parties, and intrusting the Posts of Government to *Neuters*. If he is in earnest, I beg leave to object to his Advice, that there is not a *sensible* Man, who has not conceived an Opinion upon the great Points, which distinguish Parties in this Kingdom, and there is not an *honest* Man, who will dissemble his Opinion. Who then are the *Neuters* our Author recommends? They must be Persons of too weak, or too unstable a Judgment, to form a fixed Opinion, or Persons so little under the influence of their Opinion, as to be ready to co-operate with *any* Party, for *any* Purpose, as best suits their immediate private Interest. We have experienced, that there such Men, and I need not point them out to the Author of the *Considerations*. I can truly assure him, that they are not to be found among the Persons, who have appeared in Opposition to the late Minister.

*   *   *

Having thus admitted, that the public Peace ought, if possible, to be preserved, I may justly claim from our Author a fair Concession in return; that the Persons in Opposition have as equitable a Right to ingenuous and candid Treatment, as the Persons in Administration. It is infamous, though perhaps not penal, to impute to them Transactions, in which they are known to be unconcerned; and it is a very different Offence, in the Eye of Morality, from that, which may sometimes be pronounced penal, of delivering out bold and interesting Truths, relating to a Fellow-subject in Power.

Section VII

THE SIXTIES: PARTY AND OPPOSITION REVIVED

"The outcry against the present party-disputes appears to me a little unjust. The excess to which they are carried may be blameable, but surely there can be no ill in the nature of the thing itself."

The Monitor, or British Freeholder, no. 377 (11 Oct., 1762)

The early years of George III's reign had seen a revival of partisan political writing along the traditional lines of Whig and Tory, although the fragmented state of the various connexions militated against unity either in Government or Opposition. When Tories came to Court in 1760 with the accession of George III, the days of the Whig oligarchy were numbered. Whigs out of place saw Bute's Ministry of 1762-63 as Tory, although King George sought rather a coterie of "King's friends" which would supplant both conventional parties and factions. Opposition writings concentrated initially upon those liberties of the subject endangered by the issue of general warrants. However, beginning in 1767 there appeared a number of anonymous publications anticipating Burke's famous defence of party. The best of these efforts, *A Letter to the Duke of Grafton*, was not inconsistent with the claims made in 1770 by Burke on behalf of the Rockingham Whigs. Others (extracts 50 and 53) were much more radical in tone, clearly the work of the sort of reformers then disparagingly called "political empirics".

49

An Essay on the History of Civil Society

1st edn., 1767, 4th edn. (London, 1773), pp. 212-15; 271-2; 273; 319-20; 432-4

ADAM FERGUSON[1]

The changes of condition, and of manners, which, in the progress of mankind, raise up to nations, a leader and a prince, create, at the same time, a nobility, and a variety of ranks, who have, in a subordinate degree, their claim to distinction. Superstition, too, may create an order of men, who, under the title of priesthood, engage in the pursuit of a separate interest; who, by their union and firmness as a body, and by their incessant ambition, deserve to be reckoned in the list of pretenders to power. These different orders of men are the elements of whose mixture the political body is generally formed; each draws to its side some part from the mass of the people. The people themselves are a party upon occasion; and numbers of men, however classed and distinguished, become, by their jarring pretensions and separate views, mutual interruptions and checks; and have, by bringing to the national councils the maxims and apprehensions of a particular order, and by guarding a particular interest, a share in adjusting or preserving the political form of the state.

The pretensions of any particular order, if not checked by some collateral power, would terminate in tyranny; those of a prince, in despotism; those of a nobility or priesthood, in the abuses of aristocracy; of a populace in the confusions of anarchy. These terminations, as they are never the professed, so are they seldom even the disguised object of party: But the measures which any party pursues, if suffered to prevail, will lead, by degrees, to every extreme.

In their way to the ascendant they endeavour to gain, and in the midst of interruptions which opposite interests mutually give, liberty may have a permanent or a transient existence; and the constitution may bear a form and a character as various as the casual combination of such multiplied parts can effect.

To bestow on communities some degree of political freedom, it is perhaps sufficient, that their members, either singly, or as they are involved with their several orders, should insist on their rights; that under republics, the citizen should either maintain his own equality with firmness, or restrain the ambition of his fellow-citizen within moderate bounds: that under monarchy, men of every rank should maintain the honours of their private or their public stations; and sacrifice, neither to the impositions of a court, nor to the claims of a populace, those dignities which are destined, in some measure, independent of fortune, to give stability to the throne, and to procure a respect to the subject.

Amidst the contentions of party, the interests of the public, even the maxims of justice and candour, are sometimes forgotten; and yet those fatal consequences which such a measure of corruption seems to portend, do not unavoidably follow. The public interest is often secure, not because individuals are disposed to regard it as the end of their conduct, but because each, in his place, is determined to preserve his own. Liberty is maintained by the continued differences and oppositions of numbers, not by their concurring zeal in behalf of equitable government. In free states, therefore, the wisest laws are never, perhaps, dictated by the interest and spirit of any order of Men: they are moved, they are opposed, or amended, by different hands; and come at last to express that medium and composition which contending parties have forced one another to adopt.

*   *   *

In every casual and mixed state of the national manners, the safety of every individual, and his political consequence, depends much on himself, but more on the party to which he is joined. For this reason, all who feel a common interest, are apt to unite in parties; and, as far as that interest requires, mutually support each other.

Where the citizens of any free community are of different orders, each order has a particular set of claims and pretension: relatively to the other members of the state, it is a party; relatively to the differences of interest among its own members, it may admit of numberless subdivisions. But in every state there are two interests very readily apprehended; that of a prince and his adherents, that of a nobility, or of any temporary faction, opposed to the people.

*   *   *

Under the use of this necessary and common expedient, even while democratical forms are most carefully guarded, there is one party of the few, another of the many. One attacks, the other defends; and they are both ready to assume in their turns. But though, in reality, a great danger to liberty arises on the part of the people themselves, who, in times of corruption, are easily made the instruments of usurpation and tyranny; yet, in the ordinary aspect of government, the executive carries an air of superiority, and the rights of the people seem always exposed to incroachment.

*   *   *

If national institutions, calculated for the preservation of liberty, instead of calling upon the citizen to act for himself, and to maintain his rights, should give a security, requiring, on his part, no personal attention or effort; this seeming perfection of government might weaken the bands of society, and, upon maxims of independence, separate and estrange the different ranks it was meant to reconcile. Neither the parties formed in republics, nor the courtly assemblies which meet in monarchical governments, could take place, where the sense of a mutual dependance should cease to summon their members together. The resorts for commerce might be frequented, and mere amusement might be pursued in the croud, while the private dwelling became a retreat for reserve, averse to the trouble arising from regards and attentions, which it might be part of the political creed to believe of no consequence, and a point of honour to hold in contempt.

*   *   *

Emulation, and the desire of power, are but sorry motives to public conduct; but if they have been, in any case, the principal inducements from which men have taken part in the service of their country, any diminution of their prevalence or force is a real corruption of national manners; and the pretended moderation assumed by the higher orders of men, has a fatal effect in the state. The disinterested love of the public, is a principle without which some constitutions of government cannot subsist: but when we consider how seldom this has appeared a reigning passion, we have little reason to impute the prosperity or preservation of nations, in every case, to its influence.

It is sufficient, perhaps, under one form of government, that men should be fond of their independence; that they should be ready to oppose usurpation, and to repel personal indignities: Under another, it is sufficient, that they should be tenacious of their rank, and of their honours; and instead of a zeal for the public, entertain a vigilant jealousy of the rights which pertain to themselves. When numbers of men retain a certain degree of elevation and fortitude; they are qualified to give a mutual check to their several errors, and are able to act in that variety of situations which the different constitutions of government have prepared for their members: But, under the disadvantages of a feeble spirit, however directed, and however informed, no national constitution is safe; nor can any degree of enlargement to which a state has arrived, secure its political welfare.

In states where property, distinction, and pleasure, are thrown out as baits to the imagination, and incentives to passion, the public seems to rely for the preservation of its political life, on the degree of emulation and jealousy with which parties mutually oppose and restrain each other. The desires of preferment and profit in the breast of the citizen, are the motives from which he is excited to enter on public affairs, and are the considerations which direct his political conduct. The suppression, therefore, of ambition, of party-animosity, and of public envy, is probably, in every such case, not a reformation, but a symptom of weakness, and a prelude to more sordid pursuits, and ruinous amusements.

50

An Address to the People of England:
Shewing the Advantages arising from the frequent
Changes of Ministry; with an Address to the
Next Administration [2]

printed for J. Almon (London [1767]), pp. 42-5

Thus, my loving countrymen, you see an agreeable prospect both for yourselves and posterity, enjoying this most excellent state of government I have been describing: here will be a constant emulation in the parties to qualify themselves for your service; and emulation always produces excellence: and having rivals for your favours, you may expect, like a fair lady, to be served with the utmost sincerity, assiduity and devotion. There is no guessing to what political eminence this country may arrive from this very circumstance; certainly to much greater than eye has seen, ear heard, or the heart of any man has as yet conceived.

Some timorous well meaning people, I know, are apprehensive lest such frequent shocks and changes should produce some unfavourable effects upon our excellent constitution; as if, forsooth, all changes must needs be for the worse. This is indeed a little akin to that obstinate son of orthodoxy in religion that would preclude all reasonable improvement and embellishment; but as all sublunary things are liable to alteration and suspectable of improvement, we should always avoid such principles as tend to the laying an embargo on the human mind. The changes and alterations I have been considering, will appear to an enquiring person to be analogous to a change of diet, air, garments, &c. in the natural body; all which things are frequently prescribed by physicians as conducive to health and vigor; and truly without such mutation the body politic as well as natural would have a dangerous tendency to certain lethargic symptoms, and be in a manner dead while alive.

Many of our statesmen seem to have overlooked the circumstance I have lately been considering, and to have laid their account in keeping their employments as long as was formerly the custom when one party enjoyed an exclusive privileged, if not charter, and the other was under proscription; But those circumstances have now ceased.

Our Great Commoner indeed seems (almost the only person) adequately sensible of these things, and he has accordingly conciliated himself to both parties; and this verily he might right honourably do, since, as I have just observed, they are both *now* perfectly innocent; nor do either Whigs or Tories wish any harm over our happy constitution in church and state: but certainly each contribute to give spirit and vigor thereto.

51

A Letter to ... the Duke of Grafton, on the Present Situation of Public Affairs [3]

printed for J. Almon (London [1768]), pp. 1-3; 4-13; 27-30

My Lord,

It is possible for a nation, under a limited monarchy, to be so circumstanced, that even a good man may reconcile it to his patriotism to act uniformly with his party, and, by adhering to it with firmness, deserve a certain degree of applause. The fidelity of party is not indeed to be compared to that perfect love of country, which has no other object but the public good, and of which your Grace may perhaps have seen some instances in history. Yet it is a merit of a subordinate kind, and, considering that the other is now absolutely out of date, should not be disregarded. It is also true, my Lord, that a nation may be so circumstanced, that even a bad man, who never had an idea of any interests but his own, must be obliged, if he would act consistently with those interests, to assume the appearance of a more enlarged virtue. He must break through the dependance of party and, exert himself, upon more extensive principles, to preserve the public fortune from a ruin, in which his own would be involved. Your Grace's situation gives you the best opportunity of knowing whether this country may yet be preserved by virtues of a second rate; or whether we have no resource left, but in one general united effort of pure disinterested patriotism, to save the state. Our condition, I hope, is not yet so desperate as to want such a proof of public virtue. But it is time, my Lord, we should know what we have to trust to.

*   *   *

It may seem a paradox to assert, yet I believe it will be found true upon reflection, that the distinction between the parties of Whig and Tory, while it was a real, or at least a profest [professed] distinction in principles as well as name, was of service to the kingdom. An able united opposition in parliament, ... will always have the effect of rouzing the activity, and fixing the attention of government; of perplexing bad measures, and purifying good ones. Opposition is the weight, which keeps the machine together, and makes it go. If it be steady and uniform, government will either be maintained in the same proportion of steadiness, uniformity and strength, or there will be a change of hands. If it be light, weak, and desultory; if there be no fixed general principles of opposition, experience shews us that government will soon sink down to the same level of weakness, uncertainty and disunion. The generality of men are but ill qualified to judge for themselves, or to direct their own conduct in matter of politics. Their understandings, like the navigation of the ancients, are only fit for coasting voyages, where they may have certain land-marks and beacons constantly to guide their course. Such in politics I conceive were those established principles of party, which formerly distinguished Whig and Tory from each other. When they were lost, what consequence would follow, but shipwreck to private faith and public consistency. The faith of party, to which all public virtue had been reduced, when it was no longer directed by principles openly profest and maintained, soon sunk into mere private contract and friendship; a bond too weak for modern morals. Secret stipulations are easily disavowed, and those men will desert their friends without a blush, who would be ashamed to desert both their friends and their principles at once. So much are we governed by words and forms, that when we forget our creed, religion and morals will not be very long remembered. To this confusion of parties we owe the unsteadiness and distraction, with which public councils have, for some years past, been conducted. Under the Utopian idea of a general coalition, men of all parties, sentiments, opinions, and connections were so mixed and confounded, as to form a strange heterogeneous mass, which it was impossible should hold long together.

Mr. Pitt made it his boast, though very falsely, that, under his administration, all distinction of parties was, for the first time, abolished. I am far from thinking that he would have done a service to his country, if it had been true. But in reality, it was the circumstance of the times produced that general acquiescence with which his measures were received. Public danger and distress will always have the effect of uniting parties, or at least of stifling their animosities. Any great national crisis, whether of foreign invasion or of interior convulsion, will soon oblige all parties to recede from the extremity of their principles, and meet in one point, to provide for their common safety; but in those cases it were to be wished that the union of parties were formed by the cohesion of entire bodies, rather than a confusion of parts. The conduct of the two parties, in bringing about the revolution, is a striking proof that party-spirit is not likely to be carried so far, as to endanger the great general interests of the country. They united in altering the succession to the crown, and in establishing the public security. When that great business was accomplished, each party returned to its colours, and revived that spirit of action and re-action, which constitutes the health and vigour of the state. In this light the revolution forms a glorious lesson to future princes not to depend upon an apparent animosity of one party against another, as a means of destroying the liberties of both; but rather to dread that force, which preserves its tone and activity by a constant exercise upon itself. With respect to the coalition boasted of by Mr. Pitt, it is evident that it could not be owing to his policy or management, but to some other cause; since we find, in his second administration after the peace, he has not been able to persuade any five people to agree in supporting him, or to form any thing like a strong consistent government. There is, however, too much reason to think that, by bringing together men of different parties, he laid the foundation of a mischief, which has encreased every day, and now threatens ruin to the kingdom.

It is not my design to enquire which party would have governed best, or whether the Whig or Tory principle, was best adapted to the British Constitution. I think there was no danger to the establishment from either, while a due opposition to it subsisted. What I assert is, that either party alone would have given us a government; since both have been confounded, we have had no government. The idea of forming an administration upon the broad foundation of comprehending all parties, is pleasing enough in theory, and sounds well in declamation, but has never yet been attempted in this country with success. As things are now constituted, a government by party, however imperfect and partial it may seem in speculation, is the only one likely to act with strength and consistency, and the only one that suits the temper and circumstances of this country. To complain, that an uniform opposition retards and embarrasses the measures of government, is vain and idle. A Minister, who undertakes, should be equal to the task with all its difficulties; and it is so easy for him, considering the influence and resources of the Crown to maintain a parliamentary strength sufficient for any defensible purposes, that not to have it will of itself convict him of extraordinary weakness and mismanagement. There never was an opposition supported by such abilities, or maintained with so much perseverance, as that which Sir Robert Walpole met with during the whole of his administration. Yet your Grace knows how long it was ineffectual, and that probably it would never have succeeded, if he had not given advantages against himself, by a series of measures contradictory to the spirit and temper, if not to the real interests of the people.

These observations, my Lord, will not appear useless, if they lead, as I apprehend they do, to a knowledge of the true causes of our present situation. Whether they lead to a remedy of it, will be matter for your Grace's future consideration. From this original mistake that an administration, to be firm and permanent, should comprehend different parties, all our present divisions, all the scandalous changes, which have been made in the King's servants, and confusion of broken, distracted measures, may without difficulty be traced.

In stating to the public some of the most alarming circumstances of our situation, an attempt to conceal or soften would be very difficult, and perhaps not very adviseable; to exaggerate is impossible. The same things have probably been said or thought by others; but, if we may judge by the effect, I shall repeat nothing that has yet been sufficiently considered. The most important phaenomena, in politics as well as nature, are neglected because they are constantly before us, and seem to be little observed for the very reason, which makes them most worthy of observation.

* * *

If these propositions and facts should appear to be fairly advanced and truly stated, and if it were possible for the whole to be thus represented to a great prince qualified to judge well, and anxious to do right, in what manner may it be imagined he would reason upon them? Without any great breach of probability I think he would express something like the following sentiments.

"I see plainly that I was mistaken in my first principle of government, and that by endeavouring to reconcile and unite opposite parties, I have done nothing but introduce discord and distraction into my councils. This mistake has been the source of all that weakness, inconsistency and change of ministers, which has dishonoured my government, and made my crown a burthem to me. Experience, beyond all speculation, has convinced me that it is impossible to govern this country but by a single party. I am determined, therefore, to commit my affairs for the future to that party, which, on mature deliberation, shall appear strongest in abilities, numbers, and parliamentary interests. My choice shall be made with caution, but I will adhere to it firmly; or, if I should be compelled to change my servants, the change shall be entire, for never more will I submit to patch an administration. Which ever way I turn my eyes, the necessity of forming once for all a new, a compact, and an able administration, appears to me in the strongest light. The state of the finances calls for a man of superior talents;—that of the colonies requires a man of unshaken resolution. I must have union, wisdom and firmness in my own servants, before I can hope to restore vigour to my government, or reverence to the laws. My army must no longer be sacrificed to the animosities of a Commander in Chief, and of a Secretary at war, or to the negligence of both.

"When these alterations are made, if it should then please God to make a war unavoidable, the nation will either be prepared for it, or I shall have the consolation of knowing that I have done my duty to my people."

52

The North Briton [4]

No. 99 (8 April, 1769), p. 605

But that our present ministers would willingly throw their crimes upon their master, is abundantly evident from the whole of their conduct. For, to what other motive can we reasonabliy attribute the eternal repetition, that occurs in all the addresses, of professions of loyalty to his Majesty's person, especially at a time, when no man of sense suspects the loyalty of any party in the kingdom; and least of all of that party (if indeed so great a majority of the nation can be called a party) that is now engaged in opposition to the ministry? The party engaged in this opposition are, and ever have been, the only true and steady friends to the Protestant succession, and the Brunswick family. 'Twas by their interest, chiefly, that that family was first placed upon the throne: 'tis by their interest, chiefly, that they have hitherto been supported in it; and by their interest, chiefly, that that family was first placed upon the throne; 'tis by their interest, chiefly, that they have hitherto been supported in it; and by their interest, I hope, they will continue to enjoy it till time shall be no more.

To what cause then can be possibly ascribe it, that this party, so numerous, so loyal, and so meritorious, has, almost constantly for these eight years and upwards, been in a state of proscription? Is it, that some persons, attached to the abdicated family of Stuart, have formed a design to disgust them with the present establishment, and thus dispose them for another revolution? The design is artful, but it is absolutely impracticable. The Whigs (for it is of that party I speak) well know that the preservation of their liberties, and the support of the present establishment, are one and the same; and as they can never be induced to part with the former, they will never be persuaded to overturn the latter. Is it, that others have secretly laid a plan for erecting an arbitrary and despotic government? The scheme is weak, and will certainly miscarry, and can never be productive of any other effect than the ruin of those who shall presume to undertake it. Or is it, what perhaps is still more probable, that a third set have put on a determined resolution to extirpate from the kingdom all distinction of party? This project is as absurd, and however strange the assertion may seem, is as wicked as either of the former. The spirit of party is inseparable from liberty; they follow one another as a shadow does a body; and if ever it should happen that the one is destroyed, the other will expire in the very same instant.

53

Letter signed "A Watchman"[5]

in *The London Chronicle* (18-20 April, 1769)

Sir,

An opposition to ministerial men and ministerial power, as such, however it may be dressed up in the scarecrow of rebellion, sedition, republicanism, will ever be salutary, in this country, and all countries. Few in high place have ever been able to withstand the flattering temptation of using base and undue means to enlarge or perpetuate their rule. And none should be trusted without being tied down as fast as possible, and watched, that they do no harm. It cannot then but rejoice every well-wisher to his country, to hear of the new association for the support of the rights of Englishmen, amongst which are found so many respectable names, and some honourable Members of the Senate of the nation. Such associations may produce accidental ill, as opium may kill a patient;—but this is rare, and only from mismanagement.

Clubs of honest men, publicly convened for honest purposes, strengthen the hands and hearts of others far and near, and check and intimidate men of bad designs. They are especially dreaded and hated by tyrants, who have accordingly in all times used all possible means to prevent them. And therefore in France and Spain and Portugal and Germany, men may meet together to sing and dance and game and gluttonize and get drunk as much and as often as they are able; but a *lettre de cachet* shall soon disperse them, if it be known that they intend to meddle at all with the affairs of the State.

I love the name of Supporters of the Bill of Rights. For, although the rights of the people were asserted and declared at that glorious era of our liberties, the revolution, yet unhappily those rights were not then secured, as they ought to have been.

54

Considerations on the Times [6]

printed for J. Almon (London, 1769), pp. 18-20; 31-7

I am afraid it will be very difficult to lay down a plan entirely
to make this constitution such as our patriotic ancestors first intended it, especially as I have some reason to suspect the temper
of the times to be rather to take advantage of the miseries of the
people, than to reform the state. Far be it from me, however, to
say, that corruption hath got possession of this country; but the
very suspicion of it is attended with danger. I have heard of many
remedies indeed; but the proposers seem to deal with the constitution, as physicians treat their patients, rather to prescribe than cure.
The only effectual method seems to me to be annual parliaments:
these may avoid every inconvenience; they will destroy all corruption, because no man will think it worth his while to corrupt
his constituents. Merit only will then be regarded, not pecuniary
influence: a seat in parliament will be no longer looked upon as a
pretense for a contract with government, a place or a pension, but
as a disinterested honour conferred by a disinterested people; and
I make no doubt but that there will be found a sufficient number
of gentlemen ready to serve their country on this equitable condition. There is not a man, I believe in Great-Britain, who is not convinced that annual parliaments must put an end to corruption, and
annihilate all ministerial influence in every borough; but gentlemen
who either are in administration, or expect one day or other to be
ministers, can never consent to permit the enjoyment of their
salaries to be held by so precarious a tenure. But is it not more for
the interest of this country, that ministers should be tenants at the
will of the people; and that the representatives should take annually
the sense of their constituents, who may either reject or approve
according to their merits? I have been surprised that oppositions
have not thought of this expedient; but I believe we may account
for it in this manner, that most gentlemen who are in opposition,
one day or other expect to be in administration; and they are
conscious that no one point could possibly be carried (if members
were to be annually accountable to their constituents) that infringes
upon what the subjects call their just rights; and they are likewise

convinced, that if it were once proposed in the house, those who proposed it would be joined by the general cry of the people, and of consequence, that when they had once broke asunder the chains of their fellow-subjects, in order to distress the ministers of the day, they would only forge others for themselves, when they came to enjoy their places.

*   *   *

I shall conclude these considerations with one more observation on party. Party is the natural attendant on power and riches, and the more a country has to give, the greater number of competitors there will be to receive. Several men of great authority have declared, that parties are not only natural, but even necessary, in free governments; like storms in the natural world, they serve to disperse the ill humours that are collected in it. For though as Pope sings,

> *Better to some perhaps it might appear,*
> *Were there all harmony, all concord here;*
> *That air nor ocean never felt the wind,*
> *That passion never discompos'd the mind:*
> *Yet all subsists by elemental strife,*
> *And passions are the elements of life.*

So sings that excellent poet, and this observation is equally applicable to our own constitution; for though opposition be not always grounded upon just and virtuous principles, yet is it ever a curb to administration; and though the leaders of a party may only intend to overthrow their rivals in power, yet by their attacks upon them, the public reaps much benefit, inasmuch as such contests prevent ministers from pursuing bold and dangerous measures, which, if they were uncontrolled by an opposition, they might attempt. Thus they are compelled to act with caution, both in extending the prerogative of the crown, and in disposing of the public money. The latter, in fact, only is the best ground an opposition can stand upon, as in promoting an enquiry into the disposal of the public revenues, they are sure to be joined by the people, who are the first that feel the extravagances of men in power; and the whole eyes of the nation are consequently turned upon them, and the errors they commit are not only exposed to public view, but often aggravated.

Another great advantage, says a learned author, [?Spelman] that accrues to the people from this opposition, is that each party, by appealing to them upon all occasions, constitute them judges of every contest; and indeed, to whom should they appeal, but to those whose welfare is the design, or pretense of every measure? and for whose happiness the majesty of kings, the dignity of peers, and the power of the commons, were singly instituted. This is undoubtedly the end of their institution; and this end it is their glory as well as duty to accomplish: for what greater honour can be done to the three orders of which our government is so happily composed, than to look upon them as they really are; that is, as the channels through which ease, plenty, and security, are derived to millions of people? I make a very wide difference between a faction and a party, though the word is used analogous by way of reproach, by ministers, of those who disapprove their measures: the former, I flatter myself, no longer exists in this kingdom, whatever it did in the beginning of the present century; for though the fathers of several of those gentlemen, who now are near the king's person, wished perhaps, out of principle, to see the royal family dethroned, yet I hope the sons are convinced of the imprudence of their ancestors, and will never add ingratitude towards the best of kings, to the misguided errors of their predecessors. But party is the natural consequence of liberty: in all free countries men have the privilege of speaking their minds; and it is only in free states they can do it with impunity. The freedom of the press is never allowed in arbitrary governments; and it has always been the policy of those states to keep the people in ignorance. It is only in commonwealths that books can be published without the inspection of the magistrates; and it was doubtless an infringement on the privilege of the subject when an act passed, that nothing should be acted on the stage but what was licensed by the lord chamberlain. A noble earl, in his speech on that occasion, called it "An excise upon wit;" and though wit may sometimes degenerate into scurrility and abuse, yet that is the tax a state pays for its freedom. We may venture to say that we shall never see an extinction of party in these kingdoms (I mean an opposition to the measures of ministers, for thank God his majesty has not an enemy in these realms) till the power of the crown becomes so great, either by our national debt, or the profuseness of the commons, as to enable men in power to corrupt the majority of the house: when that comes to be the case, the name of party will from that instant be unknown in England; those few, who have any remains of virtue, will then not have the resolution to oppose arbitrary measures, but will retire in despair to their country-seats; the people for a while will kiss the rod that chastises them, till liberty making her last convulsive efforts, and mankind having no protection in the laws, will have recourse to violence, and assembling together, murder, banish, and divide among themselves the land of their adversaries, till finding no security where there is no law, in their haste they will constitute a tyrant.

Every man who carefully reads the histories both of modern and ancient times, will find that a government constituted as ours must be permanent; and the wisest of legislators have contrived it to consist of king, lords and commons, that thus by uniting the excellence of a compound, they may avoid the disadvantage of a simple government. When the gladiator appears upon the stage, every grace, the excellence of each attitude, all his force, and even victory itself, depends on very part of the body bearing its just proportion to the rest. If the true poise be lost, he immediately becomes weak, his body is distorted, his strength fails him, and he tumbles to the ground. So is it with a compound government of this sort. Such a government remains firm and lasting as long as it preserves itself equally poised and balanced. But if ever the corruption of the age can seduce the commons to give up their privilege into the hands of the crown, or the spirit of faction so far infatuate the minds of the people as to encroach upon the just prerogatives of the crown, there will then be an end of government. The restoring of annual parliaments would entirely free us from any apprehension of the former; for even could we suppose men, who are chosen to be the representatives of the people, weak enough to set themselves to sale, and become the hirelings of a minister, yet their actions would soon show the livery they wore; and with what face could they return to their constituents, and desire to have their choice again confirmed, when they were conscious they had abused their trust? But there is no danger of their ever being put to such tryal, as the hands of the crown are much strengthened, and her dependents greatly increased within these few years, so that it is to be feared there is no great prospect of seeing annual parliaments restored; for the possession of power is so enticing, that few men perhaps can prevail upon themselves to resign it. I flatter myself, however, our liberties will still be secured to us, though probably not in so effectual a manner as if the sense of the people was to be taken annually. However, we shall always find some men whose virtues will not suffer them to countenance the illegal measures of ministers, and others whose motives, though they may not be quite so upright, yet will prove equally salutary and beneficial to the people; for the eyes of the world will be turned upon them, and this will oblige them to be careful how they act. The independent man will observe them, the ambitions envy them, the necessitous be dissatisfied, and the wit, on the slightest occasion, ridicule them: thus the attention of each is always turned towards administration, whilst both sides appeal to the people, and make them the judges of their respective conduct.

It happened in the last century, that the ambition of some few, instead of forming an opposition to the servants of government, made their attacks upon the crown itself, and unfortunately were too successful. Party became a faction, and the deluded people saw, when it was too late, tyranny imposed upon them under the specious shadow of liberty. This misfortune might have been prevented, had that age enjoyed annual parliaments; the people might have united in gaining a victory over an ambitious minister, but never could have joined in a conquest over their king and constitution.

55

Observations on a late Publication intitled The Present State of the Nation

(1769), in *The Works of the Right Honourable Edmund Burke* (London, 1803), Vol. II, pp. 9-10

EDMUND BURKE[7]

Party divisions, whether on the whole operating for good or evil, are things inseparable from free government. This is a truth which, I believe, admits little dispute, having been established by the uniform experience of all ages. The part of a good citizen ought to take in these divisions, has been a matter of much deeper controversy. But God forbid, that any controversy relating to our essential morals should admit of no decision. It appears to me, that this question, like most of the others which regard our duties in life, is to be determined by our station in it. Private men may be wholly neutral, and entirely innocent; but they who are legally invested with publick trust, or stand on the high ground of rank and dignity, which is trust implied, can hardly in any case remain indifferent, without the certainty of sinking into insignificance; and thereby in effect deserting that post in which, with the fullest authority, and for the wisest purposes, the laws and institutions of their country have fixed them. However, if it be the office of those who are thus circumstanced, to take a decided part, it is no less their duty that it should be a sober one. It ought to be circumscribed by the same laws of decorum, and balanced by the same temper, which bound and regulate all the virtues. In a word, we ought to act in party with all the moderation which does not absolutely enervate that vigour, and quench that fervency of spirit, without which the best wishes for the publick good must evaporate in empty speculation.

It is probably from some such motives that the friends of a very respectable party in this kingdom have been hitherto silent.

56

Thoughts on the Cause of the Present Discontents

(1770), in *Works*, pp. 329-30; 331-2; 335-6

EDMUND BURKE

It is indeed in no way wonderful, that such persons should make such declarations. That connexion and faction are equivalent terms, is an opinion which has been carefully inculcated at all times by unconstitutional statesmen. The reason is evident. Whilst men are linked together, they easily and speedily communicate the alarm of any evil design. They are enabled to fathom it with common counsel, and to oppose it with united strength. Whereas, when they lie dispersed, without concert, order, or discipline, communication is uncertain, counsel difficult, and resistance impracticable. Where men are not acquainted with each other's principles nor experienced in each other's talents, nor at all practised in their mutual habitudes and dispositions by joint efforts in business; no personal confidence, no friendship, no common interest, subsisting among them; it is evidently impossible that they can act a publick part with uniformity, perseverance or efficacy. In a connexion, the most inconsiderable man, by adding to the weight of the whole, has his value, and his use; out of it, the greatest talents are wholly unserviceable to the publick. No man, who is not inflamed by vainglory into enthusiasm, can flatter himself that his single, unsupported, desultory, unsystematick endeavours are of power to defeat the subtle designs and united cabals of ambitious citizens. When bad men combine, the good must associate; else they will fall, one by one, an unpitied sacrifice in a contemptible struggle.

*   *   *

I do not wonder that the behaviour of many parties should have made persons of tender and scrupulous virtue somewhat out of humour with all sorts of connexion in politicks. I admit that people frequently acquire in such confederacies a narrow, bigotted and proscriptive spirit; that they are apt to sink the idea of the general good in this circumscribed and partial interest. But, where duty renders a critical situation a necessary one, it is our business to keep free from the evils attendant upon it; and not to fly from the situation itself. If a fortress is seated in an unwholesome air, an officer of the garrison is obliged to be attentive to his health, but he must not desert his station. Every profession, not excepting the glorious one of a soldier, or the sacred one of a priest, is liable to its own particular vices; which, however, form no argument against those ways of life; nor are the vices themselves inevitable to every individual in those professions. Of such a nature are connexions in politicks; essentially necessary for the full performance of our publick duty, accidentally liable to degenerate into faction. Commonwealths are made of families, free commonwealths of parties also; and we may as well affirm, that our natural regards and ties of blood tend inevitably to make men bad citizens, as that the bonds of our party weaken those by which we are held to our country.

Some legislators went so far as to make neutrality in party a crime against the state. I do not know whether this might not have been rather to overstrain the principle.

*   *   *

Party is a body of men united, for promoting by their joint endeavours the national interest, upon some particular principle in which they are all agreed. For my part, I find it impossible to conceive, that any one believes in his own politicks, or thinks them to be of any weight, who refuses to adopt the means of having them reduced into practice. It is the business of the speculative philosopher to mark the proper ends of government. It is the business of the politician, who is the philosopher in action, to find out proper means towards those ends, and to employ them with effect. Therefore every honourable connexion will avow it is their first purpose, to pursue every just method to put the men who hold their opinions into such a condition as may enable them to carry their common plans into execution, with all the power and authority of the state. As this power is attached to certain situations, it is their duty to contend for these situations. Without a proscription of others, they are bound to give to their own party the preference in all things; and by no means, for private considerations, to accept any offers of power in which the whole body is not included; nor to suffer themselves to be led, or to be controuled, or to be overbalanced, in office or in council, by those who contradict the very fundamental principles on which their party is formed, and even those upon which every fair connexion must stand. Such a generous contention for power, on such manly and honourable maxims, will easily be distinguished from the mean and interested struggle for place and emolument. The very stile of such persons will serve to discriminate them from those numberless imposters, who have deluded the ignorant with professions incompatible with human practice, and have afterwards incensed them by practices below the level of vulgar rectitude.

Section VIII

THE SIREN SONG OF COALITION

"I can respect men of every different political opinion, provided they are uniform: but I have never been able to understand that eternal versatility of character which changes public debates into the venal eloquence of wrangling lawyers: . . . .

Thomas Day, *The Letters of Marius* (1784)

Frequently in the eighteenth century England was governed by a coalition. Indeed, motley administrations predominated the "broad-bottom" of the 1740s, Chatham's wartime coalition and the unsteady governments put together in the 1760s. By 1777 North's Government badly needed a transfusion of strength, although the King's refusal to have any ministers "forced" on him deprived North of the needed support. Men talked much of coalition, sometimes facetiously, as did Soame Jenyns, or earnestly, like William Eden. The horror expressed by William Pitt and his followers at the Fox-North coalition of 1783 was reminiscent of Burke's charge against Chatham's "checkered and speckled" Ministry of 1766. Disapproval of the coalition of 1783 did not necessarily imply admiration of a party system, just as some defenders of the coalition (extract 64) were also advocates of party government. The fact remains that as the reputation of any arrangement smacking of unprincipled coalition fell to a new low, party was, by contrast, gaining a good name. By the early 1780s Burke's propaganda of 1770 had a more sympathetic audience than on first publication.

57

A Defence of the Proceedings of the House of Commons in the Middlesex Election

(London, 1770), pp. 1-3

[NATHANIEL FORSTER][1]

Parties, it is said, are inseparable from a free constitution; and are also absolutely necessary to the very existence of that liberty, from which they arise. This is undoubtedly true of parties, that grow out of constitutional principles, that pursue constitutional objects, and by constitutional means only. Men formed under this standard, and cemented by these common views, cannot act with too much vigour and firmness; cannot be too much upon their guard against any encroachment on those rights, which it is their first duty to support. But the moment there is a departure from these principles, the moment men are engaged in the pursuit of an unconstitutional object, or by unconstitutional means, a total and unhappy reverse of things takes place. Every *pretended defence* of liberty upon illegal and unconstitutional ground is a *real attack* upon it; and leads directly on to those scenes of violence and disorder, in which it can have no existence. It can have no existence, but under the protection of law; of that law, which restrains every man from violating the liberty of every other man, and thereby ensures the common liberty of all.

In this view of things, the true spirit of a party depends not on the numbers which compose it. We have seen a very small part of the nation, headed by bold ambition, and uncommon ability, triumph over the united sense of the body of the people. We have seen them, subvert the constitution under pretence of reforming it; and trample upon those liberties, which they professed to defend. We have seen too (God forbid we should again see it) the body of the people, so far the dupes of their own blind zeal, as to engage, as it were, in a conspiracy against themselves, and run headlong, as in a fit of delirium, to their own destruction. The whole nation is, in such a state of things, become a *faction*; and the *voice of the people* is literally the *madness of the people*.

A spirit of discontent is of all others the most contagious. The bulk of the people are always ready to fancy themselves injured by their superiors; much more, to believe that they are so. A mere popular clamour indeed subsides, as quickly as it is raised. And unless the fermentation be constantly fed, and kept up, it will very soon exhaust itself, and cease of course. This however is very easily done. Ingredients for the purpose are always at hand. Nor does the application of them require in general much skill or address. In free governments there is commonly some popular subject of discontent. It cannot well be otherwise. The opinions of men will be different, where all are allowed to think, and to speak freely. And the passions of men are always pretty strongly engaged on the side of their opinions.

The present age has indeed shown uncommon ingenuity in multiplying these subjects of discontent. The spirits of the people have been kept in perpetual agitation by a succession of terrors and dangers held out to them. Almost every day has produced some new alarm. Private calumny has been called in to the aid of public accusation. Whatever malignity could suggest, the views of faction have propagated to every corner of the land. The voice of reason is no longer heard amidst tumult, contention, and clamour. And even the common sentiments of humanity seem to have lost all influence upon minds intoxicated by party zeal, and given up to the sole guidance of those furious passions which it never fails to excite and invenom. The administration, the house of commons, the courts of justice, the army, have been represented, as forming one dangerous conspiracy against law, liberty, and the constitution. An association has been entered into upon the avowed principle of counteracting these dark designs. And the whole nation has been called upon, in the most public manner, to rise up as one man, in defence of every thing that is dear to them.

58

A Scheme for the Coalition of Parties Humbly Submitted to the Publick

(London, 1772), pp. 9-10; 27-31

[SOAME JENYNS][2]

In order to qualify myself for this task, and forming such a coalition, I have endeavoured to recollect all the plans, which have hitherto been offered, in writing or conversation, for this purpose; and I cannot remember one, that contained any thing more, than this short proposal, to dismiss all at that time in administration, and to admit the proposer and his friends into their places, which he always calls a coalition, and recommends as the only method to restore concord to a nation, which he fails not to represent as much out of humour as himself. Although this plan may probably be perfectly right, as it has been universally adopted by all parties in their turns; yet it has of late been tried with so little success, that I would by no means have it repeated, and therefore it shall make no part of my proposal.

*   *   *

All these [grievances], I question not, will be prevented in future by my proposal; to which I have never heard any objections, except the two following, which I shall endeavour to answer.

First, that these annual changes in administration will occasion such continual changes in measures, that no system, foreign or domestic, could be pursued with steadiness and effect. To this I reply, that, under the present mode of government, this must certainly be the consequence of such frequent changes; but, under the regulations of my scheme, they will have no such operations; because the new ministry, being introduced without contest, will be under no necessity of counteracting every measure which had been adopted by the old: they will not be mortgaged to old connexions and old animosities, nor embarrassed by old principles and old professions; and therefore they will not be obliged in honor to involve the nation in a war, because the last ministry had concluded a peace; nor to relinquish taxes of which they might avail themselves, because they had formerly voted against them; nor to wink at libels, and indulge riots, because they had once been useful; nor to ruin themselves by the same arts by which they had ruined their predecessors, to prove the consistency of their conduct. This rotation of ministers will therefore be so far from changing systems, that it will contribute very much to continue them: for, if any one administration should happen to fix upon any one system, the rest, having no inducement to alter it, will probably pursue it in preference to the trouble of finding out another. But if the worst should happen, and no system at all be pursued, the nation perhaps might not suffer so much as may be imagined; for what system can we remember to have been ever strictly adhered to in this country, except this, that opposition should do mischief, and ministers embarrassed by a perpetual warfare do nothing; and yet under this we have constantly gone on, improving in wealth, trade, liberty, power and prosperity, to this hour.

The other is, that if all opposition is by this scheme put an end to, there will remain no check upon evil ministers, and the people will be left a defenceless prey to their tyranny and rapacity. This, indeed, is a formidable objection; and so tenacious am I of the liberties of the people, and so jealous of the encroachments of ministerial power, that, if I thought my proposal would be attended with consequences so fatal, I would instantly abandon it, in spite of all the parental fondness of an objector. But of this I cannot entertain the least apprehensions; for although it will destroy all opposition in parliament, where it is seldom honest, and always hurtful; yet it will leave it in full vigour amongst the people, where it is often honest, and seldom injurious to the publick: enough of it will remain in the hearts and mouths of common-council-men, liverymen, and free-holders, to watch over the conduct of ministers; here is its native soil, and here it ought always to be cultivated: but whenever it takes root amongst the great, whenever it shoots up into courts, councils and senates, it soon degenerates into selfish and angry factions, who, under a pretended zeal for the welfare of the publick, are contending only who shall first sacrifice it to the mean ends of private ambition or avarice: for true English opposition to government is like that respectable animal the true English mastiff, who, when permitted to prowl and roar about the yards and out-houses, is a faithful, honest, and intrepid guardian; but, if admitted into the drawing-room, becomes a very offensive and a very dangerous visitor.

59

Letters Concerning the Present State of England.
Particularly Respecting the Politics, Arts, Manners,
and Literature of the Times [3]

printed for J. Almon (London, 1772), pp. 198-200; 200-5

"Of Parties in England."

Of all the governments in Europe, none has been marked by such a variety of parties as that of England. I shall not attempt a regular delineation of all that have by turns honoured and disgraced our country, or enter into an enquiry after their respective conduct, their views, merits and success. These in general are pretty well known; but I shall offer you a few remarks on that very remarkable change in our constitution, for such I esteem it, which took place on the extinction of all our regular parties.

From the time of the civil wars, which gave rise to innumerable political sects, we may date the existence of those two grand parties, which were at different times distinguished by different appellations, but most commonly known under those of *Whig* and *Tory*: the most material doctrine of one was, to exalt the Crown to the possession of all those prerogatives at which Charles the First aimed: that of the other, to limit the power of the Crown as much as possible, until prerogative was so much reduced, that the nation should be in fact tho not in form a Republick. The Tories were above all other things fast friends to the House of Stewart: the Whigs fast friends to Liberty alone; which, on the Revolution, naturally threw them eagerly into the arm of the House of Hanover.

From hence it is very easy to see, that the Whigs were the true friends of their country, and deserved far better of their country than the Tories, whose principal end was ever to enslave it. Now the use of parties clearly appears in this, the existence of the tenets of the Tories did not depend on that sect; for all the friends, followers, and dependants of the Court were such in office and inclination, and regal authority in this kingdom has ever had a constant tendency towards absolute power; first from open force, and then from secret influence. The use even of the Tory party, therefore, was the giving rise to the Whigs; were it only for occasioning the being of the latter party, the use of parties in general would be clearly decided.

*   *   *

A long series of events, particularly the continued success of the Whigs, in retaining the power of administration in their hands, brought the Tories into great discredit, and at last so much reduced them, that their decline of course brought down the lustre of the Whigs, and ended in the extinction of both parties; or rather in a change of names; for instead of Whig and Tory, they were distinguished by those of Court and Country. And as either party came into power, the other regularly went into opposition; the principal men of each were known by the whole nation; and there was a great point of honour among them, to adhere strictly to their engagements with their friends.

In such a situation of domestic affairs, it was hardly possible for successful attempts to be made on the liberty of the subject; for those who were not influenced by honest and truly patriotic motives, had the incentive of mere party to animate them; which, with the strength of union ever powerful among them, formed a barrier, against which the Court, however successful in slighter matters, could not carry many acts of unfavourable to liberty.

But what spectacle have we had before our eyes since these parties have been abolished? In one period, we found the Court without the appearance of an opposition in parliament, tho' that period was the most expensive one to the kingdom that had ever been known.—And at other times, when designs extremely dangerous to the constitution have been hatching, and even executing, nothing has appeared like that firm opposition, that band of men of mutual ideas, which has so often saved this government: little miserable divisions, whose arrangements have been as varied as the chances on the dice, have by turns distracted the country, but never made three efforts in any great or manly cause, that shewed firmness or principle. No regular party existing; the breath of the day has formed, dissolved and changed oppositions: no tie or connection being found among any set of men, they have fallen by turns into the most unnatural unions imaginable one week, and betrayed them the next, until at last it is come to such a pass, that the Crown has no party to fear, or that can controul its operations, however fatal they may be in future times: no body is against the Court, but those out of power, or rather that are not influenced; so that (a few persons excepted) the measure of the Crown's adherents is the measure of its ability to influence. Every set of men, nay almost every man, has been in and out, with, and without every

other set of men; so that nothing like the principle of a party is left
in the nation. This revolution must in the end have great consequences; the present miserable disconnection among all the great
men, and their dependants in the kingdom, has thrown a greater
power into the hands of the Crown, than an augmentation in the
army of ten thousand men.

Nothing can be so shallow, as the congratulations which have
been made to the people in many publications, on the extinction of
party among us: it has been represented, as the greatest blessing
that could happen to this country, to have no more party broils
disturb it; but I will venture to assert, that all the uninteresting
debates that ever happened between Whig and Tory, had better
have continued and increased, than the spirit of the present times
have arisen among us, which, instead of a union among certain
men, that might in a day of need stand forth, and in Parliament
rescue the constitution from the evils that threaten it, has given
birth to a system of repulsion, which sets every man at variance
with his neighbour, except the league kept together under one
banner, by the influence of the Crown.

At present we have in the nation only one set of men, that can
pretend to the appearance of a party, which are those who adhere
to the Court on every question, in every business, and in every
affair; these men, who are strictly united, and under the ministerial
banner, having a principle of union wanted by every other set, are
an overmatch for all.

There has been in modern times, since our grand parties disappeared, a notion strongly inculcated by various persons, that
measures form the only object worthy the attention of Englishmen,
but that *men* are below their notice; if the measure is good, what
matters by whom it is enacted?

This reasoning is of a piece with that which makes the kingdom
flourishing, because there are no parties in it. But surely we need
only reflect on the events of our own history to be convinced, that
this is a most false and pernicious idea: the whole tenor and event
of it prove, that there are in all periods men who are to be trusted,
and others in whom no confidence can be placed. The people of
this country have not in a single instance formed a general idea of
men that was false or mistaken; patriots have deserted their cause,
and men have changed their principles; but the people have been
seldom mistaken in praising or condemning improperly; they judge
rightly of a man's actions, tho' they cannot see his heart; but from
long observance they deduce the general idea, that such and such
men are more to be trusted than others.

60

Remarks on a Pamphlet Lately Published by Dr. Price, intitled Observations on the Nature of Civil Liberty . . .[4]

(London, 1776), pp. 15-17

[ADAM FERGUSON]

It is absurd to say, as some writers have said in the course of this paper war, that there must be in every state one supreme uncontrolable power; for this never yet existed in any state whatever. The despotic Prince, in search of such a power, finds, that he changes the control of assemblies, councils, civil departments, or of men of education and virtue only, to come under the control of Serjeants and Corporals. In our government, King, Lords, and Commons are not one power, but three collateral powers; any one of which may stop the motions of all the rest. This observation, however, takes nothing from the authority of their joint acts wherever they concur, nor had any one till now, from the extreme settlements of British subjects in the old world, to their utmost migrations in the new, doubted the validity of any such act. Dr. Price seems to regret that the efforts formerly made by our fathers in behalf of Liberty are no longer repeated; he should likewise regret, that out liberties are no longer attacked in the same manner as in the times of our fathers. The contest between the prerogative of the King and the privilege of Parliament is discontinued; the King has influence enough in Parliament to obtain the necessary supports of his government, though, I hope, never to obtain the smallest resignation of the people's right. In the contest of our times, the parties are the pretenders to office and the holders of office. A noble contest, though an ignoble cause. I must call it a noble contest, as it is undoubtedly one principle of life in our constitution. It leads one party to watch the motions of administration; and the other to be on their guard because they are watched. As the matter now stands, indeed, it is more the interest of opposition to stop the ordinary movement of government, than to prevent its *abuses*. If they can stop the ordinary course of government, the minister must withdraw to make way for themselves: but in preventing abuses, they only oblige him to change ill measures for good, and by this means to take a firmer hold of his power. I know that many ill consequences might be imputed to the state of our parties; but I am not for removing any one safe-guard to freedom, until we have found a better.

61

Four Letters to the Earl of Carlisle . . .

(London, 1779), pp. 20-2

WILLIAM EDEN[5]

Amidst the humiliating weakness of our nature which I have described, it is some consolation to reflect, that to the divisions and civil contests of eminent men we owe that constitution which was wont to be our happiness and pride. The genuine use of such divisions is, to watch over the political rights of the people, and to check the irregularities of the executive power; for it must never be forgotten amongst us, that government is the business both of those who are to govern, and of those whom the constitution has instituted to controul: nor is it too much to say, that parties still continue to be salutary and beneficial, not only as a check, but as a spur to executive government; except only when they maintain opposite views, affecting the essentials of the constitution; or when they act with intemperate animosity and eagerness in times of foreign negociation and foreign wars. When the last mentioned case arrives (and it is a case which well deserves a full investigation), such divisions more or less impede every exertion of the country, and more or less accelerate every public difficulty and distress, in proportion as the parties are composed of men of rank, abilities, and personal importance. And though such men, by the advantages they enjoy in their country, are obviously most interested to promote its well-being, we find it one of the problems of history, that in every age and every nation, the most enlightened and honourable minds have been found capable of counteracting, in times of public danger, the known and evident interests both of their fellow-citizens and of themselves. An emulation for well-earned honours, a rivalship for public gratitude, the pre-eminence of intellectual faculties, the preference in wielding the national forces, are all objects which furnish just motives to the exertions of active and generous minds. But in countries where the situations of power are open to the competition of all candidates, it generally happens that the contention is not who shall serve best, but whose services shall be used exclusively of another: and, with respect to this country, your

Lordship will recollect, that considerable parties have hung like mill-stones round her neck in all her struggles with foreign powers, from the Revolution to the present hour. To allay the heat which mutual strivings have stirred up, is ever the first object in the commencement of our wars. "Peace at home, and War abroad," has, on such occasions, been the text, from Mr. Davenant down to the political Essayists of our own times: recommendations of unanimity of course accompany the royal communications of the insult received: a coalition of parties is immediately the topic of each moderate and well-meaning orator who moves the address of thanks: the lullaby of faction is forthwith sung by the Poet Laureate, and the triumphs of united Britons are anticipated by others,

> Whom the Sisters nine inspire
> With Pindar's rage, without his fire.

It is generally found, however, in the result, that the clamours of faction grow louder amidst the din of war.

62

An Argument on the Nature and Party and Faction

(London, 1780), pp. 8-11

[CAPEL LOFFT]⁶

But still, in the present *divided* state of the nation, will it not be better to sit quiet than to add to the division? To take a *decided* line, and pursue it *temperately,* is not being *unquiet.* To follow duty and conscience is as far from the guilt of making a division, as light from darkness. Do we not observe, that *political neutrality* could heal no divisions, but must leave causes to their operation that would yet more divide us? We cannot, surely, avoid distinguishing between *party* and a *faction.* FACTION, consisting of *narrow views,* selfish *interests,* and *corrupt measures,* whether of *opposition* or of *ministry;*—for every thing is a faction which is selfishly and corruptly opposed to the common good;—faction would infallibly divide and weaken; and, if continued, must ruin any nation. Nor is its guilt or its danger much diminished by such an evil proceeding from the intrusted servants of the people in the executive parts of government. But there is always a party to be formed for the general good; the party of truth, freedom, virtue. This is a party which it would be criminal, indeed, not to adopt. This is *strength,* and will eventually be *union,* if any is to be had: for there never can be union or strength but where there is *confidence* and *rectitude.* They who object to party, would alike have you of a party, the party of the minister; either *expressly,* or *virtually,* by an *affected neutrality,* which is often more to their purpose than *bad* arguments, (for what other can such a cause furnish) or a bold vote in the service of corruption.

But it is no wonder that a name like that of party, indifferent, as already observed, in its own nature, and of which the merit is to be judged by intentions, measures, and effects, in a combined view, should be drawn into reproach, and men terrified from an honest attention to the public interest by the false shame of being called *party-men;* when even names decisively honourable are held forth to *ridicule* and *abhorrence,* as if the *becoming* and the *scandalous,* as if *virtue* and *vice* had changed their nature. Thus, *liberty* is a word which ought, in the opinion of certain learned and wise men, to be expunged from the political dictionary; and *licentiousness* to be construed not the intemperate abuse of authority, not a wanton invasion on the rights, the principles, the honest manners, the sacred virtues, the just freedom of a community, but the assertion of *just* and *necessary rights,* the maintaining of that character which is essential to men and citizens.

63

Candid Suggestions; in Eight Letters to
Soame Jenyns, Esq. on the respective Subjects of
His Disquisitions, Lately Published

(London, 1782), pp. 146-9

BENJAMIN TURNER[7]

It is the glory of the present reign that the door of St. James's
has been thrown open to honest men of either party. In fact, there
ought to be some of both near the throne; the one party to prevent
the sovereign from yielding up, thro' deception or timidity, his own
essential rights; and the other to prevent his being tempted thro'
ambition to invade those of his people.

In every mixt government, like ours, there must be two such
parties as we are speaking of; and a wise monarch, who knows
that his own rights and those of his people mutually support each
other, will naturally be a compound of both. It is a mistake to say
that the House of Hanover was established on Whig-principles—it
was established on *general constitutional* principles, which are a
mixture of Whig and Tory, and which have the essence of both,
exclusive of Jacobitism on the one side, and Republicanism on the
other. The Whigs indeed brought about the Revolution, but the
Tories modified it; and since that, the Whigs have kept out a Popish
Tyrant, and the Tories have kept out a still more tyrannical
Republic, or Aristocracy.

A due contention, and equipoise of the above parties, which are
essential to the constitution, must be kept up in the nation at large,
but especially in the House of Commons, or we are utterly undone.
It is a grand and capital error to suppose that the Commons, because appointed by the people, are the guardians of their rights
only, and not equally so of the rights of the crown. They are chosen
by both parties, and ought to partake of the spirit of both.

A sense of the dangerous violence too natural to contending
parties will induce moderate men to form an independent corps of
observation, so that tho' interest or prejudice will bias many, yet

supposing one third of the House of Commons to be influenced by government (no matter how), and another third by opposition, will not this throw the balance where it ought to be, that is, into the hands of the independent party?

64

A Brief and Impartial Review of the State of Great Britain at the Commencement of the Session of 1783[8]

3rd edn. (London, 1783), pp. 62-6; 67-8; 69-72

Parties, whether generally more beneficial or prejudicial, are allowed to be inseparable from the politics of a free state. It is therefore of the highest importance to the national welfare, that they be so managed, as that the greatest possible good may be derived from them, with the smallest possible inconvenience. In order to see, how this may be best done in the present juncture, it will be necessary, to look pretty far back into the state of parties.

The two great parties, which have subsisted in this country near a century, were marked at first with the widest line of discrimination of views and principles. The prerogatives of the crown, was the great ground, on which this line of difference was first drawn. Ever since the Revolution, the first distinctions have been gradually disappearing, while others have insensibly sprung up in their place. The two parties however still retained their ancient names, though their principles and opinions had undergone an almost total change. *Whig* and *Tory* still continued to be bandied about, as the well known words of political rendezvous, though the latter had long deserted the weak and untenable ground of *prerogative,* and silently taken post behind the covert-way of *influence.* But as the change was gradual, and in the natural course of things; and entirely consistent with the spirit of first principles, the consequences were not at all disadvantageous to the interests of the public.

Things continued in this natural state of progression, from the Revolution to the commencement of the present reign. Then was begun the work of a new system, totally different from the constitution and end of both the parties, which had hitherto divided the nation. The influence of the crown, instead of being employed, as hitherto, had been usual, in giving ascendancy to one or other of the leading parties; or in bracing the vigour of a coalition of both, in trying emergencies; was now, for the first time, exerted with the impracticable aim of dissolving all parties, and abolishing for ever the national distinctions of Whig and Tory—What effect this plan must have had will be learned by looking a little into the nature of party.

Party is defined by Mr. Locke to be, *A number of persons confederated by a similarity of designs and opinions in opposition to others.* Now it obviously appears from this definition, which must be acknowledged to be a just one, that parties can only be destroyed by rendering a similarity of designs and opinions universal, or by preventing all confederacy between men of similar principles. The slightest knowledge of human nature evinces the impracticability of removing parties in the former way; the latter, therefore, is the only means by which their removal can be effected. The principle, consequently, of the new system, which had in view the extinction of all parties, must have been the destruction of every bond of union, by which men are united in a *similarity of political designs and opinions.*

The design was to appearance specious and plausible, as almost every new theory in government is, on a superficial observation. The evils of *party* were known, and had been often felt. It was therefore highly gratifying to public expectation, to hold out a prospect of entirely removing them. The popularity of the new plan, and its specious plausibility, were taken advantage of by those who had the honour of sharing the Royal confidence, to secure the approbation of a youthful, liberal-minded, sanguine Prince, highly desirous of manifesting his ardent attachment to his people by new and uncommon instances of grace and favour.

Trial therefore was made of the new theory. Then it appeared that in the ardor of the benevolent dispositions of the Sovereign, and amid the fond delusion of national hope, the most ordinary maxims of political wisdom had been entirely overlooked. It was not foreseen, that nothing short of absolute despotism could supply the loss of that energy and vigour, which necessarily attend on a *similarity of designs and opinions.*

The consequences were exactly, what might have been foreknown, did the tumult of innovation admit of a moment's reflexion. A system of court cabal and political intrigue, was substituted in the place of the open and manly spirit, which had hitherto characterised the British monarchy. Division, weakness and treachery were introduced on principle, in the place of union, strength and good faith. The ancient parties were confounded and disordered by the attacks of this irregular enemy, who without coming to a decisive action, like the ancient British charioteers, incessantly harrassed the heavy bodies of political confederacy. The Tories as being less firmly compacted were entirely broken and dispersed.

The Whigs made a long and desperate stand, but were at last disordered and obliged to quit the field.

The enemy now fully triumphant was left to his own plans and schemes of policy. Self-government is sure destruction to a lunatic. Discontents, disorders and tumults at home, weakness, pusillanimity and contempt abroad, were the first fruits of the new system.

*　　　*　　　*

Hence all the multiplied calamities and disgraces of the present reign—Hence the mighty losses of trade and territory, under which the nation is at this moment sinking. This system has achieved in the short space of twenty years, what prerogative failed to accomplish in a hundred—What influence had been labouring near a century in vain. What the united force of the power and policy of the house of Bourbon could not acomplish, a system of disunion has erected.

*　　　*　　　*

All the parties in the kingdom were broken and frittered into insignificance. Deserters from every denomination and description of men had taken a part in the new-constructed government, as interest and inconstancy had prompted. The eyes of the nation were now fully opened to its destructive tendency—Whig and Tory existed but in name—They were ranged promiscuously under the banners of the common enemy—Nothing was left from which relief could be expected, *but a renewal of confederacy on the ancient principles of the constitution.*

What is whiggism? Is it not the native vigour of the British spirit, resistant whatever is found practically dangerous to the liberties and prosperity of the nation? If this be not whiggism, it is something that does not deserve to be explained, it is a spirit which should have never existed—But that this *is* the spirit of whiggism can be easily evinced from its exertions in the cause of the constitution.

This spirit has undergone three great changes within a century. It opposed *prerogative,* as long as it was dangerous to the rights and liberties of the subject—When *prerogative* was no longer formidable, and *influence* became alarming, the *British spirit* resisted its progress—At present the spirit of whiggism is up in arms against an enemy more formidable than both *influence and prerogative united.*

The bond of union, which unites all, who deserve the name of Whigs, is a principles of resistance, to whatever threatens the constitution and welfare of the state—Let us reason of things, not of names—Is not this the bond of the *present coalition?* Their bond of union is not the antiquated maxims, which anciently united the Whigs of former times—It is a new necessity grown up within the memory of man—The impression is varied, but the bullion is the same—It is the ancient unbroken spirit of the British nation, which has triumphed on the ruins of the late system—

I am prepared for the little cavils of little men—*Is Lord North a Whig?* I will not retort this idle petulance, though I have such ample scope—But I would ask a seceding Whig, I respect the character, though under the temporary influence of delusion and error—Was not something to be relinquished by a virtuous citizen for the salvation of his country? Was the *Revolution* effected without a coalition of Whigs and Tories?

It is remarked by an elegant and judicious writer, that the generality of people are half a century behind-hand in their politics— Fatal will it be to our liberties, and remaining power and trade, should the English nation, in the present juncture, furnish an additional example of the truth of this maxim. The numerous abettors of the *late system* are still in force. Several of the most respectable Whigs in the nation have been for a while misled by the sounds of ancient names. They mean honestly, but they are bewildered in the puzzle of distinctions, which exist no longer.

I entreat these men to look narrowly into the actual state of *parties*, and to examine the real situation of things. It is not in the depression, but the revival of *parties, constructed on the spirit of ancient principles, that we are to seek the renovation of British honour and prosperity.* The only question at present is, whether those who endeavour to restore the ancient state of things under which the nation flourished for a century, are to be preferred to persons, who seek to renew a *system,* which in the space of twenty years, has reduced us from the most flourishing to our present most miserable state—It is not a little question of *station and emolument* —But a great and eventful question of *system*—It is not the cause of *men,* but of *principle*—which is now at hazard—

Section IX

PARTY IN THE AGE OF PITT AND FOX

"Party must exist in a free country. Confederacies, which are nothing more than parties on a larger scale, must exist for similar ends in an aggregate of free and independent states; since exorbitant power will equally be aimed at by the strongest, and must equally be resisted by the rest."

The Principles of British Policy Contrasted with a French Alliance; in Five Letters from a Whig Member of Parliament (1787)

It was widely maintained in the last years of the century that "ins" and "outs" would naturally organize in the form of parties. As the above quotation suggests, it was now even possible to justify the ancient notion of a European balance of power by reference to the acknowledged worth of a domestic contention between political parties. The status too of the Opposition had developed—from that of a function, possibly worthwhile, towards that of a veritable office of state. Thus while some critics condemned the Opposition secession of 1797 only because elected M.P.s had no right to desert the interests of their constituents, there occurred the further suggestion that, in leaving Parliament, Fox and his followers had ignored a public trust. Two tracts by Richard Bentley (extracts 72 and 74) testify to the fact that Government writers would continue to vacillate in their opinions about the legitimacy and dignity of an opposition party. This might be expected, especially when we recall that the rhetoric of modern parliamentary government still includes the insistence that an opposition party should not obstruct good measures.

Opposition Politics Exemplified

(London, 1786), pp. 3-5

[GEORGE CHALMERS][1]

It is a remark very trite, but very true, that the *best* institutions are liable to the *worst* corruptions. A free government naturally begets parties; and a free press necessarily engenders licentiousness of printing.

To these sources may be traced sects of every kind; which produce effects, contrary to the influences of the legislature. In proportion as political parties render the laws impotent, and create among fellow subjects the fiercest animosities, such parties ought to be detested. As far as faction tends to corrupt the heart, to vitiate the understanding, and to propagate among mankind a credulity, which fits men for any purpose, factious leaders ought to be regarded as objects of hatred rather than support.

Blessed with the freest constitution, we must be content however to endure those parties, with their consequences, which naturally spring from its forms and its checks. Other free communities have been sometimes invigorated, though oftener depressed by their parties, which arose generally from the slightest and even from most ridiculous differences. The history of party in Great Britain comprises the greatest, if not the most curious part, of our later annals: the origin of our well-known parties; the principles which they successively assumed, or relinquished; their actions, which often protected public liberty, and sometimes invaded private rights; all these are interesting topicks to a people, who enjoy the invaluable privilege of each thinking for himself, and of each giving his opposition or support, to those public men, whom he may deem most worthy of either.

A slight inspection of these annals would convince us, that whatever party principles our fathers professed, or whatever party conduct they may have held, the present generation have widely departed from both, having a right to judge and to act for themselves. The cause of this departure, in a greater or less degree, may be easily accounted for without any tedious enquiry. The Revolution, besides other felicities, in religion and government, gave a lesson of experience and of caution both to king and people. Since that aera of freedom, families have formed connections by marriage, by mutual interests, by habits of education and society. State maxims, which formerly were problematical, have been since decided either by fuller discussion, or by the experiments of a century. And a more liberal education has happily eradicated many prejudices, and freed the understanding from many narrow views both of our religious and civil establishments.

About forms of government, who now contests? From Cornwall to Caithness every one comprehends the nature of the constitution, as by law established, every one vies in admiration of it, and every one admits the reasonableness of submitting to it. Who differs now about the mere manner of administering equal right to all? Every one at present regards government as a trust, which must be carried into execution, according to known laws; a trust, which, if unfaithfully executed, may be resisted; laws, that, every one has agreed to, and all ought to obey for the common liberty of all. Who fights now for modes of faith? All wise and moderate men agree in the sound policy of toleration, which restrains the more unruly passions, and thereby promotes mutual forbearance with universal good will. The foregoing were the principal topicks about which our fathers differed: yet, about which we now all agree.

Led thus by the progress of knowledge and liberality, good citizens have, in every age, deplored our natural divisions, which are so apt to breed rancour among fellow-subjects, to destroy our internal peace, and to weaken our rational strength. But, among free men, who are born to act, divisions must necessarily arise. Disputants naturally choose leaders, who, under different pretences and under dissimilar names, form parties, which, in this country, are only to be lamented, when they are carried to immoderate lengths, and can only be dangerous, when the chiefs are influenced by improper motives. From the limited government of Great Britain spring, as its natural issue, the parties of COURT and COUNTRY; under the banners of which, various men arrange themselves, according to their usual habits of thinking, or accustomed manner of acting: the herd of each are generally actuated by principle; the heads always by ambition.

But, though PARTY can seldom in this country be very inconvenient, far less dangerous, FACTION may. Of the tree we judge by the fruit. Of associations we may decide from the *conduct* of their leaders. If a body of men, having discordant principles, coalesce for the purpose of gratifying their resentments, of seizing the emoluments of office, of perpetuating power, which had been gained by seizing on government, these men, may be regarded not as a *party* but a FACTION. If such a body of men, having by these means lost the approbation of their sovereign and the confidence of the country, should be driven from stations, which had been in some measure usurped; if such a body of men, thus disappointed in their hopes, and goaded by envy or resentment, should determine to obstruct the public good, in order to gratify their private passions; such a *coalition* ought to be deemed a dangerous faction.

The chiefs of this *new faction* assumed every appellation, which had distinguished prior parties; naming themselves the *Whigs*, the *Country*, the *Opposition*, as their purpose might best be promoted by whatever pretence.

*   *   *

Whether they ought to be regarded as a *dangerous faction*, or a *legitimate opposition*, must be determined from the principles of the Coalition and the effects of their conduct: in one sense they may indeed denominate themselves *the Opposition*, having determined to oppose every measure whether wrong, or right.

66

Comparative Reflections on the Past and Present Political, Commercial, and Civil State of Great Britain

(London, 1787), pp. 41-2; 43-4; 47-9

RICHARD CHAMPION[2]

The system which prevailed under the two first reigns of this family was the same that has been since distinguished by the name of an aristocratical government. The Administration was selected from the principal Whig families, who all concurred in the support of the person placed at the head of the Treasury, to whom they were generally united by long habits of attachment. All the other officers were made properly subordinate to, and dependent upon, his department. They yielded to him the rank of first minister, and shewed an example to their fellow subjects in the deference and respect which they paid to him.

*   *   *

Whilst the minister remained in possession of this strength in Parliament, it was not in the power of the Crown, without the utmost difficulty, to displace him. The loss of this majority was owing to the increase of the opposition to him in the House of Commons; either from his own ill conduct, or from some unpopular measure, with the weight of which his opponents overpowered him.

A strong opposition in Parliament was then considered as an accessary help to the Constitution; a necessary control over the measures of the minister. The Opposition was, therefore, no sooner become the majority of the House of Commons, than the minister was supposed incapable, from guilt or inability, and his resignation followed in course. The withstanding the power of the House of Commons was a phenomenon reserved for more unhappy times.

*   *   *

By fomenting the prejudices and provoking the passions of those men who composed the administration of George the Second, at the time of his death; by intrigues in families; by liberal promises of rewards, adapted to the several desires of those upon whom they thus practised, the Court, at length, established the truth of the maxim, "to divide is to command." They received all those who came over to them with open arms. By the accomplishment of this principle, they established the new system of government. The former steady and permanent system was thus gradually put an end to. The regularity of manners, which had distinguished the period of the two preceding reigns, insensibly followed.

The effect of this conduct soon appeared in the House of Commons. The sacred bonds of friendship and relative connections were broken down. Desertion from party became frequent. And such were the suspicions which prevailed, in consequence, amongst the remaining members in opposition, that, before the great event of the American war took place, the immediate friends of Lord Rockingham alone remained. When they were collected together, they amounted to seventy or eighty members: but their hopes were so slender from that Parliament in which the Boston Post bill, the prelude to the war, passed, that they seldom appeared together. Upon that important question, the opposition to it consisted only of the friends of that nobleman, who were men of business, and generally attended the House. Colonel Barré, Mr. Dunning, and the friends of Lord L. either absented themselves or voted for the bill. The whole number against it, as far as I can now recollect, was thirty-four.

The secret junto were now masters of both ministers and opposition. They had constantly a strong body of members in the House, composed of those who had places in the household, the secretaries or deputies of men in office, or of such others who were their immediate dependents. These were called King's friends. This body was under some known leader of the junto, who made use of frequent opportunities to shew the House the absolute dependence which the ostensible ministers had upon them.

67

Seven Letters to the People of Great Britain
by a Whig

(London, 1789), pp. 6-7

[?MAJOR JOHN SCOTT][3]

In a free state, and a mixed Government like ours, there will always be two parties; one consisting of the men who compose the Administration, and another consisting of men who want to be in their places. A very eminent writer on this subject has decided, that it is very beneficial to such a Government as this to have such parties, because they who are out of the Administration watch the conduct of those who are in; and as we enjoy the freedom of debate and the liberty of the press, the nation at large is constantly informed of the transactions of Ministers, and of the sentiments of those who oppose them. By these means we are enabled to form an estimate of the characters of each party, and to judge which is most likely to purify the interest of the country. The main point at the present moment is, how to form this estimate, and how to avoid the error of mistaking professions for principles—because most men in Opposition are apt to profess a great deal, and to promise what they never perform.

68

Speech in a Debate on the Excise, 1789

Parliamentary History, Vol. XXVIII, cols. 245-6

CHARLES JAMES FOX[4]

With regard to the popular act of opposing the present bill, which
the hon-gentleman who spoke last had sarcastically imputed as the
cause of his attendance that day, Mr. Fox denied that his attendance
was occasioned by any desire of seizing on that opportunity of
retaining popularity. In fact, if any such weak and idle motive could
influence his public conduct, on any occasion, that was an unseasonable moment for its exercise; because, so far from opposition to
the measure being popular, he had every reason to believe, that it
unfortunately happened that the reverse was the fact, and that the
people of this country were so changed in their nature, and so
altered in their feelings, that they had become, as it were, enamoured
of the collectors of taxes, especially under the excise laws, and that
they looked up with eagerness and with gratification, to invite the
most wanton exercise of power; and as if nauseated with the sweets
of liberty, were anxious to wear the badge of slavery and of despotism.—As to his not having attended the bill more closely, he had
already stated, that he had not done so, because he plainly saw, that
all opposition would be fruitless; but surely, the hon. gentleman,
and other gentlemen of the same description, had no right to expect
on every occasion, when the interests of their constituents, or some
personal motive to themselves, induced them to wish the measure
of the minister opposed, that he, and those who acted with him,
would be at their command, and ready to act as perpetual adversaries of the minister and his measures, whether those measures
should appear to them to be well or ill-founded! It should seem
as if the hon. gentleman, and those who pursued the same general
political line of conduct, but who, nevertheless, opposed the present
bill, considered opposition as the standing counsel against the
Crown in that House, ever to be resorted to in the moments of
difficulty, and therefore as necessary to exist as administration.
What was this but laughing at them? What was it but saying "We
have put you into the most humiliating situation; you shall have

no share of the power, no share of the honours, or emoluments of office; but we expect to command your public services, to profit by whatever abilities you may possess, to be joined by you and your friends, whenever we want the assistance of either." Was it not, in other words, saying, "We have raised one man to a degree of power which makes all opposition useless. By our false clamours against you, and our delusions respecting him, we have taught the public to look up to him as something more than man; hence his measures, however mischievous, however fatal, are scarcely to be resisted: but remember, we look to you to watch him. Do you take care that he does no mischief in his situation. It is your office to sound the alarm, when danger lurks beneath a plausible pretext; and to oppose yourselves to the occasion, so that the evil may be in time averted." Having deprived them of the means of resistance with any hopes of success, by putting them into so useless a situation, to call upon them to oppose, to check and to stop the minister's measures, was neither more nor less than directly laughing in their faces, and adding insult to injury.

69

Considerations on the Approaching Dissolution of Parliament, Addressed to the Elective Body of the People With Some Account of the Existing Parties

(London, 1790), pp. 5-15

[WILLIAM COMBE][5]

I do not hesitate to assert, that the Government of this country is carried on by influence; or, that I may not appear to be too reserved and bashful in my expressions,—by corruption. I must be understood, however, by no means to convey an idea that every public man who supports the measures of Government is under that influence, or fed by that corruption to which I have alluded; but that, in the present state and fashion of the higher orders of the people, no minister would be able to carry on the public business without it. This power, which no modern statesman even affects to despise, has arisen from a variety of causes, which it is not necessary for me to explain; and is so powerful in its operations, as well as necessary in its exertions, that it is, as it were, become a part of Government itself. Let the patriot of today, who has declaimed for years against it, be elevated to the seat of power,—and he will adopt it tomorrow.

Of pure public spirit, I am concerned to acknowledge, that but a small comparative portion has been seen in the parties of our day. I may declare this truth with reluctance; but my duty compels me to declare it. Without entering more at large into the question, the daily history of Parliament proves the truth of my assertion. The common business of the nation is, at times, very inadequately attended; nay, it sometimes happens, that not even forty members assemble, without which number no vote of any kind can be passed: and I am disposed to think, that the course of public business would be very much impeded, if the Minister did not possess the means of procuring the attendance of certain stationary members, to transact the common, but necessary concerns of the nation. The spirit of party may indeed occasionally croud Saint Stephen's Chapel;—but still it should be observed, that, on occasions of more than common importance, the call of the House, when every absent member is liable to the punishment of it, is thought a necessary measure, to enforce, at least, the temporary execution of a constant parliamentary duty. It appears, therefore, that this influence is not only necessary to keep a minister in power; but that, supposing him to be superior to all opposition, he would find it a very difficult matter indeed to carry on the business of the nation without it.

I cannot but foresee, that the unreflecting virtue of many of you will be startled at these propositions; and that such will not be disposed to augur favourably of my political opinions: but I am not, however, afraid to leave my sentiments to the event of your reflection. I do not affect novelty, unless it should be a novelty to relate circumstances as they are. I might sooth you with lamenting the imperfect state of parliamentary representation;—I might invoke the Genius of the Constitution to blast, in its vengeance, the venal, appropriated and uninhabited boroughs, and give their representatives to Birmingham, Manchester, and other manufacturing towns, which exceed in population, wealth, and commercial importance, many of our largest cities: I might assert, that borough property is unconstitutional property, and ought not to be possessed by any individual;—and that all contracts for the sale of a seat in Parliament, being in opposition to the spirit of the Constitution, should be void by law, and punishable by the House of Commons, whose independence is affected by them:—I might fill many a page with speculative declamation on these and similar subjects, to amuse fanciful minds, instead, as it is my duty, of stating incontrovertible facts, for the instruction of sensible men.

At the same time I do not mean to be considered as the champion of corruption; I wish with the most ardent sincerity that the purest public spirit and patriot virtue predominated in all the departments of our Government, and animated every body of men, of every denomination: nor should I dare to assert that the Constitution might not be assisted in such a manner as to enable it to bear its infirmities, or that some method might not be devised to lengthen its longevity. But it appears to me, that many years of peace must have passed away, and a considerable diminution of the national burthens have taken place, before any effectual attempt can be made to restore the palsied parts of the Constitution, or to supply those that are decayed:—But be that as it may, the Constitution will not have received a single accession of strength, or experienced the least diminution of its infirmities, when it again calls upon you to perform your constituent duties: and to point out the mode of performing them in the best manner the nature of things will admit,

is the object of this honest and disinterested address to you—the
Electors of Great Britain.

It may, perhaps, be necessary to inform many of you, that the
spirit of party is become the vivifying principle of public conduct.
—Nor can you look into the history of any public body of men in
this country, from the Houses of Parliament to the corporations
of borough towns, without discovering the truth of this assertion. In
the former, you see the ministerial and anti-ministerial cohorts
acting under its influence against each other; in the latter, you
perceive the petty divisions of subordinate interests proceeding
from the same origin. It has therefore become the general, and indeed
necessary conduct of independent Lords and Members of Parliament of the first character for integrity and good sense, to adopt
the party in whose leaders they could place the greatest confidence,
and whose principles they most approved, and to support them with
firmness and uniformity, in all the struggles of senatorial contest.

In the present state of politics in Great Britain, and indeed in
the form public affairs have assumed for a long course of years, a
neutral conduct must unavoidably render the person who adopts it
at once useless and ridiculous.

Some men, who have entered the senate with purer notions of
public virtue than the times will justify, have occasionally tried the
experiment of being of no party, and of giving their individual support to the Minister or his opponents, according to the impulse or
conviction of the moment; but, in the course of a very long experience, I never remember a single instance of one of these worthy
characters, who did not leave this amiable, but fallacious theory of
independence, for the practical adoption of a party. Nay, those
men who have, at times, enlisted and incorporated themselves under
the neutral power, with a view to give the majority to that party
whom they should favour by an occasional alliance, have always
lamented over the vanity of their project. The *flying squadron*, as
it was called, during the administration of Sir Robert Walpole, was
of this kind; and to speak in the most favourable manner of it,
answered no purpose whatever of public utlity. A similar association, during the late agitations concerning the Regency, which
adopted the title of the *armed neutrality*, must be remembered by
you all;—nor can you have forgotten what little honour that vision-
ary corps acquired to themselves, or what little service they performed for their country, in that trying crisis of public affairs.—
Like the insect of a day, its first entrance into life was but the prelude of its dissolution, and the very persons who composed it,
abandoned at once their embodied name, to acquire a reflected con-

sequence from the party, under whose wings they sheltered themselves from the mockery of the people.

I do not affect a novelty of doctrine:—The opinions I offer to your consideration have been approved by the voice, and sanctioned by the conduct of much wiser men than myself; and I might even step from modern to ancient times,—the history of which informs us of a celebrated legislator, who declares that, during the agitations of public affairs, a neutrality of conduct was a crime in the citizen, which it is the duty of the state to correct, by a compulsory mandate to take a part in the contests.

If, in consequence of my present reasoning, it should be demanded of me to explain what I conceive to be an independent, public character; or rather, to bring the question home to the subject before us, what is an independent Member of Parliament?— I shall not hesitate a moment to answer, that such a character is not due to a man because he holds himself aloof from party connexions; on the contrary, I am not afraid to assert, that a senator may attach himself to, and act under the influence of a party, on such principles as may be perfectly consistent with the spirit and honour of an independent character.

Independence is a relative term; and means nothing more, in a political acceptation of the word, than a conduct free from selfish, interested, or corrupt motives, and influenced by the patriotic desire of promoting the public good. A parliamentary representative acting under such an influence, whatever may be the party to which he has thought proper to attach himself, is an independent man, according to the most correct sense of the expression; because he has not chosen his political friends from improper motives, and is not prevented by the possession or prospect of place, pension, or title, from abandoning them, whenever they shall desert those principles which have induced him to become an associate with them.

An independent man, and a party man, are very different and opposite characters.—The former supports the measures of the party he has adopted, with general moderation and virtuous dignity, in order to serve his country; while the latter employs his forward zeal or factious outcry to serve himself. The late Sir George Savile, whose political ardour in opposing the measures of Government, during the American War, must live in the remembrance of so many of you, could not have been tempted by all the wealth of the Exchequer, or any honour the Crown can bestow,—to desert those principles, or abandon that conduct, which rendered him such a leading and conspicuous character in the party who opposed the administration of that period:—And many are there among the friends of the present Minister, who, I firmly believe, would consider an offer of remuneration for their political conduct, as insulting to the honour and integrity of their respective characters. Hampden, Sydney, Russel, and many other men of great political renown, whose names will descend to the latest posterity as examples of the purest patriotism, have supported or conducted parties in the state, and some of them maintained the principles of the parties they supported with their blood.

I might, indeed, amuse your fancy with a beautiful and correct picture of political virtue, and hold forth to your animated attention the form and progress of the perfect patriot, in performing the duties of parliamentary representation: but it would be in direct opposition to the honest zeal which I profess in your service, were I to flatter you with any other projects or modes of proceeding in your constituent capacity, than such as appear to be completely and necessarily applicable to the present state of our country, as well as the temper and manners of the people.—Your duty is well known to you all:—It is a simple operation of your understanding, as easily exerted and fulfilled as any common act of your lives: and the principles I offer to your consideration, as guides to you in the right performance of it, will, I trust, be obvious to the capacity of the meanest among you.

I have already endeavoured to press home upon your minds the necessity under which many great and good men have found themselves to join a party, if they would be of any real service to the public; and it is that very necessity which urges my countrymen, who compose the constituent body of the British people, to shape their aggregate capacity to the same conduct. You must pursue the same mode in electing your future representatives, which the best of those men, whom you have already chosen, have found it necessary to adopt, in order to fulfil the important charge with which you have entrusted them.—You must yourselves support a party.

70

A Review of the Principal Proceedings of the Parliament of 1784

(1792), in *The Works of Henry Mackenzie Esq. in Eight Volumes*
(Edinburgh, 1808), Vol. VII, pp. 393-8

HENRY MACKENZIE[6]

Though it may not be a popular doctrine, yet I believe it is one which moderate and thinking men will admit, that in Great Britain, the nature of its government, the continual superintendance of Parliament, the weight of public opinion, and the influence which all these circumstances must have on the character and conduct of persons in official situations, afford a much greater probability than in other countries, that the administration will, ordinarily, be at least right in its intentions, and will adopt its measures, from a belief, that they are such as will tend to the benefit of the nation. The men who attain the high departments of the state in Britain, are commonly such as, from their education, their habits of life, and their situation with regard to the community, have much stronger motives to purity and uprightness in their public conduct, than to the contrary. The aristocracy of Great Britain is essentially different from the aristocracy in other monarchical governments of Europe; its rights are more attached to personal merit, and less to accidental advantages; it is as much an aristocracy of talents as of rank. The term *gentleman* in Britain, is a title which is annexed not exclusively to birth, as in other countries, but to qualities generally indeed attendant on a certain rank in society, a liberal education, a well-informed mind; to elegant deportment and honourable sentiments. Hence arises a very great difference in this from other countries, both in that order of men out of which ministers are to be taken, and in that class also by which they are to be judged. The first has no privilege by which it can impose, nor the last any feeling by which it can be imposed on, in the conduct of public measures. There is in Britain no protection for the court against the prevailing opinion of the community, that could cover the dissipation, the debauchery, the capricious extravagance, the thoughtless inhumanity, which, from the interior of so many palaces, have spread oppression and ruin over devoted millions.

It is material to consider whence arises this general safeguard, which the public possesses against the malversation of ministers, against the intentional abuse, or the ignorant misapplication, of the powers with which they are intrusted. The popular nature of our government furnishes, as has been already stated, a check, of which the operation is constant, because it is excited by natural and un-ceasing causes. The opportunity which Parliament affords to the young, the bustling, the ambitious, of canvassing public measures, is one of those salutary counterpoises which our constitution affords against the weight of the executive power. The opposition in Britain is a sort of public body, which, in the practice at least of our government, is perfectly known and established. The province of this ex-official body, when it acts in a manner salutary to the state, is to watch, with jealousy, over the conduct of administration; to correct the abuses, and to resist the corruptions of its power; to restrain whatever may be excessive, to moderate what may be in-considerate, and to supply what may be defective in its measures.

In the exercise of its functions, if they may so be called, opposi-tion has advantages by which those obvious ones, often mentioned on the side of administration, are balanced; if, on the one hand, patronage strengthens administration, on the other, the discontent and envy of the disappointed are often thrown into the scale of opposition; if administration has superior opportunities of informa-tion, opposition is not restrained by official secrecy; if administra-tion imposes by its dignity, opposition wins by its familiarity with the people; and if administration enjoys active occasions of acquir-ing popularity, opposition, on the other hand, suffers none of the embarrassments which result from delicate and perplexing situa-tions. Censure has not the responsibility of action; and in debate or discussion, he who objects or blames may often object at random, and blame without certainty; the burden of proof is almost always thrown upon administration. Opposition is seldom obliged to act on the defensive, but has always the warmth, the vivacity, and the enthusiasm of an assailant.

The respect, as well as the usefulness, of this censorial representa-tive of the people, (if I may be allowed to give it that denomination) depends on the manner in which its faculties are exerted. If its re-sistance to the measures of government is unreasonable, or its ob-jections captious; if it passes those bounds within which the justice of the people would confine its censure, and departs from that con-sistency in argument, or that principle in conduct, which their understanding is always able to perceive, and which their honesty always expects, the confidence of the public is proportionally with-drawn, and the respectability of opposition diminished.

71

The British Constitution of Government Compared with that of a Democratic Republic

2nd edn. (London, 1793), pp. 26-8; 29-30

SIR WILLIAM YOUNG[7]

Thus the constitution of Great Britain hath every, and more, security against the abuse of executive power than a republic of any other form. The counsellors or ministers of executive government responsible to definite maxims, and to fixed laws which admit of no variation, distinction, prejudice, or favour, will be ever more cautious than those acting at the head of a democratic government, where conciliatory acts, and even fresh crimes, may work out a favourable decree from the assembly; where the high court of justice resembles the hustings of an election; and he is voted most innocent, who is guilty of bribing the most votes. A British sentence of judgement, founded on known principles and laws, cannot vary or bend to these or other influences.

None would advise, none would be ministers of the king's executive power under circumstances of this responsibility, and its consequences, were not advantages of power, as in a democratic republic, attached to their situation and office.

These advantages, this power, will be sought as in a democratic republic, and struggles will be made for official place: but the high and permanent office of king (as I before observed) operates as a curb on private ambition. *It is the instrument of the nation* and of the constitution of government to interpose and prevent the dangers and mischiefs arising from such struggle for power.

The king is called to raise; the king is called to dismiss. The Commons address to remove a judge, to remove a general, to remove those in trust of every department. The majority in Parliament, and of the voices of the people too, as far as their numbers can be ascertained, lose the distinctions of majority and minority as they reach the throne. It is the vote of entire Parliament; it is the voice of the whole people that calls on the king. By this operation in our constitution of government, the king is relieved from the imputations of partialities, and his appointments are never the appointments of a part, but of the whole.

Parties yet do, and must, and should exist: under these checks they cannot be mischievous; and, indeed, are most useful. That some men of leading ability and genius should ever be on the watch to acquire fair popularity, and convert their minority of support into a voice of the people in their favour, is an ambition of high advantage to the country. That in this course they should watch each occasion to discover, and show to the people instances of mal-administration in their rivals when in executive authority, must check and keep those rivals to their duty: and is of first interest and moment to the public at large. Men will become good to become great, whilst to stand well with the people at large is the only way to gain or to regain the feat of executive authority.

*   *   *

Thus, too, in the British constitution of government there is left room for competition of men of the first genius and best knowledge to struggle for the executive departments of government, without danger resulting from their success, their defeat, their exaltation, or their dismission.

Thus, too, aspiring characters neither in their elevation, or in their fall from power, disturb the national prosperity or peace. They are enforced to a middle place, and to moderation, checked by and kept between the two constitutional powers of the King and the Commons.

And thus, looking to the true and only ends of all government, the component parts of civil society, individuals, families, municipalities, are engaged as they may prefer, in their private pursuits, and yet watchfully may be looking to the conduct and characters of the constituted authority, without suffering as constituents, all those feuds and animosities; and without suffering in the private line all that loss of peace, happiness, and domestic security, which are the individual materials and form the only well laid foundation of national wealth, force, and general prosperity.

72

A Letter to the Rt. Hon. Charles James Fox, Upon the Dangerous and Inflammatory Tendency of his Late Conduct in Parliament

(London, 1793), pp. 3-5

[T. R. BENTLEY][8]

In examining into the situation of this Country, and defining the dangers to which it is exposed, it is to these that I shall frequently appeal; and in speaking of the duties of Englishmen, I shall take the liberty to remind you more particularly of yours, who have long occupied a post as honourable as any she has to confer, and as worthy of enlightened ambition to desire; a post which, if not the highest in the State, is, if I may be excused such an expression, something very superior to the second; and which offers as many occasions of deserving well of the Public, and perhaps more of uniting their admiration and esteem (occasions, Sir, which you have frequently seized, and rewards which you have often enjoyed), than, perhaps, would have fallen to your lot had you been in more complete possession of your wishes, and intrusted with the first executive office of the Government.

But to controul is at least as glorious as to direct; and the deference which your Country has almost constantly paid to your opinion was but the more honourable to you, as you were removed from the means of influence and the authority of office. The confidence of the Public seemed to attach to your person, and you held your reputation, and the power you derived from it, independent of favour, and liable only to change from causes which could alone proceed from yourself—your own neglect, imprudence, or ambition.

If such a post has its honours, and you know, Sir, they are too great to have been often well exchanged for any others, it has its duties too; and these of so much dignity and importance, of so serious and sacred a nature, that it may well be doubted, whether the occupation of any other in the kingdom be attended with so great and moral a responsibility as this is. Bound by no oath, and amenable to no tribunal, the chief of an English Opposition is called to that high pre-eminence by the silent suffrage of the Country; for they would deceive you, Sir, who would tell you, that you hold it of this House or of that, or of an union of families, or that you were elected to it by the party over which you appear to preside. Those who support the Government, as well as they who oppose it, have at least confirmed your election, and all have been ready to acknowledge your services, and confess to have profited by your advice. Not a party, but the kingdom itself have voted you to this moral chancery, where you sit to check and controul Administration on the one hand, and to instruct and enlighten the people on the other. It is but one half of your duty to oppose wrong councils, it remains for you to give vigour and efficacy to the best; for as, on the one hand, the people naturally confide in your vigilance and fidelity to resist whatever may be hostile to their interests; so, on the other, they expect that you will join in all such measures of Administration as are either necessary or beneficial to them; and that, far from opposing or retarding, from a jealousy of power, or even of benefits, you will set them the example of content and unanimity.

It is hard to say, whether the leader of a party in the House of Commons would most desert his post, and most betray the duties of his station, by assenting to illegal or dangerous measures, or by opposing such as were legal and necessary. The crime is certainly the same, and a greater crime it is difficult to imagine; but the ill consequences might be more or less fatal, according to circumstances which it is impossible to define. The Fate of Liberty and the Salvation of the Kingdom may depend upon either.

The Politician's Creed Being the Great Outline of Political Science . . . by An Independent

Vol. I (London, 1795), pp. 255-6

[R. J. THORNTON][9]

Authors enlarge very copiously on the *divisions* which proved the destruction of *Rome*, but their readers seldom discover *those divisions to have been always necessary and inevitable.*—Dissensions were not to be prevented; and *those martial spirits*, which were so *fierce* and *formidable abroad*, could not be habituated to any *considerable moderation at home.*—Those who expect in a free state to see *the people undaunted in war, and pusillanimous in peace*, are certainly desirous of *impossibilities*; and it may be advanced as a general rule, that whenever a *perfect calm is visible*, in a state that calls itself a *republic*, THE SPIRIT OF LIBERTY NO LONGER SUBSISTS.

Union, in a body politic, is a very equivocal term: *true union* is such a harmony as makes all the particular parts, as opposite as they may seem to us, concur to the general welfare of the society, in the same manner as *discords* in music contribute to the general melody of sound.—*Union* may prevail in a state full of seeming commotions; or, in other words, there may be an harmony from whence results prosperity, which alone is true peace, and may be considered in the same view as the various parts of this universe, which are eternally connected by the *operations* of some, and the *reactions* of others.—Hence the *opposition party* is no defect in the constitution of the BRITISH GOVERNMENT, unless it be desirous of *subverting the mixed form*.

A Few Cursory Remarks Upon the State of Parties during the Administration of the Rt. Hon. Henry Addington by a Near Observer[10]

7th edn. (London, 1803), pp. 71-3

[T. R. BENTLEY]

The first offering upon the altar of our country should be private rivalries, and party-hatreds. . . . At such a time, every man's knowledge, experience, and talent, is the property of the State; there ought to be no *sides* of the house, no opposition. Can it be endured then, to see all the experience acquired in the public service, all the weight and authority of past office and employment, directed to spread alarm and discouragement, or to impede and embarrass the public service? One thinks one sees altar against altar, and government against government, when the parts of an opposition are so distributed and sustained, as that the persons who have been secretaries of state, attack state papers and negotiations; and chancellors of the exchequer, the taxes. And when one observes senators and statesmen, who have scarce turned their backs on the King's Cabinet, opposing and contradicting, and thwarting their own measures and the principles of their own administration, one thinks one beholds a faction more profoundly and essentially corrupt and perfidious than there is any mention of in the history of nations.

NOTES AND COMMENTARY

SECTION I

1. *Francis Osborne* (1593-1659)
Osborne has sometimes been taken for an authority on Machiavelli, but here, as elsewhere, departs from Machiavelli's teaching. On the limitations of his Machiavellism, see Felix Raab, *The English Face of Machiavelli* (London, 1964), pp. 164-5. Examples of earlier sentiments on faction, similar to Osborne's, are Robert Dallington, *Aphorisms Civill and Militarie* (London, 1613), p. 241 (material mainly from Guicciardini) and Sir Walter Raleigh, *The Cabinet-Council: Containing the Chief Arts of Empire; and Mysteries of State: Discabineted . . .*, published by John Milton (London, 1658), pp. 81-2.

2. *The Mischief of Cabals* (1685)
This court pamphlet expresses the case for a limited religious toleration on the grounds of its contribution to political stability. The "faction" here being exposed was not any of the religious interests, but rather the Whig opponents of James II.

3 *George Savile, Marquis of Halifax* (1633-95)
Halifax has rightly been seen as a major representative of that numerous body of public men who absolutely rejected party, although the emphasis, especially on the wisdom of neutrality, varied in his different writings. See Austin Ranney and Willmoore Kendall, *Democracy and the American Party System* (New York, 1956), p. 119. *The Character of a Trimmer*, with its attractive case for limited disorder in a free country, could be interpreted as favourable to party contention. The essay was thus reprinted around 1730 with a new and misleading title. See *An Essay on Parties and a Free Government in the Character of an Ancient Trimmer taken from a Manuscript Wrote in the Reign of King Charles I* (London, n.d., [c. 1730]). The tentative date is that of the Bodleian catalogue.

4. *Maxims of State* (1693)
These maxims circulated in a number of forms prior to the posthumous attribution to Halifax in the 1700 edition. See "Maxims of the Grand Almazor", *State Tracts* (London, 1706), v. II, pp. 367-8, where the first edition is said to have been in 1693. The work continued to appear, without any acknowledgment to Halifax. See *Select Maxims Directing How to Establish the Government of any Court and Kingdom . . .* (London, 1730), sig. B- p. 8.

5. *Dr. Charles Davenant* (1656-1714)
As a much-quoted exponent of the Country attachment to public virtue, Davenant was predictably hostile to party and his towering reputation as an economist saved his political opinions from oblivion. Note however, his justification for partisanship, which sound remarkably like Burke's dictum "When bad men combine, the good must associate . . .".

6. *An Essay Towards the History of the Last Ministry and Parliament* (1710)
The "late Changes" mentioned here were the fall of the Whigs and the entry of Harley into the Cabinet. Since the author limits his proposals to a broadening of the party base of the administration, it was probably

written during the summer of 1710 when Harley was trying to form an administration which included both Whigs and Tories. Governing by a coalition was a favourite policy both of William and of Anne; the politicians often found it expedient to comply, but, on the whole, cared little for the practice. Contemporary opinion on coalitions is recorded in Geoffrey Holmes, *British Politics in the Age of Anne* (New York, 1967), pp. 48, 376-7 and 416-17.

7. *John Toland* (1670-1722)

Best known for his deistical opinions, Toland was the editor of Harrington's writings and a significant political thinker in his own right. His Old-Whig hostility to parties had softened by 1717, and with the Whigs in power, he had ceased to be very worried about party being used as a sinister device for dividing the people. Earlier writings by Toland had associated a diversity of opinions with free government, but this had not, in itself, entailed any admiration for parties. See Toland, *The Memorial of the State of England, in Vindication of the Queen, the Church, and the Administration* (London, 1705), p. 44. The same position is to be found in *Cato's Letters*, the classical formulation of Old-Whig doctrine by John Trenchard and Thomas Gordon.

8. *Matthew Tindal* (1657-1733)

This scholar and Whig pamphleteer was attacking Robert Walpole whose resignation of 1717 had split the Whig party. Tindal's authorship of *The Defection Consider'd* has always been accepted by bibliographers. One of his contemporaries asserted that the identity of the "authors" was notorious, but he then failed to name anyone. See [George Sewell], *The Resigners Vindicated*, Part II (London, 1718), sig. A2.

SECTION II

1. *John Shute Barrington* (1678-1734)

On Barrington's political thought see my "Party Before Burke: Shute Barrington", *Government and Opposition*, Vol. 3, No. 2 (1968), pp. 233-40. The Dissenters were never barred from voting or even from sitting in Parliament. However, Barrington expressed the fear that the Tory measure of an Occasional Conformity Bill would deprive Protestant Dissenters of any influence in local government and would thus destroy that local "interest" necessary to obtain parliamentary representation. A measure forbidding occasional conformity eventually passed in 1711, thus preventing those who communicated only occasionally with the Church of England from holding a number of local offices. Barrington played a role in the repeal of this legislation in 1718 and also wrote extensively against the Test and Corporation Acts—legislation which remained in force throughout the century. On the complex question of the exact nature of the civil disabilities imposed at various times on the Protestant Dissenters, see R. B. Barlow, *Citizenship and Conscience* (Philadelphia, 1962); E. Neville Williams, *The Eighteenth-Century Constitution 1688-1815: Documents and Commentary* (Cambridge, 1960), pp. 334-40 and for eighteenth-century commentary, *The Case of the Dissenters, and Others in Office, with Respect to the Laws now in Force* (London, 1712).

2. *The Rights of Protestant Dissenters* (1705)

The comment here about the power of one's political enemies being useful indicates the sophistication of the seventeenth-century tradition of *concordia discors*. Barrington wrote this work in opposition to the Sir Humphrey Mackworth, a Tory, whose tract *Peace and Union . . .* (London,

1704), was a standard plea for restraining Protestant Dissent in the name of national security.

3. *Remarks on the Letter to the Dissenters* (1714)

This was an answer to Defoe's *A Letter to the Dissenters* (London, 1713), which had argued against that permanent electoral alliance between Dissenters and Whigs which had always been Barrington's ambition to obtain. The suspicion that Barrington may have been the author of the *Remarks* rests solely on the correspondence between the argument of the pamphlet and Barrington's well-known views on electoral strategy. Of course, Barrington's characteristic defence of party as an institution does not appear here, but it was also absent from some other writings on toleration and politics which are undeniably his. The author's self-description as a "Churchman" would then be misleading, although Barrington had sometimes described himself as a "Lay-man in Communion with the Church of England". The very useful catalogue of Dr. Williams's Library, London, makes no attribution of authorship.

4. *William Paterson* (1658-1719)

Paterson, founder of the Bank of England, had good reason to be pleased with both main parties, since his advice on financial policy was sought by politicians on both sides. The proceedings of the club described here are almost certainly a vehicle for Paterson's own opinions, although such a group may well have existed at one time. A modern edition of the conversation reproduced here is available in *The Writings of William Paterson . . .*, ed. Saxe Bannister, reprinted (New York, 1968), Vol. II.

5. *Thomas Gordon* (d. 1750)

At this stage in his career, Gordon was still the advocate of rectitude in the face of that public morality exemplified by the South Sea Bubble. Machiavelli was useful to justify pressure from the people in the normal "Country" tradition, but he was not used at this time to sanction the struggle between Whig and Tory. Gordon's views in party seem to have changed when finally he became reconciled to Walpole's regime. (See extracts 31 and 43.) Later Opposition writers continued to employ Machiavelli to explain social conflict, still without finding in him support for conventional parties. See *Common Sense*, No. 315 (26 February, 1742-3).

6. *Daniel Defoe* (1661-1731)

Defoe's suppositious writings are so numerous that not even Professor J. R. Moore's valuable check list has covered all his journalism. It is impossible then to say whether Defoe actually wrote this piece in *Applebee's Journal*. Other essays in the same source, and also attributed to Defoe, present a more hostile attitude to party. It seems then, that he was just indulging in that taste for paradoxical conclusions to which Mandeville had given an impetus. For a clear indication of Mandeville's influence at this time, see the essay where the alleged connexion between private vices and public virtues is made to support the conclusion that "Faction is become Physick to the State". *A Collection of Miscellany Letters Selected out of Mist's Weekly Journal* (London, 1722), Vol. I, Letter XXXI.

Defoe's interpretation of Toland as an advocate of party must have been based on Toland's *State-Anatomy*, rather than on the work of 1701. In seeing parties as checks on one another, Defoe could rely on the fact that the king was constitutionally free to choose his ministers and would thus not normally be in danger of having a party thrust upon him. Sometimes the assumption appeared in the form that the king was to hold the balance of the parties, an idea which required reemphasis in the reign of George

III. See *A Letter from a Gentleman in Worchestershire to a Member of Parliament in London* (London, 1727) p. 5 and [W. J. Adair], *Thoughts on the Dismission of Officers, Civil or Military for their Conduct in Parliament* (London, 1765), pp. 22 & 33.

7. *Paul de Rapin-Thoyras* (1661-1725)
Rapin's *History of England* was much admired in the eighteenth century and even today he is still sometimes mentioned in the same breath as Montesquieu as a student of English government. See Nelly Girard d'Albissin, *Un Précurseur de Montesquieu: Rapin-Thoyras, premier historien française des institutions anglaises* (Paris, 1969). On the question of parties, he was far more aware of English conditions than was Montesquieu, for the latter fell into the common error of seeing political conflict through the conventional categories of mixed government. Rapin's *Dissertation* seems to have had an attentive public until late in the century, with an American edition being published in Boston in 1773. Not all observers on the Continent joined Rapin in seeing benefit in competing parties. A conventional case against party divisions is to be found in Emanuel de Cize, *Histoire du Whigisme et du Torisme* (Leipzig and Amsterdam, 1717).

Section III

1. *Henry St. John, Viscount Bolingbroke* (1678-1751)
Bolingbroke's *Dissertation* first appeared in *The Craftsman* during 1733-4. At the end of the eighteenth century, extracts from his writings still appeared in radical journals, for it was the radicals of the period whose rejection of party was most like Bolingbroke's position. A patriotic people, of course, replaced his patriot king. See *The Patriot*, No. XXII (22 January, 1793), pp. 306-11. The most ambitious attempt to attribute to Bolingbroke opinions consistent with permanent party strife is that of Kurt Kluxen, *Das Problem der politischen Opposition. Entwicklung und Wesen der englischen Zweiparteienpolitik im 18 Jahrhundert* (Freiburg & München, 1956). The argument has not found much favour, since Bolingbroke so obviously resisted any notion of a never-ending battle between "ins" and outs". Kluxen's study, and other works by German scholars following his lead, have done much to direct attention to the problem of the origins of legitimate opposition and have, in addition, clarified the distinction between opposition and resistance. Bolingbroke figures prominently in this literature. See, for example, Ingeborg Bode, *Ursprung und Begriff der parliamentarischen Opposition* (Stuttgart, 1962), and especially pp. 1-5 where the author supplies some qualifications to Kluxen's conclusions on eighteenth-century parties and Carter Kniffler, *Die parliamentarische Opposition* (Frankfurt am Main, 1967), pp. 11-14. Some of the recent literature on opposition has been more modern and analytical in emphasis. See Christian Petzke, *Das Wesen der politischen Opposition: Formen und Funktion der Opposition in staatlichen Leben* unpublished doctoral dissertation (München, 1959) and the works cited in Ghita Ionescu and Isabel Madariaga, *Opposition* (London, 1968), pp. 2 & 206. For all the undoubted importance of Bolingbroke both as actor and thinker, one wishes that the treatment by Kluxen and Bode had covered rather more of the polemical literature of the time. Dealing with such a slippery notion as the acceptance of parties and opposition, major figures can usefully be placed within the context provided by the writings of lesser people. For effective use of this approach, see Harvey Mansfield Jr., *Statesmanship and Party Government:*

A Study of Burke and Bolingbroke (Chicago and London, 1965) and Isaac Kramnick, *Bolingbroke and his Circle: The Politics of Nostalgia in the Age of Walpole* (Cambridge, Mass., 1968).

2. *George, Lord Lyttleton* (1709-73)

Prominent in the Whig opposition to Walpole, Lyttleton was a contributor to the journal *Common Sense* and probably joined Bolingbroke as one of the writers of *The Craftsman*. Writing in 1735, Lyttleton still identified party and faction, but in a sense which treated faction with more respect than was normal. An elaborate geneology was sometimes given to faction by those who, like Lyttleton, wished to cite its merits. It became the "youngest daughter" of liberty—wayward at times, but born of good stock. See, with varying emphasis, *Old England: or the Constitutional Journal*, No. 97 (16 February, 1744-5), *The Monitor*, No. 460 (26 May, 1764) and *The Universal Magazine*, Vol. XLIV (April, 1769), pp. 196-7.

3. *The Country Journal: or The Craftsman* (1730, 1739)

Although Bolingbroke and the other original writers had severed their connexion with the journal after 1735, *The Craftsman* continued to oppose Walpole largely on the basis of Bolingbroke's political theories—denying the permanence of Whigs and Tories, but defending the maintenance of a Country party as long as the Ministry had a party of its own. See, for instance, No. 667 (21 April, 1739). The more positive attitude to party, apparent in some essays by the writer who called himself "Hampden", gained unfavourable attention from the Government press. It pointed out the deviation from Bolingbroke's teaching in a journal still supposedly loyal to his principles. See *The Daily Gazetteer*, No. 1246 (19 June, 1739).

4. *The Sentiments of a Tory* (1741)

This was perhaps the earliest Tory publication unequivocally to endorse parties as a continuing aspect of public life. After the fall of Walpole, others would take up the theme. Because of the firm insistence that parties adhere to principle, the pamphlet was well received by the Government press. Obviously the Ministry was confident that Tories who based their appeal on Tory principles, rather than on issues of the day, would not expect much electoral support.

SECTION IV

1. *The London Journal* (1730-1734)

This was the chief Government paper from 1722 until 1735. The readiness with which it expressed acceptance of party conflict has been noted by Isaac Kramnick and I am indebted to his book for references to articles in the summer of 1734. See *Bolingbroke and his Circle*, p. 120, n. 30. This newspaper was without question the major outlet for views sympathetic to party in the years 1730-5 and a considerable number of contributions, not reproduced in the text, covered the same themes already recorded. See *The London Journal*, No. 711 (10 February, 1732-3) & No. 766 (2 March, 1733-4). Even *The Craftsman* was moved, on at least one occasion, to endorse the *Journal*'s claim that party was both inevitable and beneficial in a free government. See No. 187 (31 January, 1729-30). Most of the relevant essays in *The London Journal* were by James Pitt (pseudonym, Francis Osborne), an able writer, who little deserved the title of "Mother Osborne", bestowed on him by Opposition journalists. Pitt was a staunch friend to the Protestant Dissenters and wrote in favour of the repeal of the Test and Corporation Acts—once again giving rise to the suspicion that there was some connexion between an interest in religious toleration and a sensitivity to the merits of parties. Pitt's *Letters on Superstition* is his only essay which survived in the public mind, and, when reprinted, it was attributed to a much better known Pitt. However, his writings on party, opposition and the constitution were among the best the age produced. For details on his life see Alexander Pope, *The Dunciad*, ed. James Sutherland (London, 1953), p. 451.

2. *William Arnall* (d. 1741?)

Arnall was lawyer, who also found time in what seems to have been a short life to become one of Walpole's foremost writers. He wrote the notorious pamphlet *Clodius and Cicero* ... (London, 1727), a work which appalled the Opposition by its blithe acceptance of corruption as the necessary price of maintaining the right party in power. Unlike later defences of "influence" as necessary to the constitution, Arnall chose to emphasize that the best guarantee of a Whig government was for members of that party to engross the nation's riches. This somewhat Harringtonian argument had appealed to Whigs even before the time of Arnall. See *The Whig-Examiner*, No. 1 (14 September, 1710).

3. *The Landed Interest Consider'd* (1773)

This Government tract, written at the time of Walpole's unsuccessful bid to pass an Excise Bill, gave only limited support to the presence of parties. A more vigorous and cogent defence of party appeared the next year in America, where a writer in *The New York Gazette* (11-18 March, 1733-4) observed that the use of parties was to act as "spies" on one another. Although few people, apart from Shute Barrington, had made the point with comparable clarity, it was certainly not unheard of. Professor Bailyn has argued that the essay in the New York paper was unequalled by English writings of the time. See Bernard Bailyn, *The Origins of American Politics* (New York, 1968), pp. 126, 127n. This overlooks the insights of some of Walpole's writers and the fact that *The Gazette* frequently drew upon *The London Journal*, then full of such opinions, for its material. See Elizabeth C. Cook, *Literary Influences in Colonial Newspapers, 1704-1750* (New York, 1912), pp. 122-3. While I have not encountered the exact language of the American essay in any English source, the general sentiment could have been borrowed without difficulty.

4. *John, Lord Hervey* (1696-1743)

Hervey was an uncompromising enemy of the Opposition and did not deign to discuss the nature of political parties. Completely ignoring the way in which an opposition could prevent potential wrongdoing from becoming actual, he insisted that since the Opposition had carried no point in Parliament and had not supported the successful Government measures, the people owed them no thanks for any service. See *The Publick Virtue of Former Times and the Present Age Compared* (London, 1732), p. 18. The pamphlet was anonymous, but generally attributed to Hervey.

5. *Opposition No Proof of Patriotism* (1735)

At this stage in the development of opposition, it was necessary only for Arnall to emphasize that an opposition might not be carried on from virtuous motives. The point had to be made because of the long-standing assumption, common in the seventeenth century, that general resistance to arbitrary or unconstitutional measures was very likely to be both wise and virtuous. Individuals presuming to oppose the government were portrayed as gaining nothing by their efforts that was not shared with the rest of the community. At the same time, their altruistic purposes were thought to be evident in the dangers which they courted in standing up against authority. During the eighteenth century the grounds of legitimate opposition gradually extended to include action against measures which were simply unwise, though not necessarily a threat to liberty. With the growing respectability of opposition intended to capture power, party was joined to opposition. Thus a publication, equivalent to Arnall's, but appearing late in the century, contained the observation that party too was often taken to be an incontestable good—"Are not Opposition, and the party, the very echoes of virtue and genius?" [Richard Tickell], *Common-Place Arguments Against Administration. With Obvious Answers, (Intended for the Use of the New Parliament.)* (London, 1780), p. 53.

6. *Proceedings of a Political Club* (1738)

Thomas Gordon wrote the version of the parliamentary debates for *The London Magazine* and he has also been credited with writing this introductory piece. See Benjamin B. Hoover, *Samuel Johnson's Parliamentary Reporting* (Berkeley and Los Angeles, 1953), p. 17. By this time, Gordon had seemingly shed his aversion to party along with his other Old Whig prejudices. In relating the presence of parties to the need of informing the public about proceedings in Parliament, Gordon had gone beyond the first stage in a defence of party—citing their function in restraining one another—to discuss the importance of bringing party doctrines before the electorate. Of course he saw the press, not party organization, as the vehicle for this public education and he must have been aware of the limits imposed by a small electorate and the restricted sort of campaigning sanctioned by the conventions of the time. Still, this was an advance.

7. *A Word to the Good People of England* (1739)

It is not at all clear which opposition publications are referred to here, for the various writers in *The Craftsman* and *Common Sense* were generally far less well disposed to party than was *The London Journal*. It was not unusual for writers hostile to party to assume that the institution had many defenders. See *A Political Grammar Adapted to the Meridian of Great Britain,* . . . (London, 1742), p. 51. It is certainly true that the Government had become less tolerant of the Opposition, presumably because it was now more of a threat. *The Daily Gazetteer,* successor to *The London Journal* as spokesman for the Administration, had little praise for opposition in general and, by 1739, had taken to congratulating Walpole for his forbearance in tolerating an opposition. See *The Daily Gazetteer,* No. 1249 (22 June, 1739) and *The Original Series of Wisdom and Policy, Manifested in a Review of our Foreign Negotiations and Transactions for Several Years Past,* 4th edn. (London, 1739), p. 4. A factor in the changed tone of Government writers may have been the fact that James Pitt, who had been responsible for the ablest defences of party, wrote little after 1736. For information on the chief Government writers of the time see Robert L. Haig, *The Gazetteer, 1735-1797* (Carbondale, Illinois, 1960), pp. 6-8.

8. Sir Robert Walpole (1676-1745)

There is no telling whether these were Walpole's exact words, but the sentiment is consistent with his usual position. William Coxe reports another speech with the same emphasis in *Memoirs of the Life and Administration of Sir Robert Walpole, Earl of Orford* (London, 1798), Vol. I, p. 659. Further evidence of Walpole's opinions is to be found in the memoir by Thomas Pownall in Coxe, Vol. III, p. 617 and in Kramnick, *Bolingbroke and his Circle,* pp. 119-21.

9. *A Second Letter to a Member of Parliament* (1741)

The first letter from this writer had appeared in 1740. As a defence of influence, the *Second Letter* was superior to most other writings on the subject. More subtle than Arnall, the writer also managed to avoid the problems of Hume's famous essay on the subject. Hume was to reject party as an instrument of government, while accepting the necessity of influence. It seems more palatable as propaganda and more accurate as analysis to justify the bonds holding an administration together by giving a place to party both in government and in opposition. Prior to 1783, defences of influence were comparatively few and the large number which appeared after that date were quite as likely to dwell upon the power of the king as to say anything useful about party. From the fall of Walpole until the 1780s there was little discussion of influence by people in power. Arthur Onslow, the Speaker, was typical of conventional opinion in writing that opposition was best deflected when it was clear that no "combination" marred the ministerial side. See *H.M.C. 14th Report Appendix*, Part IX, p. 461.

SECTION V

1. *David Hume* (1711-1776)

Hume's thoughts on parties are quite unremarkable and, had their author written nothing else, they would surely have been forgotten. Hume's dislike of parties "from principle" did not command a large following; most men felt that if one were to have parties at all, they should be associations based on principle. That, indeed, was already the criterion for distinguishing party from faction. See, for example, the comment on Tory claims of their "party-constancy" in a tract attributed to Samuel Squire: "I am sorry to use the word Party, for what is Party without Principle? Division without Distinction?" *A Letter to a Tory Friend Upon the Present Critical Situation of Our Affairs* (London, 1746), p. 27. Squire's Whig prejudices blinded him to the quite remarkable stability of principle shown by some Tories, but that is another story. Hume's fear of parties based on principle finds a modern parallel in the opinion of some social scientists that conflict based on material interests is more readily kept "realistic" and limited than that based on ideology. See Lewis A. Coser, *Continuities in the Study of Social Conflict* (New York, 1967), pp. 33-4. For modern comment on Hume's treatment of parties, see J. P. Plamenatz, *Man and Society* (London, 1963), Vol. I, pp. 302-24 and John B. Stewart, *The Moral and Political Philosophy of David Hume* (New York and London, 1963), pp. 203-04, 387-88.

2. *John Campbell* (1708-1775)

The author was a Tory lawyer and miscellaneous writer. There were at least four other John Campbells in public life during the 1740s and all sat in Parliament. Evidence on authorship of *The Case of the Opposition* is to be found in Andrew Kippis, *Biographia Britannica* (London, 1784), Vol. III, p. 215. Campbell's pamphlet has been cited in various sources as an early example of a sophisticated position on party. It seems not to have been noticed, however, that it was reissued in 1744 under a new title as an answer to *Faction Detected*. See *The New Opposition Compared with the Old in Point of Principles and Practice* (London, 1744). Campbell was a bit premature in saying that a party with the title of "the Opposition" had existed for twenty years. In the early 1720s the term opposition had not acquired the same connotations as in 1742.

3. *John Perceval, 2nd Earl of Egmont* (1711-70)

Perceval wrote *Faction Detected* in defence of William Pulteney, who, having engineered Walpole's resignation, deserted his allies in opposition and joined the Administration. For details of the complex negotiations of 1742 see John B. Owen, *The Rise of the Pelhams* (London, 1957), ch. III. Those left in opposition were quick to recall that Pulteney had at one time been a champion of the institution of opposition [*Parliamentary History*, Vol. X (1738), col. 438] although his opinions had changed as rapidly as his fortunes. For such criticism see *A Review of the Whole Conduct of a Late Eminent Patriot, and his Friends*... (London, 1743), p. 118.

Perceval's book—it is too large to be called a pamphlet—provoked numerous answers and his comments on party and opposition continued to be quoted without acknowledgment for many years. See *A Reply to Mr. [George] Heathcote's Letter from an Honest Man*... (London, n.d. [1762]), p. 4, and, for a later use, see Archibald S. Foord, *His Majesty's Opposition*, p. 412n.

4. *The Detector Detected* (1743)

This "broad-bottom" answer to Perceval contains a number of comments quite favourable to the Tories, even coming close to the rather primitive Tory notion of opposition as a perpetual and virtuous vigilance in the wilderness. However, while the Tories remained committed to the retention of party loyalty, the "broad-bottoms" were moving towards the position—more directly stated in other writings—that the old party distinctions should be abolished. Individual men might shun the label Tory, as would whole administrations later in the century, but a stable group, adhering to Tory principles, persisted in the 1740s. The term "Whig", by contrast, meant simply "not Tory". See Owen, *The Rise of the Pelhams*, p. 69.

5. *James Ralph* (1705-1762)

The "broad-bottom" Whigs, led by Chesterfield, were equally behind this rejoinder to Perceval. This group produced two journals, *Common Sense* and *Old England*, both, at one time, edited by William Guthrie. See Laurence Hanson, *Government and the Press, 1695-1763* (Oxford, 1967), p. 119. Guthrie was bought off by the Government in 1743 and James Ralph, another journalist, seems to have assumed most of the burden of broad-bottom writing until the leaders gained admission to the Ministry in December, 1744. The evidence for Ralph as chief writer of *A Defence of the People* is to be found in John B. Shipley, "James Ralph's Pamphlets, 1741-1744" in *The Library*, 3rd series, Vol. XIX (1964), pp. 130-46 at pp. 135-6. In recognizing Ralph as the most prominent Opposition journalist of the period, Shipley has helped to rehabilitate a reputation too often dismissed with the epithet "hack". It was also in 1743 that Ralph became private secretary to Bubb Dodington, a post which would lead him into further efforts on behalf of an opposition group. See *The Political Journal of George Bubb Dodington*, ed. John Carswell and Lewis Arnold Dralle, (Oxford, 1965), *passim*. Ralph was an American and a friend of Benjamin Franklin. For details of his life, see Robert W. Kenny, "James Ralph: An Eighteenth-Century Philadelphian in Grub Street", *The Pennsylvania Magazine*, Vol. 64 (1940), pp. 218-42.

6. *Edward Spelman* (d. 1767)

As a classical scholar, removed from pubilc life and even from the universities, Spelman had no impact on the politics of his day. Following the initial publication in 1743, the booksellers brought out a further, and unauthorized, edition in 1747 and this is the one used here. The final eighteenth-century edition appeared in 1758. For the printing history, see Spelman, *The Roman Antiquities of the Dionysius Halicarnassensis, Translated into English; with Notes and Dissertations* (London, 1758), Vol. I, p. 370. If he failed to impress his contemporaries, Spelman's skilful bridging of the gap between the orders of mixed government and the parties of the eighteenth century has been appreciated by modern scholars. See Peter Campbell, 'An Early Defence of Party', *Political Studies*, Vol. III, pp. 166-7. Spelman's essay has sometimes been attributed to James Hampton, presumably because the latter also wrote on Polybius. However, Hampton's writings reveal an incapacity to relate the parties of the day to the balanced constitution; in fact he saw harmony between the various orders of the constitution as dependent on the absence of parties. See Hampton, *Two Extracts from the Sixth Book of the General History of Polybius* (London, 1764), Preface.

Section VI

1. *Ephraim Harman (fl. 1752)*
   Harman identified himself as "one of the People called Quakers". This is the only clue to his identity, leading to a comment in the catalogue of the British Museum that the name may not have been genuine. Quakers were very successful in using their political influence to best advantage by exacting the maximum number of concessions from all political parties. Other Protestant Dissenters were sometimes advised to emulate their sophisticated understanding of the competition between parties. See *Observations on the Conduct of the Tories, the Whigs, and the Dissenters; with Advice to the Latter* (London, 1739), pp. 28-9. Harman's opponent, Thomas Randolph, suffered from the common difficulty of not understanding how men, presumably equally good, could oppose one another in parties. See *Party-Zeal Censur'd in a Sermon* [on 1 Cor. III, 3] *preach'd Before the University of Oxford* (Oxford, 1752), pp. 11-12.

2. *Dr. John Brett (fl. 1753)*
   Brett, who at the time of writing his tracts was rector of Moynalty, was not nearly so original as he supposed in identifying wealth as a cause of parties. The connexion between sedition and wealth had often been discussed; Perceval in his *Faction Detected* had noted how lucrative posts in government contributed to the growth of parties and Dr. John Brown had founded a literary reputaton on his recital of the ills, including party feeling, which followed from luxury and moral decay.

3. *Political Pastime (1753)*
   In addressing this publication to himself, Brett merely epitomized the remarkable confusion in the literature produced in the crisis over Irish financial administration. Contemporaries realized, however, that the author of this tract and the previous one were the same. See *A Second Letter to a Person of Distinction . . . Containing . . . Some Remarks on a Late Pamphlet, entitled Political Pastime* (Dublin, 1753), pp. 8-9. The second pamphlet feigned sympathy for the Opposition in the Irish Parliament, but this can only have been a clumsy effort at irony. Brett seems to have been an unappealing person of no remarkable insight. His thoughts on party thus warrant reproduction here only because they contain material on the major sources on the subject which were cited at mid-century—the writings of Bolingbroke, Gordon and Hume. For background on events in Ireland at the time, see R. B. McDowell, *Irish Public Opinion,*

1750-1800 (London, 1944), and the sources cited there. Opposition was to have a hard history in Ireland, only gaining a really firm footing in the 1930s.

4. *The Protester, on Behalf of the People* (1753)
Ralph wrote this weekly in support of the opposition to the Pelhams conducted by the Duke of Bedford, ending his efforts only when the Government, following its usual practice, awarded him a pension. [See R. J. Robson, *The Oxfordshire Election of 1754* (London, 1949), p. 29.] It contains the strongest statements in favour of party that can be found in any work traced to Ralph. While his reputation as a mercenary was in no way unearned, Ralph can be credited with some of the most effective pieces against corruption since the early days of *The Craftsman*. For an early broad-bottom pamphlet which reads very much like some numbers of *The Protester*, see *The Groans of Britons at the Gloomy Prospect . . . of their Liberties and Properties* (London, 1743), pp. 38-47.

5. *The Opposition* (1755)
This would-be periodical had but one issue. It appeared at a time when the future Lord Chatham was attacking Newcastle from within the Administration, while Henry Fox, only lately reconciled to it, spoke for the Government. An allusion (not reproduced here) to inconsistency on the issue of subsidizing Hanoverion troops suggests that the inconstant orator was Chatham, for his actions in 1748 fit the description. The emphasis on the quality of oratory gives the pamphlet a disconcerting superficiality, but the 1750s was not a time of great political literature. In yielding to the temptation to put opposition in a cosmological setting, the author pursued an interest still current in the twentieth century. See C. K. Ogden, *Opposition: A Linguistic and Psychological Analysis*, introduced by I. A. Richards (Bloomington, Indiana, 1967) and Eugen Rosenstock-Huessy, *Out of Revolution: Autobiography of Western Man* (New York, 1938), p. 344.

6. *The Con-Test* (1756-7)
This strange little paper was one of two protagonists in a struggle for office involving Henry Fox and Chatham. At one time, Philip Francis was taken to be the author, but actually it seems to have been Owen Ruffhead, who wrote pamphlets in praise of Chatham's Ministry. See Howard H. Dunbar, *The Dramatic Career of Arthur Murphy* (New York, 1946), pp. 34-6. A discussion of Ruffhead's political ideas is to be found in Harvey G. Mansfield, Jr., *Statesmanship and Party Government*, p. 100. In crediting Ruffhead with being a follower of Bolingbroke's political theory, Professor Mansfield neglects the possibility that, as a professional apologist, Ruffhead probably had no philosophy at all. The *Con-Test* appeared in answer to *The Test*, written by Arthur Murphy in the interest of Henry Fox. *The Test* was consistently hostile to parties. One of the few pamphlets of the time to express sympathy for partisan feeling was by a Kentish curate. See Robert Neild, *Party-Spirit: or, An Attempt to shew both the Native Innocence and the Present Degeneracy of that Passion* (London, 1756), pp. 3-7.

7. *The Constitution* (1757)
Of the three surviving issues of this paper, this was the most hostile to Chatham. The declared aim of the publication was to watch his conduct and to criticize when necessary. The Ministerial reply was contained in an equally obscure paper which also accepted political parties, although emphasizing the need for an uncommitted group to balance and moderate

the contending parties. See *The Æquipoise, or the Constitution Ballanced,* No. I [1757].

8. *Horace Walpole* (1717-97)

On Walpole's authorship, see Archibald S. Foord, 'The Only Unadulterated Whig' in Warren H. Smith (ed.), *Horace Walpole: Writer, Politician and Connoisseur* (New Haven, 1967), p. 33n. Walpole's opponent here was Owen Ruffhead, who as a Ministerial writer in the early 1760s, seems to have lost that tolerance which sometimes appeared in the writings attributed to him in *The Con-Test*. Walpole too had changed, for his position on party and opposition was much more favourable than it had been in his pamphlet of 1747. See *A Letter to the Whigs* (London, 1747), pp. 40-2. Party feeling had grown stronger by 1763, owing to the resentment produced by the emergence of Bute as First Lord of the Treasury. A dictionary of 1760 still recorded the sentiment that Whig and Tory were names now happily set aside as significant distinctions. See John Marchant, *A New Complete English Dictionary* (London, 1760), *s.v.* party. However, the press in the early 1760s was full of alarms at the revival of Toryism, and even *The Monitor*, a responsible Opposition journal, came in 1762 to defend party disputes, after years of primly insisting that opposition be confined to measures. For opinion as to a new Toryism in the mid-1760s, see the letters in *The St. James's Chronicle* reprinted in *A Collection of Letters and Essays in Favour of Public Liberty. First Published in the News-papers in the Years 1764, 65, 66, 67, 68, 69 and 1770* (London, 1774), Vol. I.

That political tensions were growing in this period is surely undeniable and it seems equally obvious that George III strove to eliminate parties and so provoked some resentment. Of course, Chatham had already tried to accomplish the same feat in a different manner, but some writers chose to see the two efforts as very different. See *The Monitor*, No. 458 (12 May, 1764). For a spirited discussion of the difficulties of arguing for a "new Toryism" on the accession of George III, see Ian R. Christie, *Myth and Reality in Late-Eighteenth-Century British Politics* (London, 1970), ch. 7. He does, however, admit the existence of a set of "king's friends" until the year 1767 (p. 34), and this situation seems to have provoked genuine anxiety before it was exploited by the Rockinghamite propaganda. The Namierite interpretation has never involved the insistence that party labels were not used at this time, only that they fail to identify the significant problems and organizations in politics. See Sir Lewis Namier, *England in the Age of the American Revolution*, 2nd edn. (London, 1961), p. 180. However, the case against parties, and specifically two parties in 1760, is weakened by Sir Lewis's denial that the system had ever existed in England, even in the twentieth century. For if, as he said, it was but an idea, so strong as almost to become reality, the idea, it may be allowed, existed for some people even in the 1760s. See his provocative essay "The Two-Party System" in *Conflicts: Studies in Contemporary History* (London, 1942), pp. 201-6.

SECTION VII

1. *Adam Ferguson* (1723-1816)

It will be noted that Ferguson never mentions party in England; the tendency of the whole book is to provide interesting generalizations on the stages of social development, with the unavoidable cost of saying little about specific institutions in a given time and place. In the manner of so many other learned men, Ferguson approached party through the misleading experience of the conflict of orders in a mixed government.

2. *An Address to the People of England* (1767)
This was a plea for annual ministries as an alternative to the frequent calls for annual parliaments. The reference to Chatham was satirical in intent, although the rest of the tract is perfectly serious in its proposals, if unusually witty. The writer was asserting the respectability of both parties in order to allow both to compete frequently for office. He was not endorsing a coalition or a ministry above party as had been the practice of Chatham.

3. *A Letter to . . . the Duke of Grafton* (1768)
This pamphlet deserves to be thought of as one of the great documents in the history of political parties. Without any apparent party bias or reservation as to circumstances, it explains the virtues of what can truly be called a two-party system. The only statement coming close to the conventional limitations placed by the age on party and opposition was confined to suggesting that a great national crisis would see an abatement of party strife. This in no way serves as a qualification to the writer's acceptance of party, since modern democratic practice still endorses that position. It has been said that the only people between the late seventeenth century and the late nineteenth century to defend parties at any length were Burke and Bagehot in England and Francis Lieber and Philip Friese in the United States. See Austin Ranney and Willmoore Kendall, *Democracy and the American Party System* (New York, 1956), p. 146 and for a later judgment consistent with the first, Austin Ranney, "The Concept of Party" in Oliver Garceau (ed.), *Political Research and Political Theory* (Cambridge, Mass., 1968), pp. 145-7. But for the fact of the anonymity of the author, this would be a worthy addition to the list. The pamphlet was noticed in various periodicals. Some reviews were brief and unfavourable, [*The London Magazine*, Vol. 37 (July, 1768), p. 390] or limited to the specific policy proposals which were also part of the work—*The London Chronicle*, Vol. XXIV, No. 1802 (2-5 July, 1768). However, there was a full, but noncommittal statement of the argument on parties in *The Gentleman's Magazine*, Vol. 38 (August, 1768). Even the "Tory" publication, *The Critical Review*, was respectful, commenting (Vol. 26, pp. 68-9) that the work was by "no vulgar hand". This was scarcely the excitement generated by Junius's letters to the Duke of Grafton or even by the letter to Grafton published by Wilkes in 1767, but the student of political ideas will find nothing very interesting in the more famous productions.

4. *The North Briton* (1769)
William Bingley had, by this time, replaced Wilkes as editor of *The North Briton*. Earlier in the decade, Wilkes too had been concerned about a threatened abolition of party. See *The North Briton*, No. XXXIII (15 January, 1763).

5. *Letter signed "A Watchman"* (1769)
The letter-writer is not, of course, dealing with the conventional parties at all, but with a new phenomenon, heralding novel departures in political participation and the life of parties. On the reception of such associations, see Eugene Charlton Black, *The Association: British Extraparliamentary Political Organization, 1769-1793* (Cambridge, Mass., 1963), p. 5. Indicative of the difficulties faced by most associations was the complaint, not applicable to a two-party system, that a protest group such as The Friends of the People would endanger liberty. Such a "general

association" was, by definition, incapable of finding any "counterpoise". Thus it offended against the basic rule of eighteenth-century political thought—that all recognized forces had to be balanced. See John [really Fitzjohn] Brand, *An Historical Essay on the Principles of Political Associations in a State* . . . (London, 1796), p. 3.

6. *Considerations on the Times* (1769)
The generation of radicals which first sought reforms such as annual parliaments consisted of people attached to constitutional orthodoxy in other respects; only in the 1770s and after did the most ardent reformers expressly dismiss parties as weak allies and irrelevant to the needs of the country—and this at a time when Englishmen of other persuasions were coming in large numbers to appreciate the contribution party made to the political system. *Considerations on the Times* was accorded some space in *The London Chronicle*, No. 1950 (13-15 June, 1769) with special attention being given to the thoughts on parties. The Rockingham Whigs seem not to have provided any theoretical defence of party prior to Burke's *Thoughts*, and certainly they were not advocates of annual parliaments. For their opinions on these issues, see John Brooke, *The Chatham Administration, 1766-1768* (London, 1956), pp. 213-6 and John Norris, *Shelburne and Reform* (London, 1963), p. 122. Thus we have to make room for advocates of party both more radical than the Rockinghams and earlier in the field.

7. *Edmund Burke* (1729-97)
Little needs to be said on the subject of Burke and party. His *Thoughts* gained immediate public attention, but some reviews paid no heed to the remarks on party. See *The Universal Magazine*, Vol. XLVI (May, 1770), pp. 226-32. The major question raised by Burke's writings was whether he did indeed contemplate parties as permanent parts of the political scene. It can certainly be argued that he did not. See Frank O'Gorman, "Party and Burke: The Rockingham Whigs", *Government and Opposition*, Vol. 3, No. 1 (1968), pp. 92-110. Some of Burke's contemporaries also sensed the ambiguity of his position, one affirming that independence was much superior to political affiliation and then adding that he was "ready to maintain the opinion against the author of *Thoughts on the Cause of the Present Discontents*, whenever that author shall plainly assert the contrary". *The Freeholder's Supplication to Both Houses of Parliament* (London, 1779), p. 13 n. For a similar judgment, see *An Essay on the Polity of England* (London, 1785), p. 493. In Burke's defence it can only be emphasized how prone public men have been to turn doctrines about party to their own advantage. It is still widely assumed that politicians will more readily attest to the merits of a strong opposition when their political fortunes put them there. Burke expressed his ideas on party to the House of Commons at about the same time as the *Thoughts* appeared in print, but there is no verbatim account of the speech. See *Parliamentary History*, Vol. XVI (1770), col. 920. After this time, a number of Rockingham publications argued for the respectability of party. See, for instance, *Account of the Views and Principles of that Connexion of Whigs, Commonly Called the Rockingham Party* (London, 1782), pp. 1-2, 12.

SECTION VIII

1. *Nathaniel Forster* (1726-90)
Forster, who was Rector of All Saints' Colchester, was supporting Lord

Graftons Administration in its attempt to keep John Wilkes out of the House of Commons. One of Forster's other publications displays both an unusual sensitivity to the nature of social conflict and the individualist's suspicion of associations in politics. Here, in the course of discussing the landed and ecclesiastical interests, he observed that such interests, "of a middle kind", between the objects of individuals and the good of the community, were often too powerful for both. See *An Enquiry into the Causes of the Present High Price of Provisions* (London, 1767), p. 96. This classic statement of a common eighteenth-century prejudice seems to have been compatible with his accepting the conventional parties, but not the sort of popular opposition then being organized "without doors".

2. *Soame Jenyns* (1704-87)
This was a satire on one of the major foibles of the time and was accepted as such by contemporaries. Jenyns's scheme called for the assignment of ministerial posts by a lottery. It is not easy to say what Jenyns really thought about this matter, for despite his being a Member of Parliament, he was sometimes criticized for his light-hearted approach to serious problems—"While tories call him whig and whigs a tory". Jenyns was a Whig M.P., but a highly independent one. See Owen, *The Rise of the Pelhams*, p. 61 and Namier, *England in the Age of the American Revolution* 2nd edn., p. 393. Certainly Jenyns accepted parties as inevitable, if regrettable, parts of politics and also made a characteristically effective, but cynical, defence of the need for influence in order to cement parliamentary majorities. See *A Free Enquiry into the Nature and Origin of Evil* (London, 1757), pp. 143-6; *Disquisitions on Several Subjects* (London, 1782), p. 95 and *Thoughts on a Parliamentary Reform* (London, 1784), pp. 22-3.

Coalition had its champions in theory and many others applied it in practice. However, the word was more often than not one of abuse. This had been the theme of government writers in the 1730s attacking the "coalition of patriots" in opposition; it had become further debased in the humorous attacks on the "broad-bottom" Ministry of 1744 and so long before the notorious coalition of 1783 between North and Fox, "coalition" suggested the casting aside of all principle in quest of office. To some it brought visions of the wiles of diplomacy; to others, the cynical monopolizing of advantages. For an example of the first, see *The Coalition: or, an Historical Memoir of the Negotiations for Peace ...* (London, 1762), a libel on Chatham and Newcastle. The word took on the connotation of undue limiting of conflict in areas of life other than the political and so served to describe a monopoly of London theatres. See *Coalition, A Farce* (London, 1779). The broadest piece of satire in Jenyns's essay was the proposal that party struggle be confined to the public at large with the politicians remaining united in Parliament. The real complaint with coalitions had always been that they lent an artificial unity to Parliament, while ignoring real divisions within the community. See, for example, *Miscellaneous Thoughts, Moral and Political, Upon The Vices and Follies of the Present Age ... and the Coalition of Parties, or what is now Called the Broad-Bottom by a Country Gentleman* (London, 1745).

3. *Letters Concerning the Present State of England* (1772)
The writer of these letters was an admirer of Burke—"The political pamphlets attributed to him are the best this age had produced; ..." (p. 347). Reviews were unenthusiastic, *The London Magazine* suggesting

that the author had assumed a burden disproportionate to his abilities (See Vol. XLI (1772), p. 133) while *The Monthly Review* allowed at least that he was at his best on the subject of politics. See Vol. 46 (1772), pp. 438-43.

4. *Remarks on a Pamphlet Lately Published by Dr. Price* (1776)
Ferguson's tract was written on behalf of North's Administration and published at Government expense. See David Kettler, *The Social and Political Thought of Adam Ferguson* ([Columbus], 1965), p. 64. More clearly than most Government writings, this conveys the complacent acceptance of an opposition party which can oppose without constituting a serious threat to those in power. Frustration at this untenable position would lead opposition under Fox to tactics which threatened to upset the constitution.

5. *William Eden* (1744-1814)
Eden, later Lord Auckland, was a lawyer, diplomat and M.P. who served both North and Pitt. His opinion on the statesmanlike nature of coalition reflected his own answer to the difficulties of North's Ministry in 1777-8. See Charles R. Ritcheson, *British Politics and the American Revolution* (Norman, Oklahoma, 1954), pp. 241-2, 250.

6. *Capel Lofft* (1751-1824)
Lofft was a political radical and was perhaps one of the first Englishmen in the eighteenth century to call his favoured system of government "democracy". See *Elements of Universal Law, and Particularly of the Law of England* (London, 1779), Vol. I, p. 113. This same work has some excellent thoughts on the propensity of governments to call for unity—"Fools may be unanimous in the pursuit of a silly end"—and it also presents his ideal of an England where the only party was that of the people. This sentiment, which would be the watchword of radicalism, led a reviewer of *An Argument* to claim that Lofft was not arguing for party at all and that he has chosen a misleading way of conveying his message. See *The Monthly Review*, Vol. 63 (1780), p. 67.

7. *Benjamin Turner* (1750-1826)
Turner was an admirer of Lord North. His comments here would seem to suggest a liking for coalition government, but in point of fact the coalition of 1783 left him very distressed, complaining that the recent events left him no party to support. See *The True Alarm* ... (London, 1783), p. 4. His claim that all mixed governments would have a party of the people and one to support prerogative shows the lingering desire, so apparent in others, to understand eighteenth-century political parties through the categories of the orders written of by Polybius or Machiavelli. For biographical information on Turner, see *Alumni Cantabrigienses* Part II, Vol. 6 (Cambridge, 1954).

8. *A Brief and Impartial Review of the State of Great Britain* (1783)
Coalition could, in the circumstances, mean a union between Whig and Tory, as this ingenious defence of the Fox-North coalition proves. The tract received some favourable comment in the press, but I have been unable to find any suggestion as to the identity of the writer. Such defenders of the Rockingham party and the coalition found it very difficult to justify the unlikely alliance between Fox and North—but they tried. One of these writers records the new depths to which the term "coalition" had come: "The very word itself, is used by the illiterate as a storm of reproach or infamy, as if coalition were abstractly a crime in itself, ..." *Vulgar Errors* (London 1784), p. 7. This was a brave attempt to fix the crime of unprincipled coalition on the Pittites. One of the

numerous attacks on the coalition contrasted party spirit favourably with unprincipled self-interest. See *The Coalition; or an Essay on the Present State of Parties* (London, 1783), p. 37.

SECTION IX

1. *George Chalmers* (1742-1825)

   Chalmers was a noted historian and a literary adversary of Burke. In 1786 he was in the service of William Pitt. The extract shows an interesting tendency to minimize constitutional differences among the various parties. Perhaps the Tories and the bulk of the Whigs did agree as to the nature of the constitution, but with the coming of the French Revolution, it was to be made abundantly clear that there were many who rejected the prevailing ideas and, with them, the established parties. In that unhappy period Chalmers did his best to refute the argument both of the reformers and of reactionaries such as John Reeves. Chalmers also continued to affirm the connexion between party and liberty. See *A Vindication of the People, in Respect to the Constitutional Right of Free Discussion* (London, 1796), p. 76.

2. *Richard Champion* (1743-1791)

   Champion was a Bristol merchant and a Whig, who entered and left office with Burke. See G. H. Guttridge (ed.), *The American Correspondence of a Bristol Merchant 1766-1771. Letters of Richard Champion* (Berkeley, 1934).

3. *Major John Scott* (1747-1819)

   These contributions to the literature of the Regency Crisis first appeared in *The Public Advertiser* in December, 1788 and January, 1789. See *The Monthly Review*, Vol. 80 (1789), p. 180 for the attribution to Scott. The allusion to "a very eminent writer" may have referred to Burke, whom Scott, as a supporter of Pitt, had opposed on the issue of Warren Hastings.

4. *Charles James Fox* (1749-1806)

   This account of Fox's speech illustrates the painful situation of an opposition both respectable and powerless. Everything was already in place for what John Cam Hobhouse was to call in his famous *bon mot* "His Majesty's Opposition". The problem was that the weakness of the opposition party made very severe demands on that loyalty. Throughout the 1790s, Fox continued to spell out the duties of the Opposition. See the admirable speeches recorded in *Parliamentary History*, Vol. XXXIII (1797-8), cols. 20, 701-2. Owing to Pitt's strength and his own unpopularity with George III, Fox denied any ambition for office, although he did not deny that his party might rightly be seen as an alternative government.

5. *William Combe* (1741-1823)

   Not all defences of "influence" were equally friendly to party, although the two were frequently linked by people on the government side. Combe, best known for his *Doctor Syntax*, wrote a number of other political tracts, but never again gave close consideration to party. He wrote a defence of Addington's Administration which first appeared in *The Times* in 1803. Here Combe warmly endorsed government by a party, but seemingly not an opposition organized on the same basis. See *The Letters of Valerius on the State of Parties, the War, The Volunteer System, and Most of the Political Topics which have Lately been under Public Discussion* (London, 1804), pp. 16, 22-3.

6. *Henry Mackenzie* (1745-1831)

Mackenzie was a major literary figure in Scotland where he had edited several magazines. He wrote this work for Pitt and it has been taken to reflect the latter's views, since the Prime Minister himself is said to have revised it. See Rt. Hon. George Rose, *Observations Respecting the Public Expenditure and the Influence of the Crown*, 3rd edn. (London, 1810), p. 77.

7. *Sir William Young* (1749-1815)

There is something slightly naive in Young's describing the constitution as controlling the dangers of party, without his mentioning how the parties were affecting the constitution. In this respect writers on "influence" were more perceptive. However, this M.P. and supporter of Pitt at least appreciated that the constitution as it then operated was quite consistent with the existence of parties. Some of Young's contemporaries employed the existence of an opposition party to defeat proposals for parliamentary reform, it being argued that the Opposition sufficed to counteract any baneful influence of the Crown. See [?R. B. Cooper], *Remarks on the Proceedings of the Society who Style Themselves "The Friends of the People"* (London, 1792), p. 95.

8. *T. R. Bentley* (1748?-1831)

Bentley is described by some sources as a printer, but his chief occupation appears to have been that of journalist and pamphleteer, in "government employ". See *A Biographical Dictionary of the Living Authors of Great Britain and Ireland* (London, 1816). Bentley's pamphlet of 1793 was occasioned by the publication of Fox's *Letter ... to the Electors ... of Westminster*. Walpole had once given offence by being *the* minister; now Fox was coming to be recognized as being *the* parliamentary leader of the Opposition. For although Bentley was obviously feeling his way in describing the office, its nature had already become clear. As the extract shows, the price of being accepted as incumbent of such an office was to have one's opposition confined largely to Parliament. Actually, Bentley's portrait of Fox as a demagogue was grossly unjust, since Fox was, if anything, too hesitant to mobilize the "people" against Pitt.

9. *R. J. Thornton* (1768-1837)

The first edition of this work, published in 1794, was entitled *The Citizen*, and there was a further edition in 1799. Robert Thornton was primarily a writer on medicine and natural science and this seems to have been his only venture into political writing. The extract is taken from Chapter IX of Montesquieu's, *Considerations on the Causes of the Grandeur and the Decadence of the Romans*, but the favourable verdict on party is an interpolation by Thornton. This compendium of political knowledge contained little that was original—Thornton adhered, for instance, to a fairly conventional view of the balance of the constitution—and so party had taken its place with the matchless constitution in the realm of orthodoxy.

10. *A Few Cursory Remarks Upon the State of Parties* (1803)

This assault on Pitt followed his resignation of 1801. The pamphlet was widely distributed by Addington's supporters and was presumably published at Government expense. See A. Aspinall, *Politics and the Press c. 1780-1850* (London, 1949), pp. 153-4.

Specifically, as a later defence of this pamphlet indicates, the complaint was that Pitt was in fact opposing Addington's Administration but in a covert manner which refused to confess that "systematic and general" opposition which was actually taking place. See [Bentley], *The Reply of a Near Observer, to some of the Answerers of the Cursory Remarks* (London, 1804), pp. 69, 86. One of the defences of Pitt emphasized that his actions had been quite proper and that while government demanded a considerable degree of unity of purpose, opposition might best serve the country by attacking from various directions. This meant that Pitt might criticize the Ministry without feeling obliged to join any of the opposition groups in the House of Commons. See *A Brief Answer to a Few Cursory Remarks on the Present State of Parties* (London, 1803), pp. 21-2. Bentley's pamphlet remained a bone of contention; Lord Archibald Hamilton used it in the cause of opposition to drive a wedge between Pitt and Addington (now Lord Sidmouth) when the two were reunited in the Ministry. For this he was rebuked in a Government pamphlet which summed up the whole complex dispute in a way which was unavoidably tendentious but still admirably clear. See *Thoughts on Coalitions, with Reference to the Present State of Parties* (London, 1805). This publication shows very clearly that supporters of an administration might reject the contention that on a resignation the Opposition should come in as a body, while at the same time taking party and opposition as natural and valuable. See *Thoughts . . .*, sig. B- p. 5. Throughout the debate, it was very clear that there were not just two parties, which Hamilton, for instance, seems to assume, but several, and this complicated matters. The failure of British politics to conform to a manageable two-party system was still being lamented in 1858. See *A Letter to a Noble Lord on the Nature and Prospects of Political Party by a Commoner* (London, 1858), pp. 57-60.

INDEX

WESTFIELD
UNIV.
LONDON
COLLEGE

WITHDRAWN
FROM STOCK
QMUL LIBRARY